Ex Libris

The Age of Plantagenet and Valois

General Editor: D. A. BULLOUGH, M.A., F.S.A.(SCOT.),
Professor of Medieval History, Nottingham University

Fig. 1 January—John, duke of Berry seated at table, from *Les Très Riches Heures du duc de Berri* by Jean and Pol de Limbourg. *Musée de Chantilly.* (17 × 15.3)

The Age of Plantagenet and Valois

Kenneth Fowler

Photographs by Wim Swaan, Edwin Smith and others

NEW YORK

Copyright © Paul Elek Productions Ltd 1967

This edition published in USA 1980
by Exeter Books
Distributed by Bookthrift, Inc
New York, New York

All rights reserved

ISBN 0-89673-046-8
LC 79-92324

Printed in Hong Kong
by South China Printing Co.

Contents

Author's Note

It is not possible to record here the names of the numerous scholars from whose teaching and writing I have benefited, although many of them appear in the bibliography and notes at the end. I owe a special debt to Professor John Le Patourel, who introduced me to the Plantagenet Dominions, and to Professor Denys Hay, who encouraged me to extend my researches into the fifteenth century, although they will not necessarily share the views expressed in the following pages. I also wish to thank my friend and colleague Dr Anthony Luttrell for reading the work in manuscript and offering many helpful suggestions, and Miss Moira Johnston for her constant encouragement and hard work in preparing it for publication.

Edinburgh, 1967.   K.F.

Acknowledgements

The Publishers would like to thank all those organizations and individuals who have helped in the collection of the illustrations for this volume. In particular they would like to express their gratitude to those who gave their permission and assistance to Wim Swaan: front of jacket; plate numbers 2, 3, 7, 16, 17, 18, 19, 22, 25, 26, 29, 32,

The photographs are acknowledged to the following sources: Bibliothèque Nationale, Paris: plate numbers 1, 8, 9, 10, 12, 23, 24, 28, 37, 52, 58, 59, 60, 77, 80, 81, 82, 83, 88, 90, 94; text figure numbers 10, 11, 13, 14, 16, 42, 46. Wim Swaan: front of jacket; plate numbers 2, 7, 16, 17, 18, 19, 22, 25, 26, 29, 32, 33, 36, 39, 51, 61, 66, 71; text figure number 7. Trustees of the British Museum: plate numbers 4, 14, 57, 72, 76, 84, 86, 91, 93; text figure numbers 2, 3, 4, 5, 6, 9, 12, 17, 19, 20, 21, 22, 25, 37, 40, 43, 44, 47, 48, 49, 55, 56. Photographique des Musées Nationaux: plate numbers 5, 11, 20, 38, 69, 74, 75; text figure numbers 50, 59. Edwin Smith: back of jacket; plate numbers 6, 13, 27, 30, 31, 34, 35, 40, 41, 43, 46, 50, 53, 56, 63, 64, 65, 67, 68, 70, 92; text figure numbers 8, 39, 53, 54, 57, 58. Reproduced by Gracious Permission of Her Majesty the Queen: plate numbers 15, 78, 79. Kunsthistorisches Museum, Vienna: plate numbers 21, 85. Reproduced by Courtesy of the Trustees of the National Gallery, London: plate numbers 42, 44, 45. Reproduced by permission of the Syndics of the Fitzwilliam Museum, Cambridge: plate number 47. The Tower of London: plate number 48; text figure number 27. Bulloz, Paris: plate number 49; text figure numbers 28, 29, 31, 34, 52; back endpapers. Giraudon, Paris: plate numbers 54, 55, 62, 87; text figure number 1. Jean A. Fortier, Paris: plate number 73. Historisches Museum, Berne: plate number 89; text figure number 51. Victoria and Albert Museum, London; Crown Copyright: front endpapers; text figure numbers 32, 33, 38, 41. Public Record Office, London: text figure numbers 15, 18, 24, 26, 45. National Portrait Gallery, London: text figure number 23. Glasgow Art Gallery and Museum: text figure number 30. The Governing Body of Christ Church, Oxford: text figure number 35. Reproduced by permission of the Ministry of Public Buildings and Works; Crown Copyright: text figure number 36.

The maps were specially drawn for this volume by Mr T. Stalker Miller. Note: The sizes of the originals of all illustrations are given in centimetres.

List of plates

83 Fifteenth-century battle scene (Ms fr 2691, fo. 197).
84 *Danse Macabre* (Arundel Ms 83, fo. 127).
85 Portrait of the Emperor Sigismund of Luxemburg, attributed to Pisanello.
86 John, duke of Bedford, kneeling before St George (Add. Ms 18850, fo. 256b).
87 Portrait of Philip the Good, duke of Burgundy, after van der Weyden.
88 A siege, from Wavrin's Chronicles (Ms fr 87, fo. 1).
89 Detail from the tapestry *La Justice de Trajan et d'Archambault*.
90 Portrait of Louis II of Anjou.
91 Henry VI crowned king of France in 1431 from the *Life and Acts of Richard Beauchamp, earl of Warwick*, by John Rous (Cotton Ms Julius E IV Art. vi, fo. 24).
92 Portrait of John VIth lord Talbot.
93 Surrender of a town (Royal Ms 20 C VII, fo. 190).
94 Jousting, from Wavrin's Chronicles (Ms fr 87, fo. 58v).

Jacket front: The battle of Agincourt (25 October 1415); French, fifteenth century. *London, Victoria and Albert Museum.*
Jacket back: Ivory mirror-case showing a tournament; French, fourteenth century. *London, Victoria and Albert Museum.*
Front endpaper: Brasses of Sir John de Cobham of Cobham, Kent; T. de Cobham of Cobham, Kent; J. Cheyne of Drayton-Beauchamp, Buckinghamshire; and L. Cheyne of Drayton-Beauchamp, Buckinghamshire, *c.* 1365. *London, Victoria and Albert Museum.*
Back endpaper: Montage of fourteenth- and fifteenth-century arms including a sword, dagger, hand-gun, misericord, knife and crossbow.
Binding brass: The arms of France and of England as they appeared on the Henry VI *Grand Blanc* minted at Mâcon.

MAPS

Chronological table

1154 Accession of Henry Plantagenet, duke of Normandy and of Aquitaine, count of Anjou, Maine and Touraine, to the English throne. Beginning of the Plantagenet dynasty in England.

1259 *Treaty of Paris*. Henry III of England surrenders his claim to all those lands in France conquered by Philip Augustus (Normandy, Anjou, Maine, Touraine and Poitou), and agrees to hold the remaining Plantagenet fiefs in France by liége homage. This was the principal source of subsequent dispute.

1327 Accession of Edward III (1327–77) to the English throne.

1328 Death of the last Capetian king of France, Charles IV. Edward III's claim to succeed him is rejected and Philip of Valois accedes to the French throne as Philip VI. Beginning of the Valois dynasty in France.

1337 Edward III sends a letter of defiance to 'Philip of Valois, who calls himself king of France'. Beginning of the Hundred Years War.

1339 Edward III's first campaign in France, the Thiérache campaign.

1340 Edward III assumes the title of 'king of England and France' (26 January). Defeat of the French fleet at Sluys (24 June).

1345–7 English campaigns in Normandy, Brittany and Aquitaine; battle of Crécy (26 August 1346) and capture of Calais (4 August 1347).

1350 Death of Philip VI and accession of John II, 'the Good' (1350–64).

1355–7 English campaigns in northern and southern France; battle of Poitiers (19 September 1356) and capture of King John.

1359–60 Edward III's last great campaign: he fails to get himself crowned 'king of France' at Reims, is unable to take Paris and agrees to the preliminaries of a peace at *Brétigny* near Chartres (8 May 1360). A modified version of this treaty is ratified at *Calais* (24 October 1360). Peace until 1369.

1364 Death of John II and accession of Charles V, 'the Wise' (1364–80). Grant of the duchy of Burgundy to Charles' brother Philip the Bold.

1369–73 Renewal of the war and French reconquest of most of the territories ceded to Edward III at Brétigny.

1377 Death of Edward III and accession of Richard II (1377–99), aged eleven.

1378 Beginning of the Great Schism (1378–1417) in the western Church.

1380 Death of Charles V and accession of Charles VI (1380–1422), aged eleven.

1389 *Truce of Leulinghen*, renewed again and again, prevents any major campaign until 1404.

1396 Marriage of Richard II to Isabella of France, daughter of Charles VI. A twenty-eight year truce is agreed to but the two monarchs are unable to conclude a peace.

1399 Deposition of Richard II by John of Gaunt's son Henry Bolingbroke, who secures the throne as Henry IV (1399–1413).

1407 Assassination of Charles VI's brother Louis of Orléans by John the Fearless, duke of Burgundy (1404–19), and beginning of civil war in France between the partisans of the duke of Burgundy (Burgundians) and those of the duke of Orléans, called Armagnacs, after the marriage in 1410 between Charles, son of Louis of Orléans, and the daughter of Bernard VII, count of Armagnac.

1413 Death of Henry IV and accession of Henry V (1413–22).

1415 Henry V invades France. Capture of Harfleur (23 September) and defeat of the French army at Agincourt (25 October).

1417 Henry V embarks upon the systematic conquest of Normandy. The Armagnacs, in control of Paris since 1413, maintain themselves in the French capital by a policy of terror. John the Fearless and Isabella of Bavaria, Charles VI's wife, set up at Troyes a rival government to that of the dauphin, the future Charles VII.

1418 John the Fearless secures control of Paris and the dauphin escapes to south of the Loire.

1419 John the Fearless is assassinated at Montereau, where he was to have reached an agreement with the dauphin and the Armagnacs. He is succeeded by Philip the Good (1419–67), who immediately allies himself with Henry V.

1420 The *treaty of Troyes* is the result of this alliance. Henry V is to marry Catherine, the daughter of Charles VI, and become king of France on the death of his father-in-law.

1422 Premature death of Henry V, followed by that of Charles VI. There are now two kings of France: Henry VI, the ten-month old son of Henry V, and Charles VII. Henry V's brother John, duke of

Bedford, becomes regent of France, and a regency council under the protectorship of John's younger brother Humphrey, duke of Gloucester, assumes control in England.

1422–9   The English frontier is slowly pushed south: Maine is added to Normandy, and in 1428 Orléans is invested.

1429   Joan of Arc relieves Orléans (8 May), and Charles VII is crowned king of France at Reims (18 July).

1435   *Treaty of Arras.* Philip the Good makes peace with Charles VII. Death of Bedford.

1436   English evacuation of Paris.

1444–9   *Truce of Tours* suspends hostilities.

1449–53   Charles VII reconquers Normandy and Guyenne; defeat of the English army at Castillon (17 July 1453). Beginning of civil war in England.

1461   Defeat of Henry VI's army at Towton and accession of Edward IV (1461–83).

1474–5   Edward IV invades France, but settles for a pension at *Picquigny* (29 August 1475).

1485   Defeat and death of Richard III at the battle of Bosworth. Accession of Henry Tudor to the throne as Henry VII. End of the Plantagenet dynasty.

1492   *Treaty of Étaples* (3 November 1492). Henry VII makes peace with France.

1498   Death of Charles VIII and end of the Valois dynasty in France.

Note on money

Fig. 2   Coin: gold *guiennois* of the first issue of Edward III, minted at Bordeaux, 1360. *Obverse:* the king in full armour standing under a gothic-style portal; *reverse:* floriate cross with leopard and lis in alternate angles. *London, British Museum.*

Fig. 3   Coin: *demi-gros*, leopard type, minted at Piedfort. Light issue of Edward III (before 1460). *Obverse:* leopard; *reverse:* plain cross with one lis. *London, British Museum.*

References to money given in the text are to their fourteenth and fifteenth-century values. There were two types of money in the Middle Ages: money of account and actual coinage. The relationship between the two fluctuated as a result of alterations made by the public authorities of the times.

(a) *Money of account.* In both France and England this consisted of pounds (*livres*), each composed of 20 shillings (*sous*), which in turn were made up of 12 pennies (*deniers*). The *livre tournois* was the most common in France (though other systems existed, like the *livre parisis*), the *livre sterling* (£) in England, and the *livre bordelaise* in Guyenne. The exchange rate between these different systems varied according to alterations made from time to time by the kings of England and of France. During the greater part of the period under review there were 5 *livres bordelaises* to £1 sterling, and for much of the fourteenth century there were 6 *livres tournois* to £1 sterling. During the English occupation of northern France in the fifteenth century, however, there were 9 *livres tournois* to £1 sterling. Another money of account was the *mark*, of which the English variety was always worth two-thirds of £1 sterling (13s. 4d.).

(b) *Coinage.* The coins most frequently referred to in the text are: (i) the English silver penny which, since it was also a money of account, was always worth 1/240th of £1 sterling, though its silver content (18 grains in 1351, 15 grains in 1412; 1 grain = 0.064 grammes) varied; (ii) the florin, first minted in Florence in 1252, but subsequently imitated by other countries; its average gold content was 3.50 grammes; (iii) the *franc d'or,* first issued by King John in 1360, which was worth 20 *sous tournois,* and contained 3.88 grammes of gold; (iv) the *écu à la couronne,* which was worth 22s. 6d. *tournois* at the end of the fourteenth century, and contained 3.99 grammes of gold.

It is not possible to give accurate present day equivalents to these currencies; but their relative values should appear from the text where, unless otherwise stated, the figures are given in sterling. It may be of some assistance to the reader to note that in fourteenth-century England the ordinary revenue of the Crown (i.e. without parliamentary taxes) averaged about £30,000 *per annum,* and in a good year total income seldom exceeded £100,000 including parliamentary subsidies. Probably half a dozen earls had annual incomes from land of around £3,000, but the majority of knights enjoyed only around £60 from their estates. The daily pay of a knight in the king's army was 2 shillings—a substantial sum for the times, and one which had to pay for the keep of two or three horses, a page or a valet and, more often than not, both. The Statute of Labourers (1351), which attempted to fix maximum wages in the years following the first outbreaks of the Black Death, allowed 10 shillings a year for a ploughman (i.e. a skilled labourer). Though this was almost everywhere exceeded, a ploughman who earned £2–£3 a year was doing very well for himself.

I France in the later Middle Ages.

Introductory: The Hundred Years War as a historical concept

On 24 May 1337 Philip VI of France, in his court and in accordance with the law and procedure of the time, declared the French lands of 'the king of England, duke of Aquitaine, peer of France, count of Ponthieu' to be confiscate. By way of reply Edward III seized French property in England, issued a manifesto to his subjects and on 7 October once again laid claim to the French throne, as he had done nine years earlier on the death of Charles IV. Just over two years later, at a great court ceremony in Ghent on 26 January 1340, he assumed the title of 'king of England and France', which was to be borne by his descendants for nearly five centuries. He quartered the arms of France, had the fleur-de-lys engraved on his seal, furnished himself with a red and blue surcoat embroidered with leopards and lilies and dated his documents 'in the fourteenth year of our reign in England and in the first in France'. In so doing he initiated a policy from which it proved difficult for him and his successors to withdraw without losing face and creating insuperable problems for themselves, and he set in motion a train of events which were to transform a three year-old war into a conflict which lasted for more than a century. To this struggle historians have given the name 'The Hundred Years War', of which the traditional limits are 1337 and 1453.

Although the phrase does not seem to have been used before the middle of the nineteenth century, the concept of a long and distinctive struggle appeared quite early. Already in the second decade of the fifteenth century French propagandists, anxious to refute English claims to the French Crown by developing the theory of a Salic Law, traced the wars of their time back to 1328. One of them, a secretary of Charles VI called Jean de Montreuil, in a pamphlet *A toute la chevalerie de France*, even says that the hostilities had been going on *puis cent ans*—though his statement was a trifle premature. To the Italian cleric Polydore Vergil of Urbino, the first draft of whose *Anglica Historia* was completed in 1513, they were *aeternum, ut ita decam, inter se bellum*. François de Mézeray, in his *Histoire de France* (1643), appears to have been the first person to think in terms of a single continuous war beginning in 1337 and which he considered to have lasted one hundred and sixty years. David Hume, in his *History of England* (1762), wrote of a period of Anglo-French involvement 'during more than a century' and for Henry Hallam, in his *View of the State of Europe during the Middle Ages* (1818), 'it was a struggle of one hundred and twenty years'. Both Hume and Hallam thought that the period 1337 to 1453 had a distinctive unity, a view which was shared by François Guizot in his lectures at the Sorbonne in 1828. But it did not harden into a historical concept before the publication of Henri Martin's influential *Histoire de France* (1855). In this work Martin divided the period into chapters, each bearing the title *Guerres des Anglais*, and during the following six years someone in France coined the phrase *La guerre de cent ans*. Edgar Boutaric used it in passing in an essay on French military organization which appeared in the *Bibliothèque de l'École des Chartes* in 1861 and Henri Wallon did likewise in his *Richard II* three years later. It was Edward Freeman who, in the *Fortnightly Review* for May 1869, recommended its adoption in England. 'The French are perfectly right' he wrote, 'in speaking of the whole time from Edward the Third to Henry the Sixth as the Hundred Years War'. Guizot used the title for the chapter headings of his *Histoire de France* (1873) and John Richard Green, probably on Freeman's advice, did likewise in his *Short History of the English People* (1874). The extraordinary popularity of these two works did much to establish the phrase. It was used in the titles of numerous French monographs in the 1870s and first appeared in the *Encyclopaedia Britannica* in 1879.

Many twentieth-century historians, while unable to avoid using the phrase, have found the concept misleading in that it highlights the dynastic issue and a period of Anglo-French involvement that no longer seems to hold any special unity in itself. The wars of the period are seen to have formed no more than a phase of a wider conflict which had its origins in the Norman Conquest of England and the Angevin inheritance of Aquitaine, and which was not finally terminated with the loss of Bordeaux in 1453. Some historians would still prefer to see Edward III's war and Henry V's war as quite separate from one another and it has recently been pointed out that Henry VI's title to the French throne was based, not on Edward III's claim, but upon the provisions of the treaty of Troyes. No peace treaty followed the French conquest of Guyenne in 1453; Edward IV's invasion of 1474, the English intervention in Brittany in 1488 and Henry VII's invasion of 1492, although they were speedily terminated, were in the tradition of Edward III's and Henry V's wars. For a decade after the fall of Bordeaux the English government acted on the assumption that Aquitaine would be recovered, Calais continued to be held by the Crown until 1558, and the kings of England did not abandon their title as kings of France until the treaty of Amiens in 1802, though all that then remained of conquest and inheritance were the Channel Islands.

It is now generally agreed that the causes of the war lay, not merely in the disputed succession, but in the entire way in which the two countries were developing. Up to some point in the thirteenth century, the effective political, social, economic and cultural units were in many ways not England and France as we think of them today, but a Norman empire, an Angevin empire, and a Capetian empire—in so far as the word 'empire' can be used to describe groupings of territories that owed more to feudal and family ties than they did to anything else. In the early history of the two countries we are faced with a past that is Anglo-French, rather than English or French, and the process of national development was by no means completed by 1337. While in the long run the wars of the fourteenth and fifteenth centuries helped to crystallize that development, they held it up for a while and there was more than one moment in the years between 1337 and 1453 when the political map of western Europe looked very different from that which was to emerge during the following fifty years. On the other hand, already in the thirteenth century, the feudal ties established between the French monarchy and the rulers who held the English Crown were becoming incompatible with the centralization and institutionalization of political authority which occurred early in England and which gathered momentum in thirteenth-century France. It was above all else from these two ultimately contradictory processes in their development that the Hundred Years War was to spring.

Yet there is much to be said for regarding Anglo-French hostilities in the years between 1337 and 1453 as distinct from earlier and later wars. The older historians, including Mézeray, were not blind to the more distant causes of the war, indeed, they emphasized the earlier conflicts. But they also saw that Edward III's claim to the French throne inaugurated a new period in Anglo-French relations. It may be that twentieth-century historians, in unravelling the earlier history of Aquitaine and concentrating their attention upon the origins of the war, rather than on the war aims of the kings and the history of the war itself, have lost sight of the change in the relationship between the two countries that resulted from Edward's claim. For the assumption of the French royal title, as events turned out, not only made it impossible

Fig. 4 Coin: *Grand Blanc* of
Henry VI, minted at Mâcon.
Obverse: the shields of France and
England; *reverse:* cross with lis and
leopard. *London, British Museum.*

for a lasting peace to be made—even at Brétigny in 1360—but it also initiated a long period in Anglo-French relations which, up to 1492, was marked by an almost continuous state of war or truce. Prior to 1337 this had not been the case, since outbreaks of war had always been followed by a peace, however unsatisfactory or incomplete. But after 1337 an immense body of legal claims—by the king of England to the French Crown and by the king of France to sovereignty in Aquitaine—was painstakingly built up by either side and these made it very difficult to reach a compromise. Other factors also made it difficult to conclude a lasting peace. Up to 1378 the papacy played an important role as peacemaker, organizing conferences under its mediation and patching up truces at what were often critical junctures. But the advent of the Schism (1378–1417) at the moment when the chances of a reconciliation were at their highest, left no international body capable of carrying on the work of mediation; for the emperor no longer commanded the moral and political authority to carry out the task, as the efforts of Sigismund (cf. pl. 85) in 1416 only too sadly proved. Moreover, as the war proceeded and spread from province to province, it became increasingly more difficult for both the French and the English to disband the more or less permanent garrison forces which had been brought into being without creating major problems for themselves. For the Hundred Years War coincided with a period of plague, famine and economic decline, in which many men had come to depend upon war for a living and, on the English side, it was very difficult for the king to keep the peace and his throne at home unless he prosecuted active war in France.

Whilst contemporaries were not in a position to appreciate it, with the fall of Bordeaux in 1453 the war had in fact been brought to an end. Between then and 1477 the real threat to the French monarchy came not from England, but from the dukes of Burgundy; and although a number of English incursions were made into France, they did not result in extended war or military occupation. At Picquigny, on 29 August 1475, Edward IV settled for a seven years' truce in return for a sum of money and a pension from Louis XI. Thereafter, English chancery documents ceased to refer to the king of France as 'our adversary of France', and from Richard III's time they invariably referred to him as 'king of France', while at the same time giving the title to the king of England. The final turning point came with the treaty of Étaples on 3 November 1492. For, although by its terms Henry VII renounced neither the French throne nor the old English territories in France, this treaty was no longer a truce but a peace which laid the foundations of a more permanent settlement. It was ratified by all the provincial and local Estates in France and included provisions for its renewal under the successors of the two monarchs. The period between 1453 and 1492 thus saw a fundamental change in Anglo-French relations. It was also during these years that the French monarchy triumphed over the princes who had contributed so much to the length of the war by their separatist policies. With their eclipse, and with the settlement with England, the way was cleared for Charles VIII's invasion of Italy in 1494, which opened a new era in the history of France, and indeed of western Europe.

The Kingdom of France and the Plantagenet dominions

On Tuesday, 1 February 1328, the last Capetian king of France, Charles IV, died prematurely at his castle of Vincennes near Paris from an illness that had confined him to his bed on Christmas Day previous. He had no children but left his wife pregnant. After the king's burial a few days later an assembly of princes, peers and barons, assisted by a number of doctors of canon and civil law, appointed his cousin, Philip of Valois, to be regent of the realm, possibly thereby merely ratifying Charles' last wishes, since Philip appears to have been acting in that capacity during the king's illness. It was also decided that if the queen gave birth to a son, Philip was to be regent until the child's majority; but if her child was a daughter, Philip was to ascend the throne. Thus for the third time in twelve years, after more than three centuries in which the crown of France had passed in continuous and uninterrupted succession from father to son, the female descendants of the last four Capetian kings were debarred from the throne (cf. genealogical table).

There were sound reasons why the assembly should act decisively and with promptness for the situation which arose on Charles' death was not without instructive precedents. On his death in 1316 Louis X had left a seven year-old daughter of doubtful legitimacy by his first wife and his second wife was pregnant. After more than five weeks in which the country had been governed by a council of nobles, Louis' brother Philip had managed to impose himself as regent; but the assembly which gave formal assent to his regency had left the future of the succession open, should Louis' posthumous child prove to be a daughter. When the son to whom the queen had given birth died within a few days, Philip had seized the throne (though not without considerable opposition) at the expense of his niece Jeanne and his elder sister Isabella. On Philip's death in 1322 his brother Charles had likewise thrust aside Philip's daughters. Thus between 1316 and 1328 the succession had been settled, not by any predetermined law, but by a succession of *faits accomplis*. But on Charles IV's death there remained one child of Philip IV: Isabella, the mother of Edward III of England.

Isabella, notorious for her marital inconstancy, though in part excused by her husband's weaknesses, was a woman of evil character, a notorious schemer and not the person to let her claim be passed over lightly. In 1325, while engaged on a mission to her brother to try and settle the latest developments in the eternal problem of Gascony, she had eloped with the Welsh marcher lord, Roger Mortimer. Together they had led a rebellion which, two years later, had resulted in the deposition and subsequent murder of her husband and the succession to the throne of her son Edward III (cf. pl. 6) who, until the removal of Mortimer in 1330, was under the tutelage of his mother and her lover. Already after the death of Louis X's posthumous son, Edward II had at least considered claiming a share of the kingdom—presumably thereby accepting that Louis' daughter could not accede to the throne. In 1328 the incapacity of a female to succeed must also have been tacitly accepted by Isabella since otherwise her nieces patently had a better claim than she. But in the great assembly that appointed Philip of Valois regent in February, Edward III's claim was advanced by his proctors on the grounds that his mother could transmit her rights to him and that by virtue of those rights he was the nearest male heir to the late king Charles IV—a fact that is incontestable, since he was the nephew of the late king, whereas Philip of Valois was only the cousin. He may even have convinced some of the doctors of law as to the validity of this argument; but there were good and sound reasons why the assembly should reject it. For although Edward's ancestry was as 'French' as Philip's, though he spoke French, was duke of Aquitaine, count of Ponthieu and a peer of France, he was at the time only fifteen and clearly not his own master, whereas Philip was thirty-five. The prospect of the rule of Isabella and Mortimer in France was hardly likely to appeal to the assembly; nor was the power of a king who would add the domain of the English Crown and the Plantagenet fiefs in France to that of the Capetians. Moreover, to accept the argument that a woman could transmit her rights to her son spelt trouble for the future. For if one of Edward's cousins were subsequently to give birth to a son, the latter would be a grandson to a Capetian king, whereas Edward was only the nephew. The dangers inherent in accepting Edward's argument were thus very real and in part confirmed by subsequent events. For in 1332 Louis X's daughter gave birth to Charles of Navarre, who was later able to maintain that, not only was he more closely related to the last Capetians than was Philip of Valois, but that he was also more closely related to them than was Edward III. Edward's claim was accordingly rejected even before Charles IV's posthumous daughter was born and, although he vociferously resisted Philip's elevation to the throne, Philip was on the spot, well liked and in charge of the situation and there was nothing that Edward could do immediately.

The kingdom to which Philip succeeded was the richest and most populous in Europe. Extending north and west to the English Channel and the Atlantic Ocean, the eastern frontiers roughly followed the course of the Scheldt from its mouth to south of Cambrai, reached the Meuse to the north-east of Rethel, followed the upper course of that river and finally the courses of the Saône and the Rhône to their mouth in the Mediterranean. In the south they extended to the Pyrenees, save to the south-west where the kingdom of Navarre straddled the mountain range, and in the south-east where Roussillon was a sovereign possession of the house of Aragon (cf. map II). With a population perhaps five times greater than that of England and half as large again as that of Germany (they have been estimated at around 21 million, $4\frac{1}{2}$ million, and 14 million respectively), with a royal domain steadily built up by a succession of ruthless and enterprising kings and stretching over a good half of the kingdom, with a capital whose 80,000 inhabitants were more than twice as numerous as those of London, and with a steadily expanding machinery of government, the kingdom of France seemed certain to retain the hegemony in western Europe which it had achieved during the course of the thirteenth century, in particular under Saint Louis (1226–70). The Plantagenet stranglehold on the western provinces had been broken; Philip IV (1285–1314), in his conflict with the papacy, had dramatically demonstrated who was to be the master of the French Church; the count of Flanders had been brought to heel; while elsewhere, in the north and east, French hegemony was being established. A hundred years earlier all this would have been inconceivable.

It had not been an easy task. Until the end of the eleventh century the royal domain (those counties which had not been alienated and where the king was proprietor of estates, courts, mills, churches, etc.) was both small and insecure, and hardly extended beyond the cities of Paris and Orléans. It had been the task of Louis VI (1108–37) and Louis VII (1137–80) to make such acquisitions as they could and to reduce it to order, by securing control over the castellans and officials in charge of it. The increased resources which the monarchy thereby enjoyed, and the greater authority it was consequently able to exercise over its vassals, were turned to account during the reign of Philip Augustus (1180–1223), when a unique opportunity was presented by the internal divisions within the Angevin empire.

This remarkable assemblage of territories which had been brought together by inheritance, conquest and marriage, constituted the dominions of one of the king's vassals, Henry Plantagenet, who secured the throne of England in 1154. Apart from his lands north of the English Channel, Henry II was duke of Normandy, lord of Brittany, count of Anjou (to which were annexed Maine and Touraine) and, through his marriage to Eleanor of Aquitaine, the divorced wife of Louis VII of France, he was duke of Aquitaine (which included Gascony and Poitou). The whole amounted to some two-fifths of the area of the kingdom of France and occupied, in an unbroken stretch, the entire western half of the country. Fortunately for the kings of France, the extent of these dominions and the number of powerful vassals established in them (especially in Aquitaine where the ducal power was slight) posed insuperable problems of government to the Plantagenets, of which Philip and his successors were able to take advantage. Between 1202 and 1204 Normandy, Anjou, Brittany and a part of Poitou fell into Philip's hands and during the next fifty years much of the remainder of Henry II's inheritance was secured by the kings of France. The loss of most of these territories by the kings of England was recognized in the treaty of Paris of 1259 which reconstituted a much reduced duchy of Aquitaine for Henry III and his heirs (cf. below, pp. 47-8). Nor was this the only achievement of its kind during the thirteenth century. The county of Champagne was gradually absorbed by a series of politic marriages and the vast county of Toulouse was incorporated into the domain through an opportune intervention in the Albigensian crusade. This carried the royal administration into the heart of the *langue d'oc* and marked the first and longest step in the process which eventually united the south with the north.

The very success of the monarchy in enlarging the domain and in establishing its court as a court of appeal produced a rapid expansion in governmental machinery. Before the time of Philip Augustus the royal administration had been a modest enough affair. The king's main concern had been to exploit and, in some sense, govern his domain. This he was able to do through his *prévôts* and castellans, whose offices were hereditary and whose activities were closely restricted to the domain. During Philip's reign local officers known as *baillis* or *sénéchaux* came to be appointed, the *baillis* being found generally in the north, the *sénéchaux* in the south. To begin with their work was itinerant and supervisory; they were expected to see that royal officials and seigneurs having judicial and other powers were carrying out their responsibilities. Later they became sedentary and active, superseding to a large extent both royal *prévôts* and seigniorial government. Occasionally, when their work got out of hand, *enquêteurs* were sent to supervise them—a typical medieval stratification; and during the course of the thirteenth century, for the government of the more outlying parts of the kingdom, several *sénéchaussées* might temporarily be grouped together into a single circumscription under a lieutenant-general with viceregal powers.

At the centre the old undifferentiated, unspecialized and irregularly attended *curia regis* was departmentalized and largely professionalized to deal with the increasing work created by an expanding domain and the increased jurisdiction which that involved. During the thirteenth century the outlines of a *chambre des comptes* and a *trésor*, concerned with the administration of the royal revenues, began to emerge. At the same time, pressure of judicial work in the *curia* led first to regular sessions which were called, as in England, 'parliaments', then to a process of professionalization which made the judicial activities of the *curia* into a distinct institution. In France this high court preserved the name *parlement*, for the judicial business crowded out other work, whereas in England, where there were already other central courts for the discharge of ordinary judicial business and the king's first need was to raise money, the term parliament remained attached to the body whose functions were more than judicial. The remainder of the ancient *curia*, occupied in matters which were neither specifically judicial nor specifically financial, came to be known as the *grand conseil*. In the fourteenth century all three departments still reunited on occasion and temporarily reconstituted the ancient *curia*; but such occasions grew more and more infrequent and the king came to rule with a smaller body of councillors (*conseil étroit, privé, sécret*) in more or less permanent being and with a fairly well-defined membership.

There was nothing in France to correspond to the medieval English parliament. Like their English contemporaries, the kings of France in the late thirteenth and early fourteenth centuries found it necessary to supplement their revenues by *aides* which, according to universal feudal custom, technically required consent. For such, and occasionally also for other purposes, the king summoned assemblies known as *états*. But the Estates rarely, even in principle, represented the kingdom as a whole; often they were quite local. The king might even prefer to deal direct with a particular group of notables: the local nobility, the clergy or a municipality; and those consulted often appear to have preferred things that way. Meetings of provincial Estates were normally only the preliminaries to local bargaining between the king's officials and the towns or feudal lords. Their main purpose was to secure information about the resources of the localities. Larger gatherings were called together irregularly and their composition varied. From the first they offered little promise of developing into an institution which might become the basis of a constitutional monarchy.

The king ruled through and with his council, assisted in the provinces by *baillis* and *sénéchaux* working to their orders and, invariably in the south, under the direction of a lieutenant-general, usually of the blood royal, to whom the local officials acted as a council. Outside the royal domain, in those parts of France which formed part of the great fiefs, his vassals were left in charge of affairs and developed administrations of their own to carry out the work of government. Departments of government had been established at Paris to deal with the ordinary revenues derived from the domain (the *trésor*) and the extraordinary revenues or *aides* negotiated with local corporations or estates (the *chambre des comptes*). Above and beyond all, the *parlement de Paris*, the supreme judicial tribunal of the kingdom, made itself felt throughout the realm. It was a court of appeal not only from decisions reached in the courts of officials on the royal domain and from the seigniorial jurisdiction, but also from the courts of all the king's vassals and their officials, including the great feudatories.

It was a large and diverse realm, hard for the king and his contemporaries to visualize as a territorial entity, unaccustomed as they probably were to thinking of the kingdom in territorial terms and of precise linear frontiers. There were then no good maps available to give any clear idea of what assemblage of lands made up the kingdom and, before the fifteenth century, no descriptions of the different *pays* of which it was composed. But the contrasts and diversities of the landscape must have been striking, as also must the different ways of life that it supported. The rich cornlands of northern France, with their regular open-fields, greater population density and village communities, were in marked contrast to the poorer and more sparsely populated territories of the central regions, to the enclosed fields of Maine and the confines of the Massif-Central with their more scattered communities, and to the Bordelais with its vineyards and irregular open-fields. Within each of these regions the contrasts between plateau and valley, of settlement, wealth and employment, must have been equally striking. The plateaux of Burgundy and Poitou were also lands of rich harvests, but in the west the marshlands of southern Brittany and the Vendée, for all the great work of drainage that had gone on in the thirteenth century, supported a very different way of life, especially in and around Guérande, then the centre of a prosperous salt-extracting region, and the anchorage of the great northern fleets which carried cargoes to England and had contact with the herring fisheries of southern Sweden. All along the Loire valley, in Anjou and the Orléannais and in Burgundy, as in the south-west, around Bordeaux and in the region of Entre-Deux-Mers, the countryside was dominated by the vine.

The contrasts between north and south, between Languedoïl and Languedoc, contrasts of climate, language, customs, traditions—of two ways of life—must have been the most marked of all. For although the old civilization of the south had now passed away, its influences were everywhere to be seen and heard. A reasonably educated Englishman would have had no difficulty in making himself understood in most places north of the Loire valley, however odd his French may have sounded to Parisian ears; but south of the Loire he would have found most of the people he met incomprehensible, as would any native of northern France. Even the buildings were strikingly different in the south-east. In Languedoc and up the Rhône valley as far as Lyons many of the houses were built of stone and were perhaps several stories high. They were more akin to those of Italy than to the timber and wattle dwellings of the north.

'In distant and foreign countries', wrote the chronicler Jean Froissart, 'one may well marvel at the noble realm of France, therein are so many towns and castles, both in the distant marches and in the heart of the realm'. Froissart was clearly impressed with the wealth of the country but it was, of course, a predominantly rural land rather than one of urban communities. It was a kingdom, he also tells us, 'full of large villages, fine country, sweet rivers, good ponds, fair meadows, mellow and full-bodied wines, and of a temperate climate'. Paris apart, there were no towns to rank with the great Italian cities in size; but there were several with around 30,000 inhabitants: Rouen, Bordeaux, Toulouse and the great Flemish cloth-making towns of Ghent, Ypres and Bruges, swarming with artisans and humming with looms, the centres of a great international trade. By English standards they were veritable metropoli. 'And the town is larger than any town in England save London', Michael de Northburgh wrote of Caen in 1346, and he makes other comparisons: Barfleur which was as large as Sandwich, Carentan which was as large as Leicester and Saint-Lô which was greater than Lincoln. But large and numerous as the towns of France undoubtedly were in comparison with those of England, by our standards they were little more than overgrown villages. The majority of the population lived in country parishes, working on the estates or paying rents to a landholding noble class, which resided in castles and manors to be found throughout the country.

The nobility were distinguished by their landed wealth, by the inheritance of property in both land and jurisdiction which the noble family passed on and hoped to augment from generation to generation. They were, however, neither a large nor a homogeneous section of society but showed great differences in wealth and standing. They may be very arbitrarily divided into two categories: a higher nobility and a lesser nobility or *petite-noblesse*. The former, around sixty families or so, but varying in number from one period to another according to new creations and the fortunes of existing families (marriages, lack of heirs and the like), had the title of duke, count, or, in the south, *vicomte*. Some of these were very powerful men for, unlike their contemporaries in England, their territorial holdings coincided with the duchies, counties and *vicomtés* that gave them their titles. The latter category were designated knights (about 2,000 or so) and enjoyed the titles of *messire, seigneur* or *dominus*, deriving from their possession of one or more castles, the exercise of seigniorial rights and jurisdiction or both; or else they were esquires (about 15,000 or so; *écuyer, damoiseau, domicellus* were the names commonly given to the sons of knights who had not been dubbed, but also to other men who never attained knighthood). The words 'knight' and 'esquire' were used throughout the country, but in some parts such men might be referred to simply as *noble* or *noble homme*.

Le duc de bretai
gne seu vint a
baugency sur
loire z sa ordon
na vne partie de ses besongnes
pour venir vers paris. En cel
lui mesmes temps entra a
paris auant que le duc de
bretaigne y entrast la royne
de secille z de iherusalem qui
femme auoit este au duc dan

dame pour ce en faisie men
tion ameuoit son ieune fil
lois en sa compaignie lequl
on nommoit ia par toutte
france roy des terres dessus
En leur compaignie estoit
iehan de bretaigne frere a sa
dame z venoient a paris.
Auant que sa dame entrast
a paris elle signiffia au
duc de berri z de bourgoigne

By far the most important of the higher nobility were the four great feudatories: the dukes of Brittany, Burgundy and Guyenne, and the count of Flanders, all of them peers of France. These men controlled such extensive territories and had such wide powers of jurisdiction that it is appropriate to think of them as princes and their fiefs as principalities. Already by the beginning of the fourteenth century each of them had built up within his principality a machinery of government in various stages of development; some were more precocious than others, but all were closely modelled on that of the king. Each had a *curia* in a more or less advanced state of specialization into *conseil, parlement* and *chambre des comptes* (though the names varied from one to another), and each had an organized system of local government.

These developments had been fostered and aided by a variety of circumstances. The county of Flanders had a Germanic population at the core and the duchy of Brittany a Celtic nucleus. The former was a region of exceptional economic development and the latter held a strategically vital position adjacent to the sea routes. All four principalities were situated on the frontiers of the kingdom and had interests outside it: Flanders and Burgundy held territories within the Empire, and Brittany in England. The duke of Guyenne was also the king of England, his dominions tied together by an economic reciprocity centred on the wine trade; and the county of Flanders was dependent on English wool to supply the industries of her great cloth manufacturing towns. Other nobles, like the counts of Forez and Beaujolais and the *vicomte* of Béarn, also had a machinery of government with which to administer their territories, though for the most part less complex and in a less advanced state of development than that of the great fiefs. On the morrow of the accession of Philip of Valois, only five very small *apanages* (grants of lands to members of the royal family on terms of relative independence) remained, for by a freak of chance most of the *apanages* created by thirteenth-century kings had reverted to the royal domain, either because their possessors inherited the crown, or because they died without issue. The holders of these remaining *apanages* were on a level with the little dynasties of counts, such as those of Blois, Rethel, Bar and Nevers, and they were of no great danger to the monarchy.

The lesser nobility were a mixture of old-established families and *parvenus* who had attained their rank through royal or comtal service, the acquisition of rural lordships, the holding of fiefs, or marriage into the group. As with the higher nobility, they were not a homogeneous class, and there was a great disproportion of wealth and standing between them. The wealthier of them, those who held several castles and lordships, were nearer to the less well-to-do comtal families than they were to the relatively poor knights and esquires who constituted the majority of the *petite noblesse,* many of whom led a life not very different from that of their tenants, except that they did not till the land they possessed. We cannot yet make a detailed survey of this group for the whole of France. However, a study of the county of Forez shows the following: The count enjoyed an income of £2,400. Of the remaining 215 noble families two or three important barons (those holding several castles and fairly extensive lands) enjoyed incomes of between £200 and £400 and the holders of single castles (perhaps 20 or so) had an annual revenue of between £20 and £100. A large number of the remaining noble families enjoyed incomes of only £5 a year, from small demesnes no greater than the larger peasant holdings, and a few rents and tithes due from neighbouring tenants. Entry into the local nobility was not restricted. Technically, all sons of nobles were themselves noble and the status could only be conferred upon others by the king or a prince of the blood; but this seems to have been little more than a legal fiction. In Forez the noble families died out, through failure to provide heirs or through sheer poverty, at the rate of about half their number a century. They were replaced by men hailing from widely differing strata of society—fairly easily by the count's retainers and officials, less easily by merchants

2. The main façade of the Papal Palace, Avignon (1344–52).

23

and burgesses, more commonly by lawyers and, above all, by prosperous peasants. Such men did not require any formal act or letter conferring noble status, but merely acceptance by the local gentry of their right to call themselves *domicelli*.

But although the wealth and standing of the nobility varied widely, noble families were drawn together by mutual dependence, a number of privileges which set them apart from other sections of society, and a certain way of life. Above all they were drawn together by the noble profession of arms, by a knight's ability to fight on horseback with lance, sword and heavy armour, and by the income necessary to sustain these things. Knighthood also involved a code of chivalric behaviour, an obligation to observe the contemporary law of arms, whether on the battlefield or in the lists. The chroniclers of the period—Froissart, Monstrelet, Wavrin, to mention but a few—are full of the wars in which the nobility fought and they provide an invaluable commentary on their interests and their prejudices. Their self-consciousness as a privileged group was also displayed in their coat of arms, blazoned on their seals and shields. We still have a number of rolls of arms, manuscripts giving lists of knights who were present at a particular tournament or military enterprise, with coloured paintings of the armorial bearings which they carried into battle (cf. pl. 47).

Society was not divided up into neatly parcelled strata. Even the condition of the peasantry was not static or everywhere the same. Unlike England, where the process was far from complete, by the beginning of the fourteenth century most French lords had abandoned direct farming of their broad acres and instead collected rents from their tenants. Labour services on the manor, which the peasantry performed in return for their holdings, were everywhere giving way to paid labour and rent. Serfdom had almost disappeared in many parts of northern France, but in other regions it was still predominant, and in some places—like the Paris basin and the Bordelais—there were sharp contrasts. The fortunes of the peasantry differed as much as those of the nobility. Some families had secured manumissions, others had not. Some men of servile condition were making modest fortunes through renting part of a lord's lands and making a profit out of their labours. Others who were technically free were worse off. Between the prosperous manumitted tenant farmer, accumulating rents, with a foot on the ladder that led up into the nobility, and the man of servile condition, performing labour services on the lord's manor and with but a small personal holding, there was all the difference in the world. But these were only the poles of an unprivileged class and the way was open to the ambitious on the long road in between.

At the heart of the kingdom, in all but geography, was Paris, and the Ile-de-France, already acting as a magnet to neighbouring and to some outlying provinces (cf. pls. 1, 69). A political and cultural centre, though hardly an industrial or a commercial city, Paris was nevertheless the centre of a region which provided it with the wherewithal to support a growing court and bureaucracy and a large and cosmopolitan crowd of students at the University. To meet the demands of these sections of the civic population a multitude of crafts had been brought into existence, ranging from the manufacture of more commonplace articles to that of stained glass, musical instruments and illuminated manuscripts. By comparison with other French towns it was heavily peopled, as was the whole of the Ile-de-France. Taken together the population density amounted to more than four times that of the entire realm and even without Paris it was double that of the kingdom. By comparison with some of the leading Italian towns—Genoa for instance—this was not outstanding, for like many other north European cities Paris contained much of the neighbouring countryside within her walls. There were gardens and enclosures on the islands in the Seine, which had willows along its banks, and there was the open area of the Pré-aux-Clercs where tournaments were often held. To the south there were warrens

3. La Grosse Cloche, Porte St-Eloi, Bordeaux.

4. View of London from the *Poems of Charles of Orléans* (late fifteenth century). *London, British Museum Royal Ms 16 F II, fo. 73.* (18.8 × 15.9).

5. Portrait of King John (1350–64), attributed to Girart d'Orléans. *Louvre, Paris.* (59.8 × 44.6).

ēs nouuelles Dalbion
il vous en plaist escou
on tex 2 mou tōuli

Jehan rey de .auc.

at Saint-Germain, and the lanes of Saint-Sulpice wandered between vines. Viticulture was indeed an important industry throughout the Ile-de-France, which also provided grain and other produce to meet the needs of the city, as did the more distant fields of Picardy (grain), Beaune (wine), Perche (livestock) and, in times of scarcity, Normandy (hay, apples, corn)—goods which came by mule pack or in boats along the rivers. For the king and his court the Ile-de-France offered everything they required, not least some of the best hunting the country had to offer and this was their chief relaxation. The prosperity of the region had for long attracted immigrants from the poorer parts of France; but the unity of the area depended upon Paris, a regional capital which had become the capital of the kingdom. The Capetians had made Paris, but Paris had also made the French monarchy.

At the beginning of the fourteenth century the Plantagenet kings ruled over a much smaller realm than their contemporaries in France, for they were still far from controlling the whole of the British Isles and recent attempts in that direction had been but imperfectly fulfilled. Although Wales had been subjected (1276–95) under Edward I and was in future to give little serious trouble, ten years fighting in Scotland (1296–1307) had produced only fleeting success and, when Edward II's forces were defeated at Bannockburn in 1314, Scottish independence was dramatically proclaimed. Even in Ireland, theoretically conquered during the reign of Henry II, English authority rarely made itself felt outside the area around Dublin (the Pale) and further south around Cork and Waterford. Elsewhere, the chiefs of the Celtic clans, particularly powerful in Connaught and Ulster, and the Anglo-Irish families long settled in the country, took little notice of the king's lieutenants.

Within these somewhat restricted boundaries, the ability of the king to govern effectively ultimately depended upon his relations with the magnates of his realm. The development of political consciousness among the baronage had come early in England, as had the development of a royal administration that had in part provoked it, but which also formed its instrument. The king might enjoy the benefits of the latter or suffer the humiliations of the former and the climate of his reign would depend much upon his personality and his ability to get on with his magnates. The reign of John (1199–1216) and the later years of Henry III's reign had been turbulent and vindictive and, with the removal of Edward II, the beginnings of a long history of deposition were added to the history of rebellion. Some monarchs had maintained law and order by ruling firmly but wisely: Henry II (1154–89) and Edward I (1272–1307); or because of their martial successes enjoyed the support of their people: Edward III (1327–77) and Henry V (1413–22). But the intervening periods were often years of bloody strife. 'They have a way in England', wrote Jean Juvénal des Ursins in 1444, 'of not thinking twice about changing their kings when it seems convenient, to kill them or evilly bring about their death'—'something which the good and loyal people of France have never done', commented Jean de Rély forty years later. These Frenchmen wrote with the removal of English kings fresh in their memory; but the violence in high politics which lay behind the depositions they referred to had its origins in the earlier history of the island.

The England of the early fourteenth century was not only a smaller kingdom than was France, it was also poorer and more thinly peopled; a land of farmers, fishermen and sheep graziers, an exporter of raw materials and an importer of manufactured goods. Its four-and-a-half million inhabitants, unevenly distributed among some 8,600 parishes (by comparison with around 32,000 parishes in France) were also unequally spread throughout the land, for the ancient distinction between highland and lowland zones was still a very real one. North and west of a line drawn roughly from York to Exeter there were no towns of any size and relatively few villages; the country population was scattered and small. Outside Wales with its four bishoprics, three dioceses sufficed for the province of York, as opposed to

6. Gilt copper effigy of Edward III (1327–77), Westminster Abbey, London.

fourteen for the province of Canterbury. Within the south-eastern lowland zone, East Anglia, south Lincolnshire and the Midlands between Sherwood and Oxford (which were the chief wheat-producing areas) were the most heavily populated, though nowhere densely. Surrey, Sussex and Hampshire, the counties of the Weald and the New Forest, on the other hand, may have been little more populous than Shropshire and Herefordshire. Apart from London with around 35,000 inhabitants and York with around 11,600, it is unlikely that any town had a population of more than 10,000. Indeed, it has been calculated that by 1377 the population of London, although small by comparison with Paris, outnumbered that of the next four largest cities (York, Bristol, Plymouth and Coventry) put together and that no other English town had a population of more than 6,000. It was in every sense a sparsely populated land.

London was precocious in more senses than one. Although still confined, as it was to be for centuries, to the city north of the Thames, the recent growth of the borough of Westminster (where most of the government departments were established) and the construction along the Strand of fine seigniorial mansions were rapidly turning it into a true capital (cf. pl. 4). It had commercial dealings with many parts of the continent and was capturing an increasing share of the cloth trade. Under Edward III and Richard II it became the social and literary, as well as the political and administrative, centre of the kingdom. During the law terms, and when parliament and convocation were in session, its population was swollen by students, retainers, clerks and lawyers, as well as by lay and ecclesiastical magnates, an increasing number of whom maintained permanent town houses. Like Paris, the city had a high population density, but still retained many of the characteristics of a country town. The bells of Bow church (St Mary de Arcubus or St Mary Arches) sounded the curfew for those benighted in the fields as well as for city workers and only the proximity of the countryside can have saved the closely-packed inhabitants from deadly disease. Open channels for refuse ran through the streets into streams and ditches, pigs rooted in the garbage, butchers slaughtered their beasts in Fleet Street. Yet London alone recruited her population from all parts of the land and fear of disease did not prevent the steady flow of countrymen and townsmen, of artists and craftsmen, soldiers and adventurers from coming to swell its population.

Outside London there were great contrasts in the landscape and in the types of husbandry, tenurial arrangements and peasant status that the land supported and conditioned. During the course of the thirteenth century, the classic period of high farming, demographic and economic expansion had led to the clearance and settlement of a good many areas. By 1300 a large proportion of ground under cultivation had been wrested from woodland of various degrees of density. Parts of the Lincoln-shire fenland had been enclosed and drained. On the moors of Cornwall and Devon small pastoral farms had been established, most of them by peasants. In the north the slopes of some of the hills had been brought under cultivation. Yet for all this work of colonization there remained a great contrast between the rich agricultural regions of the Midlands and the east, and the lands of moors, heaths and woods. Everywhere the wild life of the woods pressed closely on the homesteads and the fields. 'From rising ground, England must have seemed one great forest . . . an almost unbroken sea of tree-tops with a thin blue spiral of smoke rising here and there at long intervals'—rather like much of Scandinavia today. Great royal forests (like the New Forest, Savernake, Arden and Sherwood), the Lancastrian forests (in Lancashire, Yorkshire and Derbyshire) and innumerable smaller private chases and thick woodlands, covered much of what has since become arable land. Most of the land under cultivation was open-field country and the majority of people occupied in tilling it lived in villages, that is in one of a number of houses grouped

Fig. 6 Privy Seal of John of Gaunt. *London, British Museum Harleian Charter 43 E 14.*

7. Effigy of Charles V (1364–80), Abbey of St-Denis, near Paris.

8. The naval battle of Sluys (1340); Froissart's Chronicles. *Paris, Bibliothèque Nationale Ms français 2643, fo. 72. (31 × 43).*

9. The battle of Najéra (1367); Froissart's Chronicles. *Paris, Bibliothèque Nationale Ms français 2643, fo. 312v. (32 × 31.4).*

10. The capture of Charles of Blois at La Roche-Derrien (1347); Froissart's Chronicles. *Paris, Bibliothèque Nationale Ms français 2643, fo. 180. (32 × 44).*

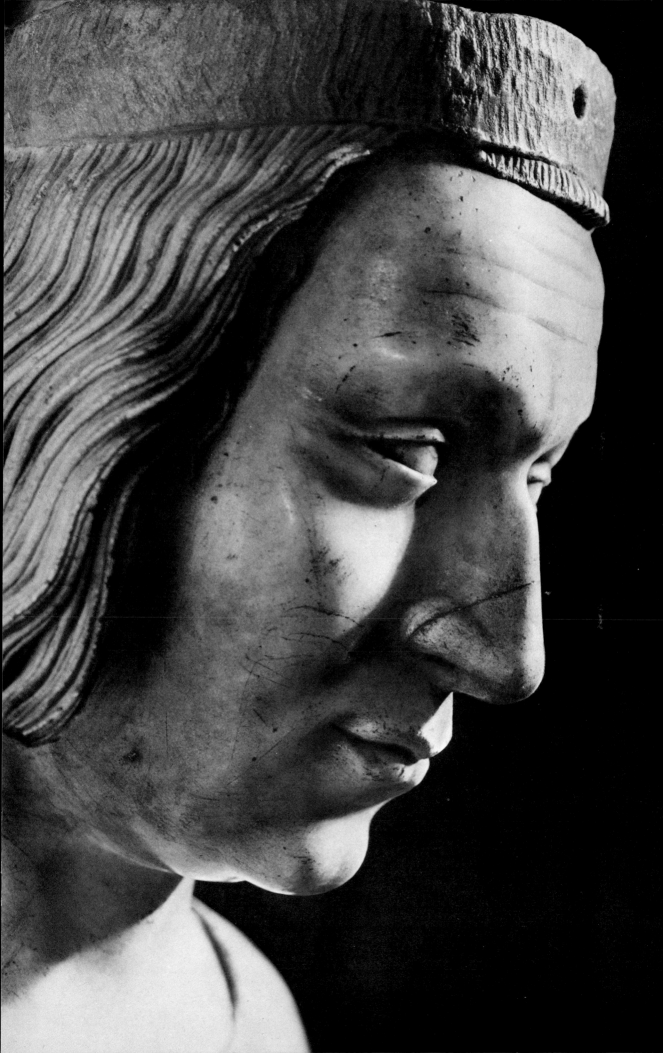

Uant le roy dan
gleterre z ses ma
reschaulx eurent
ordonnees leurs
batailles et leurs nauires
moult richement z paignent
Ilz furent tendre et tiaire
les voiles contremot et vin
drent au bent de quartier
sur deytre po, au sanätaige
du soulcil qui en benant
leur estoit ou bisaige. Si
saufferent que ce sez puoit
trop muyre et detyrient bng

vii et tournoyent tant qlz
eaurent a leur boulente. Les
normans qui les boyoient
tourner se merueilloient
poz quoy ilz se faisoient z
disoient ilz resongnet et
reculent Car ilz ne sont
pas gens pour combatre a
nous. bn bxoient les nor
mans vir les banieres q le
roy dangleterre y estoit per
sonnelement. Si myrent
leurs bausseaulx en bõ estat
Car ilz estoient saiges en

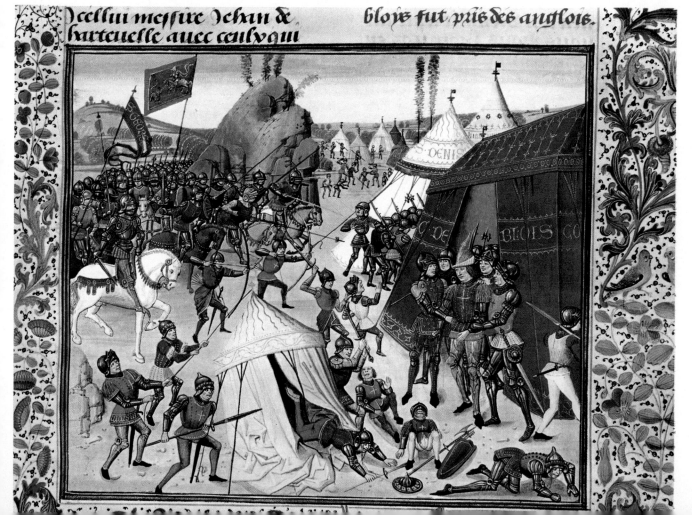

11

PHILIPPE LE HARDY FIX DV ROX IEAN DVC DE BO̐

Jhā dit de malə Conte de fendrə, 1346
Conte d'arrvā 1382   ob 1384

12

Fig. 7   The arms of John of
Gaunt; stained glass. *London,
Victoria and Albert Museum.*

11. Portrait of Philip the Bold,
duke of Burgundy (1364–1404).
Musée de Versailles. (42 × 30).

12. Drawing of Louis de Male,
count of Flanders (d. 1384). *Paris,
Bibliothèque Nationale, Receuil d'Arras.*

around a church, a mill and possibly a manor-house. The fields belonging to the village were split up into a large number of unfenced strips, of which each tenant, the lord of the manor and the parson held several, often widely dispersed in different fields. Such nucleated settlements were typical of the Midlands, where half of the villages coincided with a single big manor of anything from 500 to 750 acres. For reasons of geography they were not normal in the hilly country of the Pennines and the Lake District, Cornwall and the Welsh marches, where the population was frequently scattered in small hamlets rather than grouped in villages, although there were also a number of open-field villages. Nor were they normal in much of East Anglia and Kent. There were consequently great variations in the condition of the peasantry. The essential distinction between free and unfree, and the institution of labour services, were to be found in varying degrees almost everywhere. But in eastern England, in the lowlands of Yorkshire and the old Mercian Danelaw, the seigniorial lands were greatly dispersed and only the more accessible 'inland' tenements were directly exploited, whilst the more distant 'outland' holdings were leased. In East Anglia there was a high proportion of freemen with extensive lands and little connection with the manors, but also a number of large manors whose villeins owed heavy labour services. Moderately sized manors, with small demesnes and generally light services, were characteristic of the Midland counties. In Kent there was little villeinage. But the most striking feature of the English scene must have been the widespread sheep-farming that took place and which provided the country with its single great export commodity, the wool which was shipped to Flanders and as far afield as Italy, which brought prosperity to many farmers, and was particularly rewarding to the Crown.

As in France, the majority of the population spent their lives working on the estates and paying rents to a not very large landholding noble class and in many of its essentials the daily life of both lord and peasant were much the same in the two countries. The nobility may be divided into the same two general groups: a higher nobility of twelve to fifteen earls and between twenty and thirty greater barons and, at the beginning of the fourteenth century, a lesser nobility or gentry of around 1,500 knights and a rather larger group of esquires, about 1,500 of whom were of sufficient standing to have become knights. Entry into the lesser nobility was certainly no more difficult than it was in France and may even have been easier for men of bourgeois origin. The higher nobility also had ministers, officials and a more or less elaborate machinery of government for the exploitation of their estates. The noble way of life, a regard for all the trappings of chivalry, blazonry and romance, were also common in England, as was a preoccupation with the immediate business of the estates. But in spite of the many similarities between the nobility in the two countries, there were some marked differences.

To begin with, in England an earl's title did not imply territorial possession of the county from which he derived his name. The thirty-nine shires of unequal size of which the country was made up were administrative units and not feudal entities. From the time of the Norman Conquest the fiefs, manors and honors of the higher nobility had been scattered throughout the country, never forming vast estates. There remained only two palatinates into which the royal officers did not penetrate: that of Chester, which had however reverted to the royal domain, and that of of Durham, in the hands of the bishop. In 1351 the county of Lancaster was to be erected into a palatinate for one of the king's most trusted and experienced lieutenants, Henry of Grosmont, who was given the title of duke, and after his death the grant was renewed in favour of the king's second son, John of Gaunt. But even the dukes of Lancaster cannot be compared with the great feudatories in France, for their palatinates hardly gave them such extensive powers and they did not, nor did any of the earldoms, even those of the marcher lords, correspond to a region with an individual identity or a long history of provincial separatism.

There were also significant differences between the lesser nobility in the two countries. In England the knights of the shires, as local landowners and men of influence if not of affluence, were actively employed in the work of local government and administration and some of them also came to play a vital role in greater affairs of state as representatives of the shires in parliament. Because these duties were often found to be onerous, because of the expense of maintaining the military status of a knight, and doubtless because of the increasing preoccupation of many landowners with the business of estate management, the knightly class greatly diminished in numbers, though there was a vigorous group of esquires and potential knights. Edward I and his successors persistently but unsuccessfully tried to impose on this latter group (all landowners of a certain income) the obligation to take up knighthood, irrespective of their social origin. There was nothing like this in France. Even the legislation on mortmain in part differed in its purpose and its consequences. The only purpose of Edward I's statute of 1279 was to put a brake on the indefinite extension of Church property, which was diminishing the income of the feudal lords as well as depriving them of military service. But in France, the ordinances of 1274 and 1290, whilst their purpose was much the same, also imposed a heavy tax on religious bodies and non-nobles who acquired fiefs, in order to compensate the lords for their lost profits and because the clerics and non-nobles were supposedly unable to do military service for these lands. These differences may have been due to the different obligations of feudal society rather than to divergencies over the legal definition of nobility; but as the fourteenth century wore on the differences became more marked. By 1400 the French nobility, because of their obligation to do military service, had largely gained exemption from extraordinary taxation, whereas in England, where that obligation had faded out, only those lay barons receiving a writ of summons to parliament (some 51 in 1436) were technically noble.

Another difference was the more rapid development in England of the non-feudal contract whereby a great lord was able to build up an affinity of servants, officials, friends and dependents of all kinds who were paid and fed by him or had taken his livery. All the great magnates had to maintain a household staff befitting their station in society, officials to run their estates and an entourage to defend their persons and maintain their dignity. For much of the thirteenth century it had been possible to do this by investing such persons, according to the service they performed, with lands upon the baronial estates; but since the statute of *Quia Emptores* of 1295 had put a stop to sub-infeudation it had become necessary to devise some type of contract with a cash nexus. This was done by means of indentures of retainer and the granting of annuities, both of which might be for a period of years or for life. To have accepted a lord's fees or taken his livery was a mark of connection with him. In this way a man might gain the protection and patronage of a great lord and the lord was able to secure the service and support of all kinds of men who were not necessarily his vassals, ranging from knights and esquires, councillors and lawyers, to cooks, barbers and menial servants. A great magnate like John of Gaunt contracted at one time and another to pay fees in return for services to some hundreds of men and these contracts were embodied in various forms of indenture and letters patent. With lesser men life retainers were not so numerous, for they constituted a burden on the estate and it was cheaper to offer fees and liveries on a temporary basis to neighbours, tenants and others in search of a patron. The forms, purpose and extent of retaining and connection varied from time to time and from magnate to magnate; they were given a fillip by the advent of the Hundred Years War, but they were in existence long before its outbreak.

In France the transition appears to have been less abrupt and, for much of the fourteenth century, both the king and the magnates continued to secure the service

36

Fig. 8   Effigy of Sir Oliver de Ingham (*d.* 1344), seneschal of Aquitaine (1325–7 and 1331–43) and lieutenant of the duchy (1338–40), Ingham Church, Ingham, Norfolk.

and support of men not settled on their estates by granting money fees (*fiefs-rentes*) which, since they involved homage, were still essentially feudal even though it was feudalism of a decayed form. But by the late fourteenth century a non-feudal contract, the *alliance* concluded between men describing themselves as *alliés*, was taking its place and played much the same part in bolstering up the relationship of lord and servant as it did in England. Many such contracts were already being concluded in the 1370s by Gaston Fébus, count of Foix and vicomte of Béarn, and they were commonly employed by the duke of Orléans and even by lesser men at the turn of the century. There were also other means by which a lord might secure service beyond that provided by tenure. He could grant pensions and offices which bound their recipients more closely to his person, or secure support through the foundation of a chivalric order, which might have much the same effect upon its members—there was a proliferation of such orders in France in the Late Middle Ages (cf. below, pp. 144-5). In these and other ways a magnate was able to secure an affinity of which the nucleus was made up of familiars, officers and courtiers who might or might not have concluded a formal contract with him. He had an outer circle of *alliés* in court and country bound to him by *alliances*. He could rely on the support of pensioners, of well-wishers and simple hangers-on. Connection operated at all levels of society. Many baronial families concluded *alliances* with each other and with the more important ducal and comtal families and the latter concluded *alliances* between themselves. These might involve fees and annuities, more often they did not and their effect was much the same as that of the indenture of retainer in England. But in the *alliances* concluded between equals, especially between territorial princes, with all which that involved, the development of the non-feudal contract had perhaps been taken a step further. At least the conditions of Late Medieval France made it that much more potentially dangerous.

There were also great discrepancies in the wealth of the English nobility, though it is difficult in the absence of complete and reliable evidence to see precisely what the over-all position was. An investigation of the income-tax returns of 1436 suggested that the baronage were distinctly less wealthy than had once been imagined and that the income of the gentry was comparatively greater. According to these returns, the English aristocracy was at the time made up of fifty-one lay barons with an average income of £865, 183 greater knights with an average income of £208, 750 lesser knights with £60, 1,200 esquires with £24, and 5,000 others (gentlemen, merchants, artisans, but largely yeomen) with incomes of between £15 and £19. Ten non-baronial families had incomes comparable with the average baronial income and an even larger number had incomes comparable with the smaller baronial incomes. Much learned dispute has taken place over the validity of these statistics and on the general question of baronial incomes, and it is unlikely that a complete picture will ever be obtained. What is clear is that the returns of 1436 understate the income of many baronial families and may overstate that of some of the knights; but they also suggest that, even allowing for the differences in total population, the number of esquires was considerably less in England than in France, and this may once again have reflected the differences in the general character and composition of the nobility in the two countries.

The Plantagenet kings at the beginning of the fourteenth century had by no means extricated themselves fully from their French origins. They were still bound closely to France by family ties, language, taste, culture, and above all their territorial possessions. For their dominions were by no means limited to their island kingdom. They still held a part of the old duchy of Aquitaine, the Channel Islands and, since 1279, the county of Ponthieu in northern France. In Henry II's time the continental territories had formed the greater part of the king's dominions and it was only slowly during the thirteenth century that they had come to be considered as territories of the English Crown in France. To begin with, the conquests of Philip Augustus and Saint Louis, by changing the entire territorial balance, had shifted the centre of gravity from France to England and during the course of the thirteenth century other changes followed. The king-duke's lengthening and ultimately permanent absence necessitated the creation of a more sedentary form of government in his remaining French possessions. In granting what remained of them to his eldest son in 1254, Henry III invested them in the English Crown for ever, and so made impossible their alienation to a younger son of the royal family. In the treaty of 1259

13. Effigy of Richard II (1377–99), by Nicholas Broker and Godfrey Prest, Westminster Abbey, London.

he acknowledged the loss of the greater part of Henry II's dominions and the duchy of Aquitaine, which he retained, was reconstituted on the basis of liege homage and the acknowledgement of the sovereignty of the king of France in the mid-thirteenth-century sense which that had come to imply. This involved the notion that the king of France had no temporal superior but was 'emperor' in his own realm and its development coincided with the common acceptance of the fact that imperial claims to universal overlordship were no more than a legal fiction. In practical terms it gave the king of France judicial sovereignty within his kingdom and it offered a legal basis for the development of the claims of the *parlement de Paris* as the highest court of appeal in the land. This greatly complicated the king of England's task of governing his duchy, the more so since during the course of Edward I's reign its administration was being subordinated to what were primarily English institutions and by the beginning of the fourteenth century English chancery clerks were referring to the duchy as part of the king's 'dominions overseas'. For while the king of England could give concrete form to his claims to sovereignty within his kingdom, his vassalage to the king of France for the duchy of Aquitaine made it impossible for him to do the same in the lands he held in France. Moreover, since at the same time both kings claimed cognizance of disputes which occurred between merchants and sailors in the marches of their realms and at sea, another source of conflict was added by the requirement that the king of England should do liege homage for his French lands. Thus although a revolution had taken place in the different constituent parts of the Plantagenet empire, owing to the sovereignty of the king of France in the continental territories, it was a revolution that remained incomplete.

As it existed towards the end of the thirteenth century, the duchy of Aquitaine consisted of most of the ancient duchy of Gascony, the Bordelais, the Agenais, Saintonge south of the river Charente and certain lands in Limousin, Périgord and Quercy. Sporadic warfare with the French and repeated confiscations led to many changes in its frontiers, so that by the beginning of Edward III's reign not only had Limousin, Périgord and Quercy been lost, but the Agenais and, beyond the river Garonne, Bazadais, were occupied by the French. A maritime strip without any deep hinterland, stretching from the mouth of the Charente to the Pyrenees, was all that by that time remained of the Plantagenet dominions in the south of France.

It was a land of contrasts, with the sparse and difficult mountain terrain of the south giving rise to a remarkably free and independent way of life, even amongst the peasant villagers of the mountain valleys such as Aspe and Azun, the economically useless and strategically vital marshy wasteland of the Landes that separated the two principal towns of Bordeaux and Bayonne, and the rich and fertile vine-growing districts of Entre-Deux-Mers. Each of these districts might have its own customs and fiercely-held local traditions, but they were bound together by a common independence of spirit, a common language and a common allegiance to their duke. In its entirety Gascony formed a territory as distinct from the rest of France in language, race and customs as was England, and in some respects more so. But between England and the duchy, although even in normal times they were separated by eight to ten days' sea travel, a political, administrative, military and above all an economic symbiosis had been created during the thirteenth century that was to withstand each threat to its existence for another hundred and fifty years.

Bordeaux was in a very real sense the capital of the duchy, a great fortified city whose fourteenth-century walls came close to the quayside and encircled the commercial and administrative centres of the greatest wine exporting region in the world. Within the walls stood the cathedral of Saint-Andrew, the castle of the Ombrière, several religious houses, a mint, factories producing vessels for the transportation of wine, warehouses and all the buildings needed by the merchants, shopkeepers and other members of a trading centre which, with a population of hardly less than

14. Battle at the gates of a city. *London, British Museum Stowe Ms 54, fo. 83. (25.5 × 16).*

41

30,000, was much larger than any English provincial town and not much inferior to London itself. Outside the walls flowed the Garonne, far wider than the Thames, and used for transport between the many riverside towns both on the Garonne and the Dordogne. The city had a double defence line: seigniorial castles like Lesparre, Blaye, Fronsac, Benauges, Langoiran and Blanquefort, royal castles like La Réole (the Château Gaillard of the Garonne) and rectangular castles of the fourteenth century, like Fargues, Roquetaillade, Villandraut, Budos and Landiras, formed a solid line of defence behind the frontier fortresses and *bastides*.

It was from here that the duchy was governed by the king's chief officer, the seneschal of Aquitaine, who resided in the castle and was responsible for civil and military affairs, assisted by a council of barons and officials, of which the constable of Bordeaux, who was in charge of the financial administration, was a permanent member. Local government was in the hands of sub-seneschals, *prévôts*, *baillis* and castellans appointed by the seneschal and responsible to him and for this purpose Gascony proper was divided into three administrative districts (Bordelais, Bazadais and the Landes), while such other territories as were in English control were formed into separate *sénéchaussées* (Saintonge, Agenais, the three dioceses of Limoges, Cahors and Périgeux, etc.). The seneschal and the constable were appointed by the king and council in England, from whom general directives were sent out, and from the outbreak of war in 1337 they were almost without exception English. So also was the mayor of Bordeaux, whose office gave him such extensive powers that the right of the city to elect him frequently had to be suspended to prevent authority falling into the hands of anyone who might provoke instead of suppressing disorder. Some of the sub-seneschals (for instance of the Landes) were also, though not always, English, as were the captains of some of the royal castles, particularly in the fifteenth century. But although the top civil and military appointments came increasingly to be held by Englishmen, Aquitaine was never in any sense 'colonized'. No Englishman ever held the see of Bordeaux and there were few who were granted lands in the duchy. Except when an expeditionary force was sent out, English administrators and soldiers cannot have exceeded a few hundred. There were probably more Gascons in England than there were Englishmen in Gascony, younger sons of noble families who went to fight in the Scottish wars as they had previously done in Wales, and merchants in London occupied in the multifarious activities connected with the wine trade.

Viticulture had never really prospered in England, for both the climate and the long connection with France discouraged it. During the twelfth and early thirteenth centuries wine had been shipped to England from many parts of the Plantagenet dominions, but with the loss of Poitou, much of Saintonge and other parts of Aquitaine, the vineyards of the Bordelais secured a virtual monopoly of the English market. Quite apart from political factors there were good reasons why they should. Geography not only made the Bordelais particularly suited to the cultivation of the vine, but water transport along the Garonne and by the sea to England made the latter a very favourable market. It also meant that the wine could be easily taxed and provide valuable revenues for the Crown. The wine trade was in fact second only to the wool trade and the customs revenues that were derived from it were substantial: approaching half of the £17,000 sterling received in Gascony in 1282 — a substantial sum when the ordinary English revenues of the Crown seldom exceeded £30,000. It is hardly surprising therefore that the kings of England promoted the wine trade by granting privileges to English merchants in Gascony and to Gascon merchants in England. They favoured the merchants of Bordeaux, which was the centre of the traffic, by prohibiting the sale of wine from the *haut-pays* (upstream from Saint-Macaire) before the growers further downstream had sold theirs. The resulting monopoly made viticulture something of a monoculture in the Bordelais. During the fourteenth century the region gave up trying to meet its

need for wheat locally and came to rely on England for supplies of grain, salted fish, wool and later cloth. Nor was Bordeaux the only town to benefit from the English link. The smaller inland towns were mostly engaged in the wine trade and were thus bound to Bordeaux, where the wine was collected, taxed and shipped. Bayonne, the second town of Gascony, built and manned most of the ships in which the trade was carried out; although with the advent of the Hundred Years War they were rapidly ousted from that function by armed naval convoys sent out from England, which secured a virtual monopoly of the overseas trade of Gascony during the course of the fourteenth century.

The economic benefits of the English link were in fact felt most strongly in the towns and it was upon their loyalty and that of the Gascon seigneurs that the extent of English control in Gascony ultimately depended. The duchy was indeed noted for its large number of towns and castles and a much impressed Froissart enumerates some twenty-six towns along the Garonne between Bordeaux and Toulouse and twelve castles along the Dordogne, 'some English, some French'. Some of these were old foundations but during the course of the thirteenth century there had been a considerable expansion of the colonization of the countryside, which had been going on all over France since the eleventh century, and which in Gascony resulted in the foundation of numerous small rural towns known as *bastides*. Increasingly after 1259 the kings of England and France, and the Gascon seigneurs, fortified many of these places in the frontier districts. By the outbreak of the Hundred Years War they stretched in an unbroken line from the Pyrenees to Périgord. A double military defence line had been organized (cf. maps I, V).

Some of these places were in the hands of royal castellans, but the majority were in the hands of the Gascon seigneurs. On the eve of the outbreak of war the most powerful noble families included the counts of Armagnac, Astarac and Pardiac, the vicomtes of Lomagne and Auvillar, and the lord of Isle-Jourdain, all of them territorial princes whose allegiance was firmly French. The nobles of the Bordelais, whose allegiance varied with their fortunes but who were for the most part pro-English, included the lords of Lesparre, Fronsac, Montferrand and Budos, the Albret family, and the family of Grailly who had settled in the country in the thirteenth century and had become vicomtes of Benauges and Castillon and one of whose members was the captal of Buch. The king and his seneschals had to pick their way amongst these rival interests, jurisdictions and loyalties with infinite care. Almost from the beginning the duke had been faced with warfare in Gascony, either from the king of France or from his rebellious subjects. The Gascon barons were proud, turbulent and often treacherous and they had to be treated with a mixture of firmness and leniency to ensure their allegiance. The loyalty of the towns, the most important of which by the mid-thirteenth century had evolved quite advanced and independent forms of government, had to be bought by the confirmation of existing privileges and the granting of new concessions.

Over this explosive territory conflict had frequently broken out. The settlement of 1259, which was designed to put an end to future disputes by defining the limits of the Plantagenet dominions in France and the manner in which they were in future to be held, created more problems than it solved. While Saint Louis agreed to surrender rather more territories to Henry III than the king of England then possessed (Gascony, diverse fiefs and domains in Limousin, Périgord and Quercy and the promise of several others in the Agenais and Saintonge), the boundaries were virtually impossible to determine. Neither side knew precisely what was being ceded, since the territorial extent and the manner of tenure of many of the fiefs had never before been determined and numerous lords who held land upon the royal domain, the *priviligeati*, could technically never be alienated from it by treaty or otherwise. Ultimately more important was the stipulation that the duchy, thus

18. Statue of John, duke of Berry, *c.* 1390, by Jean de Rupy of Cambrai, Bourges Cathedral.

reconstituted, was in future to be held by liege homage. Only simple homage had been done before and not even that, it seems, for Gascony proper. This new relationship, as it was being defined, obliged the duke to perform military service, to provide troops for the king of France in his foreign and domestic wars and not to support his overlord's enemies. And yet consideration of the wool trade made it essential for the king of England to keep on friendly terms with Flanders; it was through alliances with Castile that some defence was afforded to Gascony; the king of France was from 1295 allied to Scotland, and in all of these places the French pursued policies which were quite opposed to English interests. Moreover, the sovereignty of the king of France entitled him to receive appeals not only against decisions reached in the courts of the duke's Gascon officials, but also in cases of dispute between their respective subjects. The very real effect of the treaty of 1259, in its stipulation of liege homage alone, was to wreck any attempt which the kings of England might try to make to govern their duchy without interference from Paris or to conduct an independent foreign policy. Slowly but inexorably, and perhaps with only an imperfect knowledge of the consequences of what they were doing, the kings of France in the thirteenth and early fourteenth centuries were reducing the duke's lordship to landlordship, erecting their suzerainty into sovereignty, and changing the notion of *nulle seigneur sans terre* into *nulle terre sans seigneur*.

It was an impossible situation for the king of England. The performance of liege homage, quite apart from the conditions it imposed upon him, was onerous in itself, resented because of the obsequious position in which it placed him, and because the territorial provisions of the treaty which had stipulated it had not been fully honoured by the king of France. He therefore sought to defer or escape doing homage, to do it in an ambiguous form, to get his son to do it in his place and this in turn led to a further deterioration in Anglo-French relations. He sought to avoid its implications by reorganizing the administration of the duchy, attempting to reduce the number of appeals being taken to Paris by making the seneschal of Aquitaine responsible for appointments to local offices, appointing lieutenants in the duchy with supreme judicial powers and hearing appeals himself in England. His lawyers even sought to escape the implications of French sovereignty by declaring that Gascony was an *allod*. But he could not stem the tide of change that in France was making a centralized monarchy out of an old feudal kingdom and which was also transforming the basic relationship between his kingdom and his territories in France. War broke out in 1294 when Edward I refused to appear in Paris to answer to a dispute that had arisen between a number of Gascon and Norman sailors, and again in 1324 when one of the duke's vassals burnt down a *bastide* at Saint-Sardos, in territory disputed by the French. On each of these occasions the duchy was confiscated and only partially restored after a number of years had elapsed. The various treaties that were concluded between 1259 and 1337 only added to the problems which they sought to solve, and such attempts as were made to settle outstanding differences by judicial process—at Montreuil in 1306, at Périgeux in 1311, and at Agen in 1322–3—were doomed to failure by the incompatibility of the claims of either side, for the French commissioners insisted on acting as judges by virtue of their king's claims to sovereignty. There could be no easy solution to Anglo-French relations as long as the king of England, sovereign in his own isle, was a vassal of the king of France for the duchy of Aquitaine. If in theory it was possible to distinguish between his separate capacities, in practice it was not.

In 1328, the problems arising from a disputed succession were added to the complexities of the situation occasioned by French sovereignty in Aquitaine. In the next decade Anglo-French relations were further aggravated by events in Scotland, where Edward III's open intervention to secure the pretender, Edward Balliol, on the throne in 1333, provoked a chain reaction which threatened and ultimately

48

dissolved the peace of western Europe. In 1334 Philip gave a warm reception to
David II, the exiled nine-year old son of Robert Bruce. Giving substance to the by
then ancient but recently renewed Franco-Scottish alliance, he insisted that David
should be included in any general settlement with England, he attempted to
arbitrate between Edward and the Scots and in the following year he fitted out a
number of ships for the exiled king to make an abortive attack on the Channel
Islands. When, in 1336, Pope Benedict XII cancelled the Crusade (in which the
French king's interest was possibly no more than financial), Philip transferred the
fleet (which was ostensibly to have taken him to the East) from Languedoc to
Normandy and Edward seems to have been convinced that a large-scale intervention
was intended on behalf of the Scots. In the belief that war had become inevitable,
he began to look for allies. In May 1337 an elaborately equipped embassy, with
apparently unlimited financial resources, was sent to Valenciennes, the capital city
of his wife's native county of Hainault. Within a short time the counts of Hainault,
Gelderland, Berg, Cleves and Marck, the count palatine of the Rhine, the margrave
of Juliers and the elector of Brandenburg, promised their support—though at a price.
Moving on to Frankfurt, the ambassadors negotiated an agreement whereby the
Emperor Lewis also promised military assistance and when, just over a year later,
Lewis created Edward his imperial vicar-general *per Alemanniam et Galliam*, Philip of
Valois was ousted from a prize he too had sought. The effect of this appointment was
to give Edward sovereign rights in Germany and in all imperial lands west of the
Rhine. It empowered him to enforce service against France from the subjects of
the Empire, associated him with a German policy of revindication of imperial
rights in the west and was the crowning achievement of his diplomacy, duly
celebrated by a great ceremonial meeting in the market-place at Coblenz in
September 1338.

Fig. 9   Troops in a *melée*; from a
late fourteenth-century manuscript.
*London, British Museum Royal Ms
20C VII, fo. 30.* (7.8 × 7.8)

While Edward's ambassadors were thus busying themselves, Philip declared
Gascony confiscate and by July 1337 an army commanded by the count of Eu, then
constable of France and Philip's lieutenant in Languedoc, had been sent into the
Garonne valley and had taken the key fortresses of Saint-Macaire and La Réole.
By way of reply, Edward seized French property in England, issued a manifesto to
his subjects and on 7 October once again laid claim to the throne of France. But
engaged in feverish preparations and diverted by papal diplomacy, it was not until
July of the following year that he sailed for Antwerp, where, short of money and
supplies, he had to wait until September 1339 before he could get his allies to move.
When his troops entered the Cambrésis the first major campaign of the Hundred
Years War, the Thiérache campaign, had begun.

The protagonists

While it is now agreed that the causes of the war were diverse and inextricably interwoven and that the main burden of blame for its outbreak cannot reasonably be attached to either Edward or Philip, the war aims of the protagonists are by no means clear. It is not easy to unravel Edward's motives and ambitions, cloaked as they are in the chivalrous preoccupations of contemporary chroniclers and the mountain of propaganda issued by his government departments. Some historians have discerned in his martial exploits and urbane conventionality 'a prince who knew his work and did it'. For others they were the psychological reaction of a humiliated child to the weaknesses and failures of his father and the unspeakable deportment of his mother. For others he was obsessed with the crown of France which his uncle had worn, and which he believed to be his 'by most clear right, by divine disposition and through the death of Charles of famous memory', which implied a duty to his French subjects, and to which, in the final instance, he could not withdraw his claim. Still others have seen his assumption of the French royal title as no more than a tactical device, never taken really seriously and easily thrown over for territorial concessions, and have argued that his real aim was no more than an enlarged and sovereign Aquitaine. Did he seriously envisage his own elevation to the throne of the Capets or, recognizing from the start that his dynastic claim was unrealistic, did he put it forward in order to rid himself of the obligation to do homage for Gascony? In the nature of the evidence, it is unlikely that a final answer can ever be given to these questions. It has been suggested that 'the conquest of the whole of France' and 'the complete surrender of the French monarchy and people' were impossible objectives; but such conceptions themselves presuppose the existence of national consciousness of a sort that was clearly lacking in fourteenth-century France, and a complete misunderstanding of the nature of fourteenth-century warfare and the military and financial resources at the disposal of the protagonists. The rule of two kingdoms did not necessarily imply the subjection of the one to the other, as the recent precedent of France and Navarre had shown and, in the fifteenth century, the dual monarchy of Henry VI was to some extent to prove. 'Conquest' and 'surrender' imply subjection, and there is no evidence that in fourteenth-century terms Edward's accession to the French throne, if that was his aim, would necessarily have resulted in any such condition. It has been pointed out that the destruction wrought by Edward's armies was hardly likely 'to impress provincial opinion' in France; but that is to apply a twentieth-century viewpoint. The behaviour of 'French' troops within their own country left a lot to be desired. Of necessity, Edward's war aims must be deduced from his actions and what we know of the way in which he conducted his war.

Philip VI remains a much more shadowy figure. His correspondence and his actions reveal a cool and calculating mind, though one which was occasionally overcome by outbursts of temper. It has generally been presumed that his policy was essentially defensive since it was taken for granted that the war would be fought in France. But in its early stages, as later in the 1370s and 1380s, that must have seemed far from inevitable to most Englishmen. Did Philip ever take the Crusade seriously and why did he move the fleet that was being assembled in the Mediterranean to

19. The house of Jacques Coeur, Bourges.

20. Portrait of Charles VII (1422–61), by Jean Fouquet. *Louvre, Paris.* (85.7 × 70.6).

21. Portrait of Cardinal Albergati, by Jan van Eyck. *Kunsthistorisches Museum, Vienna.* (34.1 × 27.3).

LE·TRESVICTORIEVX·ROY·DE·FRANCE·

CHARLES·SEPTIESME·DE·CE·NOM·

the Norman ports in the summer of 1336? Was his ordinance for the invasion and conquest of England (dated 23 March 1339, and discovered by Edward's troops during the sack of Caen in 1346) merely intended to divert Norman indignation away from Philip, as has been suggested, or is it to be taken at face value? Plans to send twenty armed Provençal galleys round to Rouen and to hire a further twenty from Genoa to be based on Bruges, which were drawn up in the summer of 1337 and the autumn of 1339, certainly suggest that they are to be taken seriously, as do proposals for a blockade of the English coast and the destruction of English shipping. It has generally been assumed (from the account of Froissart and the evidence put together by De la Roncière at the end of the last century) that the great French fleet anchored in the Zwin in the summer of 1340 was intended to intercept Edward's forces, that he unsuspectingly ran into it and gained a great naval victory. But from a letter subsequently written by Edward, it appears that the encounter was positively planned by the English government and that it was intended to deliver England from French invasion. As in 1386, the majority of the French naval forces was Norman and the assembly port was Sluys. On the latter occasion, French intentions are much more obvious because there were then no allied troops concentrated in northern France. Up to the summer of 1340 the possibility of a French invasion was very real and there were good reasons why Edward temporarily jeopardized the wool trade to push the Flemings into an alliance, set up the *garde de la mer*, a kind of home guard to protect the coastal districts, concentrated his forces in the Low Countries and left the defence of the duchy of Aquitaine to his Gascon subjects and the much-taxed resources of the English Exchequer.

Fig. 10   Execution of the Norman seigneurs in 1356; *Grandes Chroniques. Paris, Bibliothèque Nationale Ms français, fo. 398.* (7 × 6.3)

The fundamental factor in any appraisal of Edward's war policy is that he had support in France from the start. This is obvious in the case of Aquitaine; but it shortly became true of Flanders, and subsequently of Brittany and Normandy, where revolts against the French monarchy resulted in the landing of English troops and the recognition of Edward as rightful 'king of France'. Some historians have seen the ghost of the Angevin empire asserting itself in these developments, a protest against the predominance of men from eastern France among the counsellors of the first two Valois kings, and even a reaction to the centralizing policy of the French royal house over the course of the previous century. Certainly, both Philip VI and John II acted foolishly in regard to the provincial liberties of some of their subjects and the entrenched interests of a number of their vassals and their actions had a decisive influence on the subsequent course of events.

The revolt in Flanders occurred in 1337. It was led by a wealthy artisan of the patriciate of Bruges called James van Artevelde. Its cause was an English embargo on the supply of wool to the Flemish cloth-manufacturing towns; it resulted in the removal of the pro-French count Louis de Nevers and it placed Flanders under the hegemony of the towns of Ghent, Ypres and Bruges, whose inhabitants first agreed to be neutral in the war with France and then (3 December 1339) recognized Edward as the rightful king of France.

The revolt in Brittany occurred in 1341, consequent upon a dispute over the succession to the duchy on the death of Duke John III. On this occasion the French royal candidate was Charles of Blois, who claimed the succession by right of his wife, while the English supported John de Montfort. When war broke out between the partisans of the two claimants, Edward offered Montfort his support. The immediate result was that a number of Breton nobles recognized him as king of France and several English garrisons settled in the duchy to make sure that they continued to do so. Then in 1356, when King John surprised a dinner-party being held by his son in Rouen castle and took Charles of Navarre prisoner and executed four of his associates out of hand, Charles' brother Philip, together with an influential Norman seigneur called Godfrey d'Harcourt, immediately got in touch with Edward and, having secured a promise of military assistance, recognized him as 'king of France and duke of Normandy'. John's action was very ill-judged since Charles of Navarre held considerable lands in Normandy and had recently been conspiring with the English. Although at the time he was still only a youth, he was an attractive one, a glib talker, cunning, energetic, madly ambitious and he had been harbouring several grievances which had boiled up into a feud against the Valois dynasty.

Whatever the motives of the rebels, there can be no doubt that the support secured by Edward in the French provinces vitally affected his strategy and the whole manner in which he fought the war. In the initial stages his plan was formed on traditional lines. At Valenciennes in May 1337, he attempted to hire the princes of the Low Countries through the distribution of money-fiefs and other pensions (as John had done in 1214 and Edward I in 1294) and the first major campaigns took place in the north, not in Aquitaine. He invaded France from the north-east; his forces crossed to Flanders in 1338 and endured the long and frustrating winter and spring of 1339 there, while he could neither pay nor induce his Netherlandish allies to move. He blundered into the country, devastating the countryside and looking for a French army to fight. This was the Thiérache campaign of 1339, when the two armies were drawn up at Buironfosse for a battle that never took place. He even offered to settle the quarrel by issue of personal combat between the two kings. All this was frustrated by the French king's refusal to risk a battle. It was a wise refusal and it was the complete answer to Edward's invasion.

The only positive achievement of these years, though a significant one, was the naval victory at Sluys in 1340 (cf. pl. 8), which prevented an invasion of England, gave Edward control of the Channel and made possible landings in France wherever and whenever he wanted during the next twenty years. But nothing immediate had been gained, and he was reduced to a somewhat futile siege of Tournai. His Netherlandish allies had cost him dearer than he could afford; he ran into debt with his creditors, the Italian banking houses of Bardi and Peruzzi; he was detained in the Low Countries for the payment of his debts; and he faced a ministerial crisis at home as a result of his financial demands.

23. The return of King John to London in 1362; *Grandes Chroniques. Paris, Bibliothèque Nationale Ms français 2813, fo. 438.* (7.5 × 14.5).

24. Soldiers in the service of the town of Paris; *Grandes Chroniques. Paris, Bibliothèque Nationale Ms français 2813, fo. 409v.* (9.3 × 6.8).

Fig. 11 The battle of Crécy; Froissart's Chronicles. *Paris, Bibliothèque Nationale Ms français 2643, fo. 165v.*

23

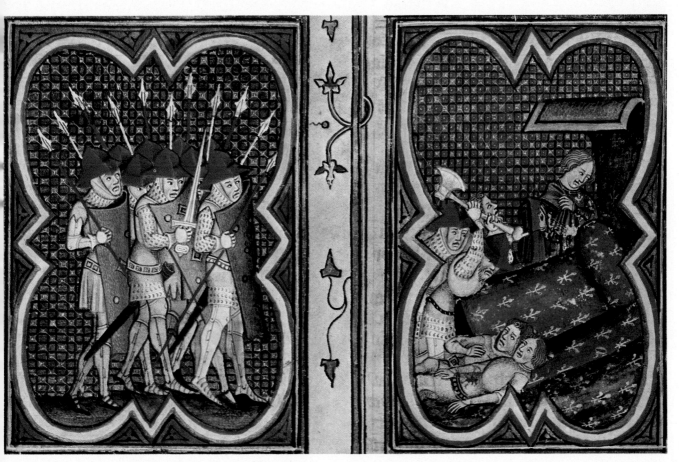

24

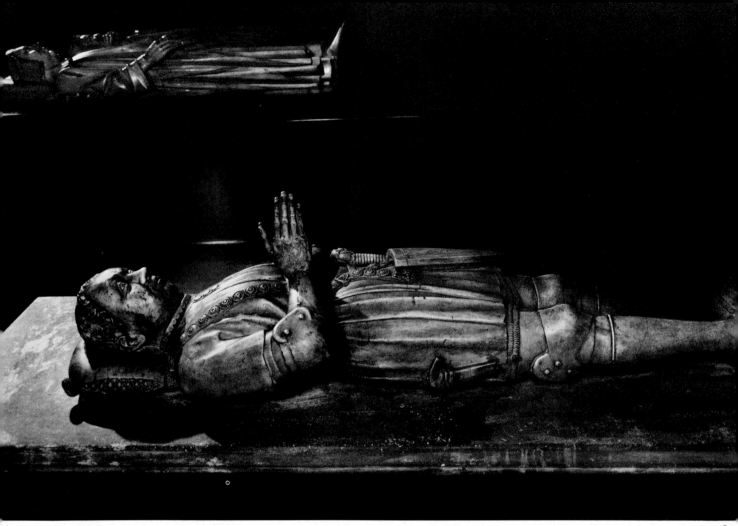

LOUIS II DE SANCERRE, +1402
Connétable de France, Maréchal de France,
Fils de Louis Ier de Sancerre

But the revolts in France led to a completely different way of directing the war. To take advantage of local conditions it was often necessary to have two or even three armies operating at once, either independently or in concert and to delegate command of some of them at least. Herein lay the opportunity for profit and fame that was open to nobles like the earls of Lancaster and Northampton, as later to the Black Prince and John of Gaunt, and occasionally even to men of much more humble backgrounds, like Walter Mauny, Walter Bentley, Robert Knowles or Hugh Calveley.

The first campaigns under the new strategy were carried out in 1345. Simultaneous commissions were issued to Lancaster and Northampton: Lancaster was to operate in Gascony, Northampton in Brittany (significantly in co-operation with the claimant, John de Montfort). Both were designated king's lieutenants, with what were virtually vice regal powers (cf. below, pp. 120-3), Northampton in 'Brittany and the kingdom of France', Lancaster in Aquitaine and Languedoc. A year later, when a large French army had been drawn into the south under the command of the king's son John, Edward under the guidance of the Norman renegade, Godfrey d'Harcourt, landed in the Cotentin, captured Caen (cf. pl. 81), eventually defeated the main French army at Crécy (26 August, 1346) (cf. fig. 11), and sat down before Calais (cf. map VIII). There can be no doubt that these three campaigns were linked by a general plan. They were hammered out in the king's council early in 1345 and it seems perfectly clear that Edward's landing in Normandy was intended to relieve Lancaster in the south. It is sometimes said that all the territory won by Edward in the huge military effort of 1346–7 was the town of Calais; but if these three campaigns are regarded as strategically interdependent, Lancaster's considerable gains in Aquitaine and those of Northampton in Brittany must be added to the credit side of the account—and this amounted in all to a great deal.

Not until the summer of 1355 was the war once more actively pursued. There were several reasons for this: the plague, lack of credit facilities with which to finance any major campaign, and papal diplomacy, were among the most important. After the fall of Calais, a truce was drawn up between the protagonists and this was renewed again and again, the papacy constantly endeavouring and failing to convert it into a firm peace. But from the summer of 1355 to the spring of 1357 the same general strategy of a group of simultaneous campaigns was followed as ten years earlier: Lancaster co-operated with the Navarrese in Normandy, and the Black Prince conducted operations in Aquitaine. This is not the place to enter upon a discussion of the raids led by these two lieutenants; but it is to be noted that in September 1356, when the Black Prince was moving down the south bank of the river Loire, Lancaster advanced through Brittany and Anjou to meet him. There can be no doubt that a junction of the two armies had been arranged; but no meeting took place. Lancaster failed to cross the Loire at Les Ponts-de-Cé, just south of Angers, and the Black Prince continued his retreat to meet glory alone at Poitiers on 19 September 1356 (cf. map VIII and fig. 13).

There are many similarities between this victory and that of the prince's father ten years earlier. Both were gained against considerable odds, while the English forces were in retreat, and through much the same tactics. In 1346 Edward's troops moved east from Normandy towards Paris, then turned north. Beyond Abbeville they were trapped by the pursuing French forces under Philip and forced to an engagement in the open field, though outnumbered by perhaps as many as three to one. Ironically enough, the strength of Edward's army lay in its numerical inferiority, which enabled the king to choose a strong position, forced him to fight a defensive battle and make good use of his archers who, like the men-at-arms, dismounted for combat. Dismounted horse-archers, combined with dismounted men-at-arms occupying a defensive position, had been used to good effect against the Scots at

Fig. 12   Coin: *demi-gros* of the Black Prince, minted at Agen. *Obverse:* the prince holding a sword. *London, British Museum.*

25. Effigy of Bertrand du Guesclin, constable of France (1370–80), Abbey of St-Denis, near Paris.

26. Effigy of Louis de Sancerre, constable of France (1397–1403), Abbey of St-Denis, near Paris.

Halidon Hill in 1333. The tactics of the English were to extend their wings forward, so that the advancing French cavalry met fire from three sides. Philip's mistake was to assault a very strong position. The attack was launched by the Genoese cross-bowmen in his service who suffered heavy losses; it was ill-disciplined and appallingly costly. The English archers and men-at-arms had become well trained in fighting together during the Scottish wars and the longbow, the principal English weapon, though it had a much shorter range than the crossbow, had a rate of fire almost five times as great. In the conditions of close combat that prevailed at Crécy the longbow had the advantage. The engagement was an indescribable *mêlée*.

The Black Prince's victory at Poitiers was a much narrower thing than the battle at Crécy. King John had pursued the prince's forces (heavily laden with booty) southwards in a brilliant flanking movement which cut off Prince Edward's line of retreat to Bordeaux. On this occasion it is probable that the French forces were hardly double those of the prince; but, like his father in 1346, Edward had the good sense to take up a well chosen defensive position and adopt the tactics used at Crécy, placing his archers on the wings and dismounted men-at-arms in the rear. On the French side, there was a dispute in the preliminary council of war between the marshals Clermont and Audrehem, which resulted in a rash initial assault before the army units known as battles had been ordered (cf. below, pp. 100-1). In their over-hasty attack the French advance guard repeated Philip's mistakes at Crécy, charging straight into the line of fire of the English archers. Although in the subsequent battles which were sent in to engage the English, the French men-at-arms were dismounted, they were not combined with archers and, weighed down in

Fig. 13   The battle of Poitiers; Froissart's Chronicles. *Paris, Bibliothèque Nationale Ms français 2643, fo. 207.*

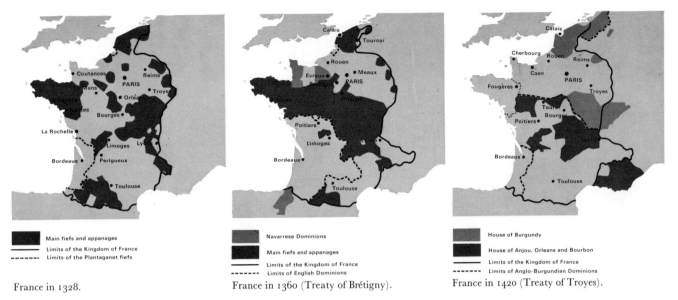

France in 1328.

France in 1360 (Treaty of Brétigny).

France in 1420 (Treaty of Troyes).

II France during the Hundred Years War.

armour, they had a hard trudge to reach the English positions. The first of these battles, under the dauphin, suffered heavy losses and retreated; that of the duke of Orléans fled the field. When John moved in with the final battle, the prince sent a force of Gascons under the captal of Buch around to its rear, while the greater part of Edward's forces mounted and charged the remaining French troops who were advancing on foot.

The capture of King John and a considerable section of the French higher nobility had a decisive effect upon subsequent events—but not immediately. During the course of 1358 and 1359, two draft treaties were drawn up while John was captive in London. The first (8 May 1358), concluded while Paris was in revolution and only a few weeks before the peasant rising known as the *Jacquerie* broke out, was already dead in late autumn, by which time the revolts had been quelled. The second (24 March 1359), concluded when preparations for renewed military intervention were well under way, was so preposterous that it is difficult to believe that it was ever intended seriously, and it was firmly rejected by the French Estates. King Edward could now without conscience proceed to his grand design.

The campaign of 1359–60 was intended to deliver the *coup de grâce* and its aim was a great coronation ceremony in Reims cathedral. With the king of France a prisoner in London, with the Valois kingdom torn by civil strife, with Anglo-Navarrese forces swarming in Normandy and up to the gates of Paris, with half of Brittany and most of Aquitaine in English hands, with garrisons establishing themselves in Anjou, Maine, Touraine, and even in Burgundy, it really seemed as though Edward's great moment had come. The strategy of provincial opportunism had done its work, and the time had come to revert to the single great army marching straight to its goal, a goal that could now be defined.

But in the event Edward was not ready to move until late in the autumn and by then the climax of his fortunes had passed, for the situation in France was a good deal less advantageous to him than it had been in the spring and early summer of the previous year. The dauphin's authority was beginning to make itself felt and he had reached an understanding with Charles of Navarre. Edward's security had been very bad and Reims was prepared to meet him. After a month or so the siege of the great fortified city had to be abandoned and the army moved into Burgundy and then turned back on Paris, which it dared not assault. When they saw that he was in retreat, the French opened negotiations and a draft peace treaty was drawn up at Brétigny (8 May 1360) (cf. fig. 15), a tiny hamlet a few miles south-east of Chartres.

To those historians who believe that Edward's war aims were no more than a sovereign Aquitaine, this treaty represents his moment of triumph; to those who believe he wanted the French crown, it registers his defeat. For although by its terms he was given more than a third of France in full sovereignty (cf. map II), he was to renounce his claim to the crown of France, and to the sovereignty of Normandy, Touraine, Anjou, Maine, Brittany and Flanders, where allied forces occupied towns, castles and fortresses in his name. But the treaty still had to be ratified. When that happened at Calais in the following autumn (24 October 1360), the clauses touching French renunciation of the sovereignty and *ressort* (the right to give judicial decisions which could not be challenged before a higher court) in the territories assigned to Edward, and those providing for Edward's renunciations, had to be taken out of the treaty and embodied in a separate clause which provided for them to be made at a later date, after the transfer of certain specified territories; but the renunciations were never made.

It was once suggested that these changes were the result of an astute diplomatic manoeuvre on the part of the French negotiators, though the only argument offered in favour of that assumption was that they later proved to be advantageous to the king of France. More recently, it has been convincingly demonstrated that, since the transfer of territories could not be completed within the envisaged time schedule, it was inevitable that the renunciations should be legislated for separately. On the other hand, to judge from Edward's hurry to get things moving at Calais and from his actions in the following years, it seems fairly clear that it was his policy to try and secure the territories assigned to him as quickly as possible, with or even without the French king's renunciations, and before he was prepared to make his own. If this was his policy, was it dictated by a wish to see that the territories assigned to him by the treaty were actually handed over, or was it because, in the final instance,

Fig. 14   King John pardons Charles of Navarre; *Grandes Chroniques. Paris, Bibliothèque Nationale Ms français 2813, fo. 395.* (7 × 6.3)

27. Effigy of Sir John de Hardreshull, lieutenant of Brittany (1343–4), Ashton Church, Northamptonshire.

Fig. 15   Part of the principal document of the treaty of Brétigny, 1360. *London, Public Record Office.*

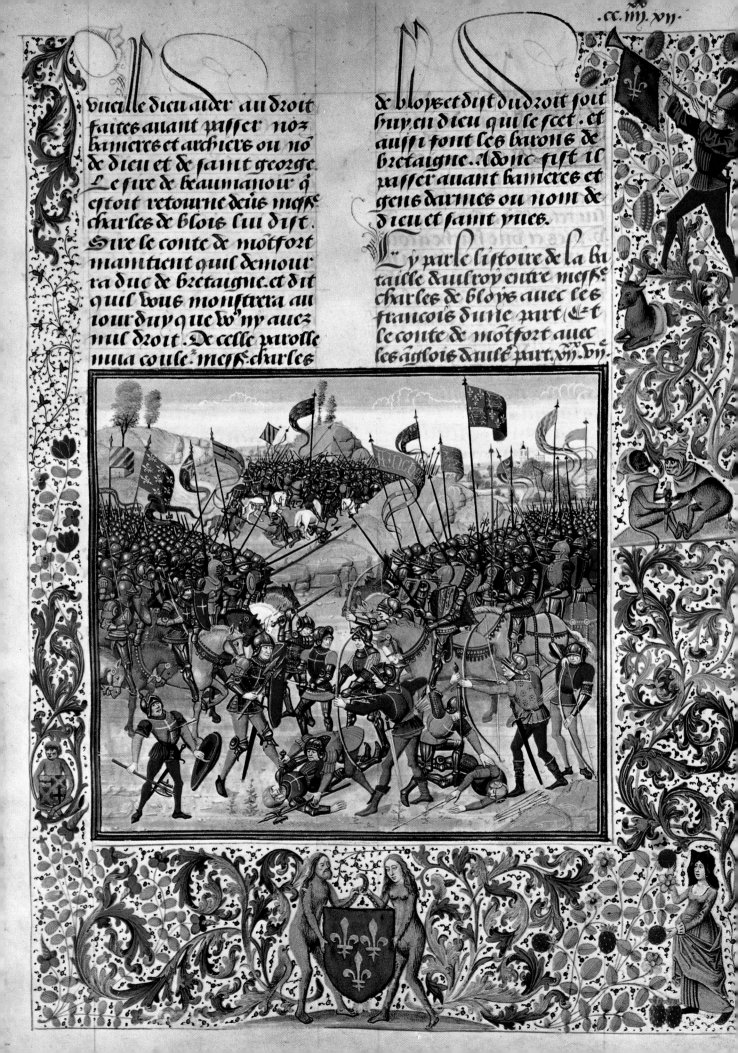

vueille dieu aider au droit
faites auant passer noz
baineres et archiers ou nõ
de dieu et de saint george.
Le sire de beaumanoir q̃
estoit retourne de9 mess̄
charles de blois luy dist.
Sire le conte de moffort
maintient quil demour
ra duc de bretaigne.et dit
q̃ il vous monsterra au
iourduy q̃ le v̊ ny auez
nul droit. De celle parolle
ruia co9le9 mess̄ charles

de blois et dist du droit soit
huy en dieu qui le scet. et
aussi font les barons de
bretaigne. Adonc fist il
passer auant baineres et
gens darmes ou nom de
dieu et saint yues.

Ly parle listoire de la ba
taille du roy entre mess̄
charles de blois auec les
francois dune part. Et
le conte de moffort auec
les aglois dune part.xv.biij.

he could not surrender his claim to the throne? Did he genuinely fear that, if he renounced the Crown, the French would hold up the cession of the remaining territories indefinitely, or was it because the treaty of Brétigny had not given him what he wanted? The documents tell us no more than those for the peace negotiations at Avignon in 1344 and 1354, which do not reveal why a settlement was not reached and who was responsible for the breakdown. In the final analysis, we can only surmise the aims and motives which lay behind the king's actions.

Fig. 16   The king of Navarre at the Pré-aux-Clercs; *Grandes Chroniques. Paris, Bibliothèque Nationale Ms français 2813, fo. 405v.* (7.6 × 6.3)

28. The battle of Auray (1364); Froissart's Chronicles. *Paris, Bibliothèque Nationale Ms français 2643, fo. 292.* (32 × 43).

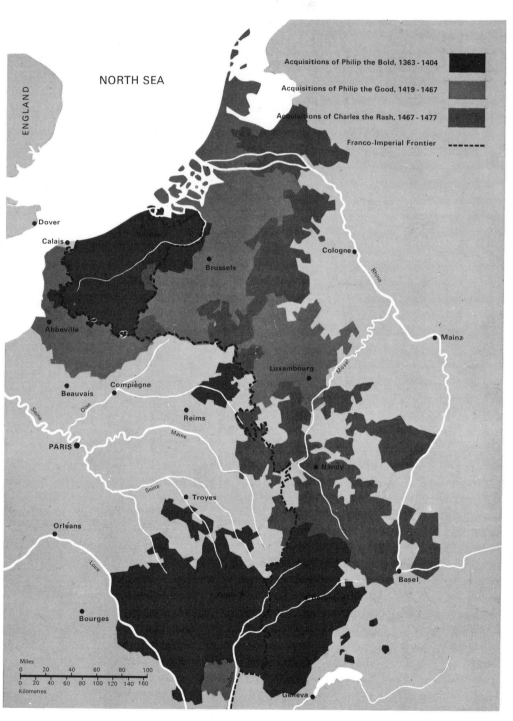

Acquisitions of Philip the Bold, 1363 - 1404

Acquisitions of Philip the Good, 1419 - 1467

Acquisitions of Charles the Rash, 1467 - 1477

Franco-Imperial Frontier   - - - - - - -

NORTH SEA

ENGLAND

Dover

Calais

Brussels

Cologne

Abbeville

Luxembourg

Mainz

Beauvais

Compiègne

Reims

Nancy

PARIS

Troyes

Orléans

Basel

Bourges

Geneva

Miles
0   20   40   60   80   100
0 20 40 60 80 100 120 140 160
Kilometres

III   The growth of the duchy of Burgundy.

On the face of it, there is no evidence that Edward was anything but satisfied with the considerable territories which he received, most of which were subsequently formed into an impressive principality for his eldest son, the victor of Poitiers. Nor is there any sign of his wish to renew the war in the years after 1360, in order to secure more. It was Charles V of France who, once he had established himself firmly on the throne, was determined to see that the treaty of Brétigny was undone. It is possible that Edward was willing to settle for peace in 1360 because in the years after Poitiers he could not control the war as he wished. Unable to pay the English, Breton, Gascon and Navarrese forces who were ostensibly fighting in his name, he had progressively less control over the fortresses they occupied throughout France; for it was in these years that the free companies were being formed (cf. below, pp. 169-71). There was more than one captain who, like Robert Knowles, could boast that he fought 'neither for the king of England, nor for the king of Navarre, but for himself'. Moreover Charles of Navarre was by then in his mid-twenties, a popular figure with a considerable following, and a dangerous rival. On whose side were his forces? Extensive territory in Aquitaine, together with Calais and Ponthieu, must have appeared a very solid prospect in view of the increasing anarchy in France. Edward had already lost much since the summer of 1358. Had he not settled quickly in 1360, he was likely, as the duke of Lancaster is said to have told him, 'to lose more in one day than we have gained in twenty years'.

Must we presume that his war aims were consistent? To judge from his actions he was a remarkable opportunist. His interventions in Scotland, Flanders and Brittany; his flirtations with Charles of Navarre; his claim to Hainault, Holland and Zeeland by right of his wife; all seem to point in this direction, even his motto: 'It is as it is'. Up to 1358 the war went exceedingly well for him and he could place his stakes high. But in the years of victory, circumstances were everywhere against him. He left for Reims when it was already too late, his good fortune had broken and he was wise to make a peace on terms that were still good.

Peace lasted only nine years—hardly more than the period of truce that followed the fall of Calais. They were far from inactive, in both the military and the diplomatic spheres. Although the treaty of Brétigny had left the issue of the Breton succession to be resolved by the rival claimants without outside interference, nevertheless both French and English troops took part in the wars in Brittany, which was finally secured for John de Montfort when his rival Charles of Blois was killed and his army defeated in battle at Auray on 29 September 1364 (cf. pl. 28). English and French troops also found themselves in opposite camps in the war south of the Pyrenees, where Peter the Cruel was driven from the throne of Castile by his half-brother Henry of Trastámara, assisted by Du Guesclin and an army of *routiers*. The Black Prince's intervention on behalf of Peter was not as pointless as was once supposed, for the French intervention in Castile was intended to lead on to a Franco-Aragonese invasion of Aquitaine and, as early as February 1365, the prince was aware of Charles V's plans. Prince Edward's famous victory at Nájera on 3 April 1367 (cf. pl. 9) enabled him to restore Peter to the throne and once again demonstrated his abilities as a commander; but his political ineptitude was apparent in his refusal to surrender to Peter those of his political opponents whom he had taken prisoner. Within two years, these men had murdered the king and opened the way for the usurpation of Trastámara and the reassertion of French control over the Castilian fleet. Meanwhile, since Peter failed to reimburse the prince for his expenses, the latter was obliged to try and raise his men's wages from the already overtaxed Gascons.

A new *fouage* provoked widespread resentment and the resistance of two of the prince's leading vassals: the count of Armagnac and the lord of Albret. Charles V encouraged them to lay their grievances before him. He made the most of the prince's

Fig. 17 Coin: gold *guiennois* of the Black Prince, minted at Bordeaux; similar to those issued by his father. *Obverse:* the prince in armour under a gothic-style portal; *reverse:* floriate cross. *London, British Museum.*

29. La Grosse Horloge, Rouen.

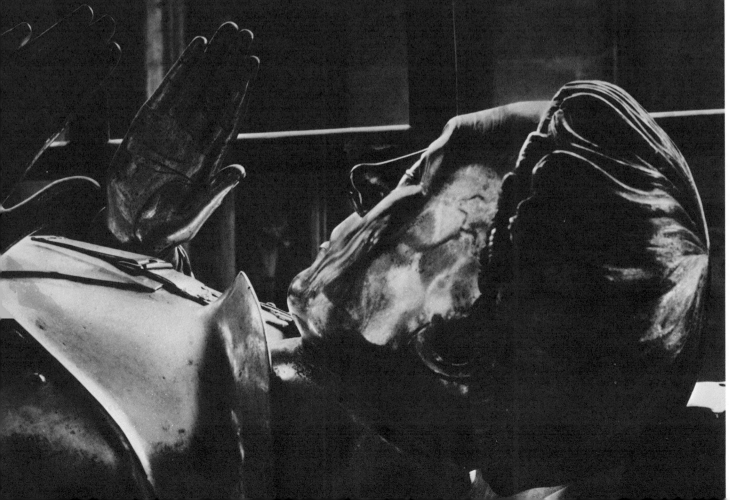

embarrassment and, after making a great show of seeking the advice of eminent jurists, on 3 December 1368 he declared his right to receive their appeals. Edward III took up the challenge. On 3 June 1369 he resumed the French title and on 30 November following Charles V pronounced his French lands confiscate. During the course of the next six years, the principality of Aquitaine was once again reduced to the coastal strip between Bordeaux and Bayonne, with a number of isolated garrisons along the Dordogne valley as far as Bergerac; most of Brittany was overrun by French armies; Ponthieu, Saint-Sauveur-le-Vicomte and Bécherel were also lost. How had this been achieved so quickly?

There can be no doubt that most of the credit goes to the dauphin Charles, who succeeded to the throne on King John's death in London in 1364 (cf. pl. 7). Charles 'the Wise', as he was known (1364–80), was a first-rate politician and diplomat, an able man of only twenty-nine at the time of his accession and whose comparatively early death at forty-five was to cost his country very dear. He had proved his mettle in the years after the battle of Poitiers, first as lieutenant and then as regent for his father during the years in which John was a prisoner in London. He had weathered the Parisian revolution (when he was forced to flee the capital), the *Jacquerie*, and the invasion of 1359–60; and he had already done much to restore the fortunes of his country before John's release. He was no soldier, he had a delicate constitution, he suffered from ulcers, and had a bad circulation; but he kept a regular routine, possessed fantastic energy and a capacity for delegating work and choosing the right men to carry it out. He sought and received sound advice from intimate councillors like the clerk Raoul de Presles, the knight-administrator Philip de Mézières and the scholar Nicolas Oresme. The work of government was greatly facilitated by good administrators like the chancellors Jean and Guillaume de Dormans, the *prévôt* of Paris Hugues Aubriot and Bureau de la Rivière. Not the least important was the good generalship which he found in soldier-administrators like his brother Louis of Anjou, lieutenant in Languedoc (1364–80), the constable Du Guesclin (1370–80) (cf. pl. 25), the admiral Jean de Vienne (1373–96), and the marshals Audrehem (1351–68), the elder Boucicaut (1356–68), Moutain de Blainville (1368–91) and Louis de Sancerre (1368–97) (cf. pl. 26).

The years between 1360 and 1369 witnessed military and financial reorganization made necessary by the activities of the Navarrese and the free companies and the need to find the money to pay John's ransom. The Navarrese threat was eliminated when Du Guesclin, at the time little more than an unpolished Breton knight, secured his first victory at Cocherel in Normandy (16 May 1364). By intervening in the dispute over the throne of Castile, and by maintaining a standing field army in the years after 1364 (cf. below, pp. 134), he either eliminated the majority of the *routier* captains or brought them into his pay, and he also thereby secured the support of the Castilian fleet in the war which he renewed against England in 1369. Thereafter, Charles concentrated the entire French effort on the reconquest of the territories ceded at Brétigny. The military and naval arsenal in the *clos des gallées* at Rouen was reorganized, Franco-Castilian naval raids were mounted on the English coast and simultaneous attacks were made on the English positions in both northern and southern France.

On the English side the war lacked central direction. The strategy of simultaneous and interdependent landings in France was abandoned, or else seemed inappropriate to the king and the victor of Poitiers in what was essentially a defensive war. An expedition entrusted to Robert Knowles in 1370 turned itself into a futile plundering raid, relief intended for Aquitaine came to nothing when a fleet under the earl of Pembroke was sunk (with the soldiers' pay on board) off La Rochelle by a Castilian fleet in 1372 (cf. pl. 80), and Gaunt's fantastic campaign across France in 1373, while it showed immense daring, bore no fruits. Charles V, adopting the tactics

30. Gilt copper effigy of the Black Prince (d. 1376), Canterbury Cathedral.

31. Effigy of Richard Beauchamp, earl of Warwick (d. 1439), Beauchamp Chapel, St Mary's, Warwick.

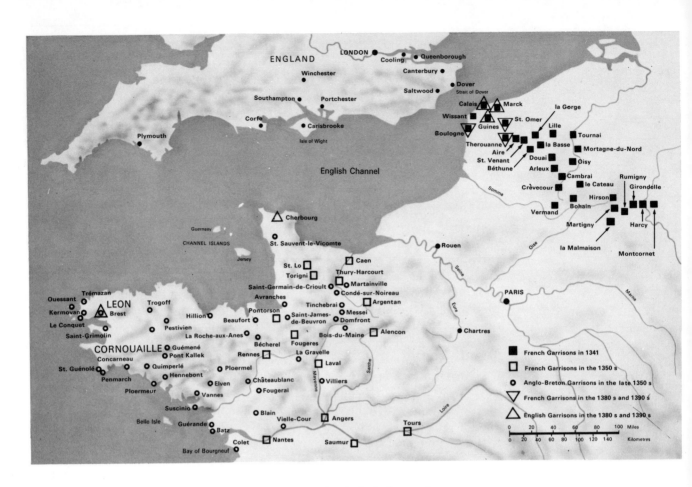

IV Brittany and the northern frontier in the fourteenth century.

which he had learned in the crisis of 1359–60, practised a scorched earth policy and forbade his generals to risk an engagement with the enemy. Moreover, Edward III was ageing fast. The Black Prince returned home in 1371, his health broken and his reputation tarnished. With his death in 1376, followed by that of the king a year later, the era of Crécy and Poitiers came to an end.

Divisions in council, which became evident in Edward's last years, were reflected in military policy. In 1375, when the earl of Cambridge and John IV of Brittany were promoting military operations in the latter's duchy, John of Gaunt was busy negotiating a truce at Bruges. When this expired, within a matter of days after Edward's death, French naval raids on the English coast were intensified. Organized by Jean de Vienne, these aimed to inflict as much damage as possible, to secure command of the Channel and so prevent military aid being sent to Brittany and Guyenne, and as a preliminary to a sea and land blockade of Calais. The latter was undertaken by the duke of Burgundy, using much of the latest equipment collected by Vienne at the *clos des gallées*. Military assistance was also sent into Guyenne, where an Anglo-Gascon army was defeated and the seneschal, Sir Thomas Felton, captured at the battle of Eymet (1 September 1377). But the final crunch did not come in 1377. Calais and the Bordelais held out and during the course of that year Cherbourg and Brest were ceded to the English government, for the duration of the war, by Charles of Navarre and the duke of Brittany. This was the situation when Charles V died in 1380, the year of the last great English expedition of the fourteenth century, led by the earl of Buckingham.

70

Much of the subsequent period between 1380 and 1415 was taken up by uneasy truce. Garrison warfare from frontier posts and piracy in the Channel were the chief military characteristics of these years. Not until the accession of Henry V was the war once again actively resumed. There were several reasons for this. To begin with, the kings of both countries were children and this fact made it difficult for a vigorous military effort to be attempted. Richard II (cf. pl. 13) was only eleven on his accession in 1377 and Charles VI (cf. pl. 16) was the same age on his accession three years later. Divergent interests in the councils of both kingdoms prevented either effective military policy or peace negotiations from being pushed forward. John of Gaunt, becoming daily more absorbed in his Spanish ambitions, advocated no consistent policy towards France. Gloucester and Warwick seem to have sponsored an energetic anti-French policy as soon as they ascertained that Richard was decidedly inclined towards peace. Similarly in France, the all-powerful duke of Burgundy subjected the

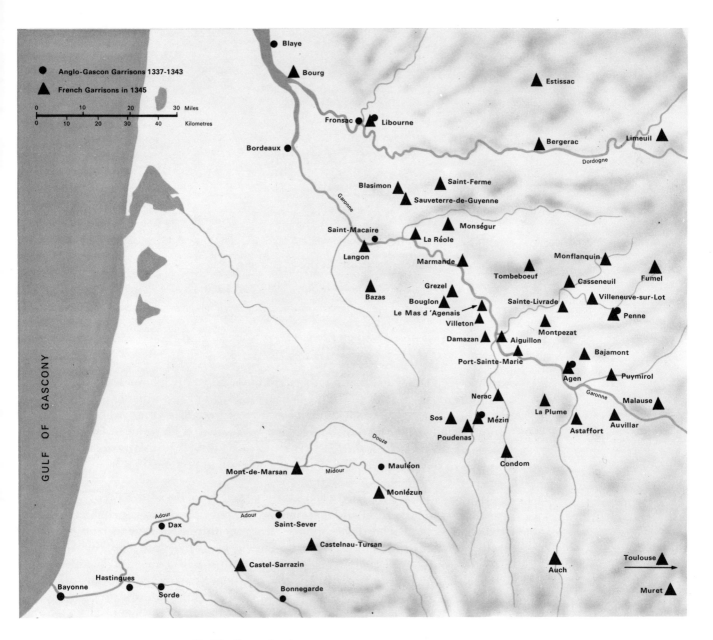

V   The Gascon frontier, 1337–45.

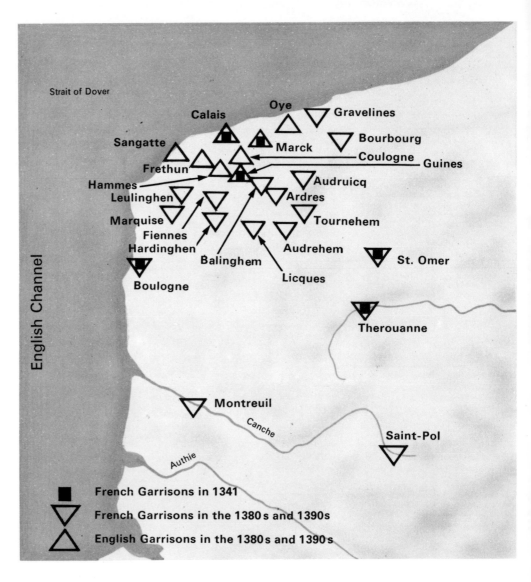

Strait of Dover

Calais

Oye

Gravelines

Sangatte

Bourbourg

Marck

Coulogne

Guines

Frethun

Hammes

Audruicq

Leulinghen

Ardres

Marquise

Tournehem

Fiennes

Hardinghen

Audrehem

Balinghem

St. Omer

Licques

Boulogne

Therouanne

English Channel

Montreuil

Canche

Saint-Pol

Authie

French Garrisons in 1341

French Garrisons in the 1380s and 1390s

English Garrisons in the 1380s and 1390s

VI   The Calais frontier in the fourteenth century.

king's foreign policy to his own interests in Flanders where his aim was first to secure, and then to protect, the Flemish heirloom. Hope of a permanent reconciliation seemed near in 1393, when a provisional treaty was drawn up whereby a reconstituted duchy of Aquitaine would have been created for John of Gaunt and his successors, to be held from the French Crown. But since there was resistance in Gascony to the prospect of a ruler in Bordeaux and of alienation from the English Crown, the scheme had to be abandoned.

In 1396 Richard married Charles' daughter, Isabella, and a twenty-eight year truce was concluded. But the two monarchs were unable to conclude a treaty of peace and, when Richard was removed from the throne three years later, it seemed likely that all his efforts in that direction might be thrown into jeopardy. Henry IV was, however, too preoccupied in securing his throne at home to make any effort to acquire that of France as well and in subsequent years he was not in sufficiently good health to undertake large-scale military operations. Internal divisions made it difficult for the French to exploit Henry's domestic embarrassments, although they made notable encroachments in Guyenne during the early years of his reign. After 1392 Charles VI underwent recurrent periods of mental illness and later became

32. Part of the medieval fortifications at Carcassonne.

72

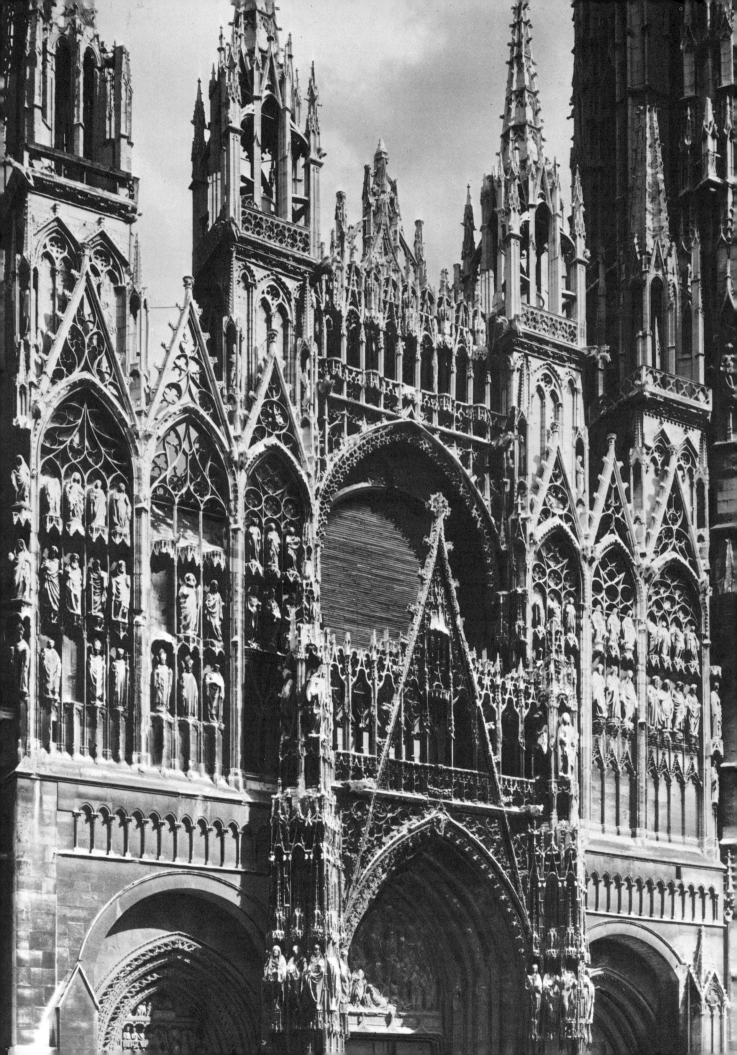

incapable of carrying on the business of government. The length of his life (he died in 1422) was as unlucky for France as was the brevity of his father's. The most important development of these years, not least for its future bearing on the relations between England and France, was the increasing power of the dukes of Burgundy.

The history of the Valois dukes of Burgundy began when the infant Philip de Rouvre, the last Capetian duke, died in 1361. The inheritance was split up and the duchy passed (though not without subsequent dispute) to Philip's cousin King John, and the imperial county of Burgundy (Franche-Comté), together with Artois and Champagne, went to Margaret, the daughter of Louis de Male, count of Flanders (cf. pl. 12). In November 1363 John secretly promised the duchy to his fourth son Philip (cf. pl. 11) and the grant was confirmed by letters patent of Charles V in June 1364. To bar English pretensions in the Low Countries, royal support was given for Philip's marriage to Margaret, who was the only surviving child of Louis de Male. Margaret had been betrothed to Edmund of Langley, son of Edward III, but Pope Urban V had given aid to the French cause by refusing a dispensation for this marriage which was within the prohibited degrees. Her marriage to Philip took place in 1369, her father having finally given his consent in return for a considerable money payment and the return to Flanders of the territories lost to France in 1305 (Lille, Douai, Orchies), which he had long coveted. When Louis died in 1384, Philip succeeded to the counties of Flanders, Artois, Nevers, Rethel and Franche-Comté, and a number of smaller but important lordships (cf. map III). These acquisitions were at the time seen to constitute an important extension of French power and during the following years Philip built up his influence in the Low Countries through a number of opportune marriages and family alliances.

It seems unlikely (though it has recently been suggested) that Philip was already thinking of building up an independent Burgundian state. If he was thinking in these terms, it is difficult to see why his lands were divided up between his three sons on his death in 1404. For although the two Burgundies, Flanders and Artois were kept together for the eldest son John the Fearless, Antoine, count of Rethel until his father's death, received the duchies of Brabant and Limbourg and the lordship of Antwerp, and the youngest son Philip secured Nevers, Rethel and the lands of Champagne. At this point, it looked as if the Burgundian inheritance would go separate ways and it was largely a matter of chance that John's son Philip the Good (1419–67) was able to bring together all of the lands which the family had held under his grandfather and a good deal more besides. For although John the Fearless had eight children, he only had one son, and there was therefore no question of the division of the inheritance in 1419. It is from this date that we can confidently perceive a policy of deliberate expansion to the north and east and for the junction of Flanders and Burgundy proper. Up to 1419 it was the policy of the dukes to seek domination in France and of the French monarchy and only thereafter that they sought a political capital outside France. To the achievement of both of these ambitions there were dangerous opponents.

During the reign of Charles V, Philip the Bold's preoccupations, as those of his other brothers Louis, duke of Anjou, and John, duke of Berry (cf. pl. 18), lay in the prosecution of the war with England and the giving of counsel to his royal brother. On the accession of the infant Charles VI the duty of counselling his nephew became a yet more pressing obligation. A council of regency was formed dominated by the royal uncles, who dismissed Charles V's ministers and who exploited their hold over their nephew and diverted royal resources to their own ends. The duke of Berry exploited his tenure of office as lieutenant in Languedoc to increase his own revenues. Philip the Bold used royal troops to suppress a revolt in Flanders at Roosebeke in 1382 and he was able to consolidate his interests in the Low Countries and Germany through Charles VI's marriage to Isabella of Bavaria. Between 1382 and 1403 he

Fig. 18 Privy Seal of the Black Prince. *London, Public Record Office.*

33. The west front of Rouen Cathedral.

received one and a third million *livres* from Charles in 'gifts' alone and towards the end of his life nearly half of his revenues were drawn from the French Crown in the form of pensions, gifts and grants of royal taxation. In the later years of his life, and under John the Fearless, this reliance of the Burgundians on French financial sources became more pressing.

Meanwhile, the king's madness brought to a head the struggle for control of the French government between Philip the Bold and Charles' younger brother Louis, who became duke of Orléans in 1392. The two dukes found themselves rivals in Italy and Germany, over the Schism, the policy to be adopted towards England and above all for control of the kingdom. Broadly speaking, Orléans proved the most influential when Charles was sane, and Burgundy when Charles was mad. The rivalry between them prevented France from exploiting the English domestic troubles in the later years of Richard II's reign and the dynastic change of 1399, and the conflict between the two houses was further intensified with the succession of John the Fearless. John made skilful use of demagogy to win the people of Paris over to his side and the competition for control of government culminated in November 1407 in the murder of Orléans by an armed gang at the behest of the duke of Burgundy. Three years later civil war broke out, the Orléanist vengeance being organized by the count of Armagnac, whose daughter married Louis' son and successor Charles in 1410. When the fighting began (almost everywhere, but especially in the Ile-de-France) the two sides inevitably competed for English military support. At first, the English hesitated between Burgundy and Armagnac, then played off the one against the other in order to secure the most handsome terms. Henry IV was unable to intervene in person, but two thousand English troops sent to Calais in October 1411 assisted Burgundy to raise the blockade of Paris and the king's second son, Thomas of Clarence, was sent with an army to support the Armagnacs in the following year. With the accession of Henry V on 21 March 1413, full scale intervention was inevitable.

By a singular irony of fate, the first king of England who had some English blood in his veins and who started having some of his chancery deeds written in English was also the man who achieved for his son the dream of his Plantagenet predecessors: the union in one person of the Crowns of England and of France. To succeed where Edward III had failed took outstanding qualities and in these Henry V (cf. pl. 15 and fig. 19) was not lacking. King at the age of twenty-five, as a boy he had seen service in Ireland with Richard II, had served a hard military apprenticeship in the Welsh campaigns at the beginning of his father's reign and had subsequently shown himself eager to exercise the royal power. A good soldier he was also, like his ancestors Henry II and Edward I, a businesslike bureaucrat, a sound administrator and a stern judge. To one French historian his devoutness has seemed hypocritical, his conduct deceitful, his sense of justice pretentious, even false, his revenge cruel, and his ambition overwhelming. Yet there seems no reason to doubt his piety or his conviction in the justice of his cause. In that his claims were ambitious and his diplomacy deceitful he was a true son of his times. That his Victorian biographer found it necessary to explain away his debauched youth as being out of keeping with the piety which marked him when he became king, does not necessitate that we should find the two incompatible any more than did his contemporaries. His popularity among his countrymen was hardly less, and was possibly greater than that of Edward III; and his premature death at the peak of unprecedented fame, while it may have contributed to his posthumous esteem, was a tragedy for the nation.

It seems clear that a full-scale renewal of the war was Henry's policy from the beginning of his reign; but the *voie de fait* which he had in mind had to have its diplomatic preparation if it was to seem just. There were two possibilities: he could go the whole length and demand the French Crown, or he could fall back on the

Fig. 19 Henry V with a sword. *London, British Museum Cotton Ms Julius E IV Art I, fo. 8v.*

34. Window in Henry IV's Chapel, Canterbury Cathedral.

76

unfulfilled treaty of Brétigny. An embassy sent to France in 1414 went far beyond the latter in its demands. It suggested that if Henry were to be given the king's daughter Catherine in marriage, he would be satisfied with full and independent sovereignty in Normandy, Touraine, Maine, Anjou, Brittany, Flanders and Aquitaine—territories amounting to more than the Plantagenet dominions when at their greatest under Henry II. When the French tried to separate the question of Henry's marriage from his territorial claims, they found that the English had actually increased their demands to include half of Provence and the castles and territories of Beaufort and Nogent. The fact that Henry was simultaneously negotiating with both the Burgundians and the Armagnacs was undoubtedly intended to enhance the price of his support to each of them. That his demands were rejected was probably no more than he expected for, as with Edward III in 1359, the French refusal made it possible for him to use the army which he had long been assembling.

The invasion, the destination of which was even to the hour of departure a closely guarded secret, took place at the mouth of the Seine in Normandy during the second week of August 1415 (cf. map VIII). The king's intention was probably no more than to make a reconnaissance march and to secure a port of disembarkation to act as a bridgehead for the subsequent conquest of Normandy. In this, and in much more than he had bargained for, he was successful. After a somewhat protracted siege of Harfleur in which his forces suffered heavy casualties, he was proceeding northwards to Calais when he was forced to battle at Agincourt on the plateau of Artois (25 October 1415) (cf. jacket front). The French repeated the mistakes of Crécy and Poitiers in mounting a cavalry charge across unfavourable terrain on dismounted English men-at-arms supported by a wedge of archers and infantry. Once more, against all odds, the English victory was overwhelming and the French losses were very considerable. But although Henry's victory established his military reputation and allowed him to proceed to Calais unmolested and with his mission amply fulfilled, it was not until a second invasion in 1417 that the systematic conquest of Normandy was begun and only three years later that his troops were sufficiently firmly entrenched for him to bring the French to terms. On 21 May 1420 a treaty was concluded at Troyes (cf. fig. 24) which would have more than satisfied the ambitions even of Edward III. By its terms, Henry was granted Charles' daughter Catherine in marriage, and it was agreed that the Crown of France should pass to Henry and their children on Charles' death. Meanwhile, in view of Charles' illness, Henry was to act as regent and he undertook to bring into royal control the territory then recognizing the Armagnacs, asserting that along with Normandy it would be absorbed into the French kingdom when he became king of France. The dauphin was thus disinherited by the mutual consent of his parents and the way was paved for the establishment of a dual monarchy of England and France. How had this been achieved so quickly?

There can be little doubt that Henry's personal ability contributed actively to his triumph. He was masterful and competent, unwilling to endure opposition, but clear and firm in his decisions. This sense of authority made him liked as well as respected. He forbade his soldiers, with much more success than might have been expected, to loot or otherwise ravage newly conquered territory. There was a touch of genius in his command, especially in the regard accorded him by his own men, which made him a good, if not an outstanding general. But he was better at redeeming than exploiting a situation. Thus, although he was out-generalled before Agincourt, he won a dramatic victory which allowed him to get his army to Calais and to prevent the relief of Harfleur. He was fully aware of the strategic importance of Normandy in any attempt to secure France and his systematic conquest of the duchy, which he accomplished piecemeal behind frontier posts established between Caen and Mantes, and in the marches of Maine and Alençon, showed a strong grasp of

Fig. 20   The siege of Rouen in 1418; *Life and Acts of Richard Beauchamp, earl of Warwick,* by John Rous, *c.* 1485. *London, British Museum Cotton Ms Julius E IV Art VI, fo. 19v.* (22.8 × 20)

Fig. 21   The siege of Caen in 1418; *Life and Acts of Richard Beauchamp, earl of Warwick,* by John Rous, *c.* 1485. *London, British Museum Cotton Ms Julius E IV Art VI, fo. 19.* (21.5 × 20)

35.   Interior of the Chantry Chapel, from the Chancel, Higham Ferrers Church, Northamptonshire.

the military situation. Together with treaties which secured the neutrality of the dukes of Anjou and Brittany, these frontier fortresses effectively sealed Normandy off from east, south and west, and enabled him to secure full control of the duchy.

However, the most important factor in his favour was undoubtedly the political situation in France. While Henry proceeded with the conquest of Normandy, John the Fearless occupied Paris and secured control of the king and queen; but they were still operating independently and, if a reconciliation had been achieved between Armagnac and Burgundy, the story would have been very different. But instead of agreement being reached on the bridge at Montereau (cf. pl. 58), John the Fearless was murdered by the Armagnacs (10 September 1419) and as a result his son Philip the Good determined to give his full support to Henry. It was their alliance, rather than the victory of Agincourt or the conquest of Normandy, that made possible the treaty of Troyes.

Two years after the treaty of Troyes, both Henry and Charles VI died; the latter within two months of his son-in-law. The infant Henry VI was solemnly proclaimed king of England and, on his grandfather's death, king of France. In conformity with the provisions agreed to at Troyes, a dual monarchy of the two realms was set up; but in reality it was an Anglo-Burgundian *condominium* that was established. After 1422 there was no kingdom of France as it had developed over the centuries. There was a northern, Plantagenet Anglo-French state, a Burgundian state (partly in France and half, or rather more than half, in the empire) and a Valois, southern French state. Up to 1435 the government of northern France was managed by the duke of Bedford (cf. pl. 86), as regent for Henry VI, working in conjunction with Philip the Good, duke of Burgundy (cf. pl. 87). After their co-operation came to an end in that year, the English dominion was reduced to those parts of northern France

Fig. 22 Coin: gold *salute* of Henry VI, minted at Rouen. *Observe:* arms of England and France and above the Annunciation, showing the Virgin and Angel; *reverse:* Plain cross with lis and leopard and letter H below the cross. *London, British Museum.*

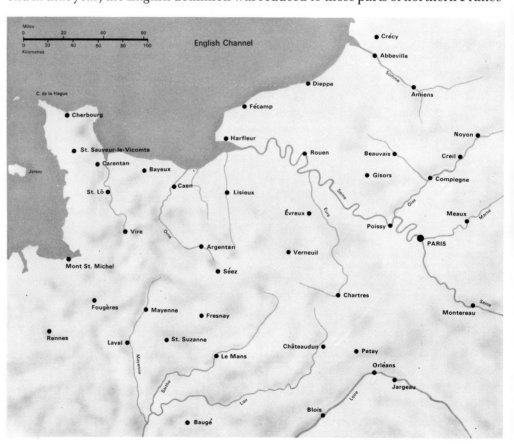

36. Bodiam Castle, Sussex (1386).   VII   Northern France in the fifteenth century.

36

Coment le duc de lancastre et le duc de breline vindrent a paris pour eulz combatre deuant le Roy. mais le roy print le fait

N lan. mil en fa main trois cens cinq̃te deux la veille de la uye dame miaoust le combati monseigneur Guy de Neelle Seigneur dou remout lors mareschal de france en Bretaigne. et fu le dit mareschal occys en la

dicte bataille. le Sire de Briquebec. le chastellain de Beauuais z plulieurs autres no bles tant du dit pays de bretaigne come dautres maires du royaume de france.

Item en icelui an . ccclij . le mardy quart iour de decembre se dot combatre a paris un duc dalemaigne apelle le duc de brelme contre le duc de lancastre pour pa roles que le dit duc de lancastre deuoit a uoir dites du dit duc de breslue dont il appella en la court du Roy de france. Et uni occupied by English troops, and what remained of the ancient duchy of Aquitaine. By the time these were lost in 1453, Charles VII's authority had been long established; but it was not until the death of Charles the Rash in 1477 that the Burgundian stranglehold was finally broken and the integrity of the Valois French kingdom finally re-established.

Bedford's achievement as regent for Henry VI was undoubtedly considerable. He realized the importance of the Burgundian alliance and during his lifetime he managed to keep it intact against considerable threats, including the foolish machinations of his brother Humphrey. In the government of northern France he showed a wise respect for native institutions and personnel, and his efforts to achieve the maximum publicity for the dual monarchy seem not to have been without rewards. But the government of Normandy and the *pais de conquête* (that part of the Seine valley beyond the Norman frontiers which Henry V had conquered before the treaty of Troyes), and subsequently of Anjou and Maine, was kept separate from the government of those areas (notably Paris and the Ile-de-France) which had been secured by the treaty of Troyes. In the former, the source of Bedford's authority was Henry's conquest. In the latter it was the Burgundian alliance and the Burgundian *coup d'état* of 1418. Thus, while Paris became the undoubted capital of the Anglo-French state, and while all the central organs of government (conciliar, judicial, financial) continued to function in Henry VI's name along traditional lines, a separate administrative machinery based on Rouen was maintained as the surest guarantee of English power. While he technically satisfied the claims of the treaty of Troyes, Bedford consolidated the Anglo-French administration in Normandy so that even the fall of Paris in 1436 did not shake it.

Nearly all the government offices in the capital were filled by Burgundian personnel. The most important of these was the *grand conseil*, which made policy decisions and sent out general directives to all branches of the administration. Although its members were chosen by Bedford, with whom the most important decisions (particularly concerning military affairs) finally rested, the majority of them were Burgundian protégés or partisans. Frequently, during Bedford's absences from Paris, it acted on its own initiative under the direction of chancellors like Jean de Luxembourg and Pierre Cauchon. In Normandy, on the other hand, although some of the government departments set up by Henry V were suppressed, contrary to the provisions of the treaty of Troyes the council of Normandy (now called the council in Normandy) was made responsible for governmental and judicial affairs, a separate financial administration under a receiver-general was maintained and the moribund Estates were revived. In effect, the council in Normandy rather than the *grand conseil* in Paris directed the affairs of the duchy and the *pais de conquête* and it acted as a sovereign court, successfully resisting the claims to jurisdiction of the *parlement de Paris*. Nevertheless, this council was overwhelmingly French in composition and in local administration a clear distinction was made between civil and military affairs. Thus, although the five *baillis* were always English, their civil functions were exercised by *vicômtes* who were for the most part French. The former were chiefly responsible for military affairs, particularly the supervision of the mustering of the troops; the latter were responsible for local justice (including disputes arising between the troops and the civilian population), the summoning of the Estates and the collection of taxes. Doubtless a conciliatory policy was expedient from both a military and financial standpoint: the occupation would be facilitated by the minimum of resentment from the native population, and their willingness to vote upkeep costs. But it seems clear that Bedford sought, through sound and just government, to gain widespread support for the dual monarchy. The co-operation of the inhabitants and the testimony of the Norman chronicler Thomas Basin, leave us in no doubt that he had a fair measure of success in that task (cf. below, p. 151).

37. Institution of the Order of the Star; banquet of the Knights of the Star; *Grandes Chroniques*. Paris, *Bibliothèque Nationale Ms français 2813, fo. 394.* (7×6.3).

Alongside these two fairly distinct administrations, the dukes of Burgundy had built up a machinery of government for their by now considerable territories. Although a mass of principalities which had been brought together by inheritance, purchase, marriage, diplomacy and war, and which were held together by a variety of ties, the Burgundian state—the grand duchy of the west—was developing central institutions based on those of France. These derived from or were superimposed upon the local institutions of each province; but under Philip the Good and Charles the Rash, really central organs emerged. Until that time there were three fairly distinct groups of territories for the purposes of administration: the duchy and the county of Burgundy (the former in France; the latter in the empire) together with the other southern territories; the county of Flanders; and the Low Countries (cf. map III). But centralizing tendencies and institutions were there from the start and they became progressively more important.

Thus, although the provisions of the treaty of Troyes were not strictly adhered to, the government of northern France was in no sense Anglicized. If anything, the contrary was the case. During the years of the Anglo-Burgundian *condominium*, the beginnings of what might be described as an Anglo-French secretariat were being formed. French administrative organization, in many fields in advance of its Plantagenet counterpart, was beginning to influence English practice, as it moulded Burgundian development. Secretaries like Jean de Rinel and Laurence Calot, who began their careers in Burgundian service, played significant roles not only in government departments at Paris and Rouen, but also in London. They held properties in each of these centres, and acted as intermediaries between their respective government personnel. In financial organization, the first systematic English budgeting was undertaken as part of a comprehensive survey of the entire resources of the dual monarchy in France and England in 1433–4 and it may have owed something to French methods of forward planning which crystallized during these years into the practice of drawing up an *état général des finances*. Even in military administration, the English achievement in Normandy owed much to the development of muster and review in French military organization during the previous century, adapted to English needs in the occupation of northern France by French financial personnel. Up to 1435, and for a while beyond, the dual monarchy of Henry VI was being given concrete form behind a comprehensive, if not always subtle, propaganda. Without Charles VI's disinherited son, it might well have led to the emergence of a lasting Anglo-French state.

Recognition of Henry VI was, however, limited to those provinces of northern France occupied by English troops or which were under Burgundian control, and to a few of the fiefs, notably Brittany. South of the Loire, apart from that part of Guyenne in English control, the country overwhelmingly favoured the Armagnacs and a provisional government had been set up under the dauphin at Bourges (cf. map II). Thus, an area amounting to more than half of the kingdom remained to be reduced to the obedience of the dual monarchy in conformity with the treaty of Troyes. Had Henry V lived longer, it is conceivable that resistance to his rule might have broken; but the succession of his eleven-month old child to the Valois throne hardly favoured a monarchy established by treaty in a France which harboured an ambitious duke and a dispossessed royal heir approaching manhood.

The dauphin Charles was almost twenty when his father died in 1422; but it was not for another eleven years, after the murder of his grasping adviser George de la Tremoïlle, that he finally shook off the control of the evil counsellors in his entourage and showed himself capable of being a king. For although the kingdom of Bourges (as those lands which recognized him came to be known) was superior to the Lancastrian government by virtue of the area under its control, its financial potential, its support by the appanaged princes, and the ability of its civil service, nevertheless a lack of morale at the top and the influence of dishonest officials and greedy courtiers for long prevented a bold military effort. The dauphin's greatest weakness lay in his own personality and those of the men who advised him or sponged on him. Charles was not a prince fitted to evoke enthusiasm, to defend what for long looked like a lost cause and to play the part of leader and then king. A puny young man, with a blank face and unpleasant features (cf. pl. 20), he was both physically and mentally weak. Unlike his grandfather Charles V, he was no judge of character, was unable to delegate responsibility effectively or to inspire good service. He doubted himself, his followers, even his rights; and after his father's death he relapsed into apathy, of which his entourage were quick to take advantage. Not until his later years did he reveal his capabilities.

Meanwhile, Bedford consolidated the English position in Normandy and the Seine valley and added Anjou and Maine to the territories secured by Henry V. While the relief of Orléans in April 1429 was undoubtedly important in that it prevented the Anglo-Burgundian forces from pressing further south, neither it nor the dauphin's coronation at Reims on 17 July following immediately compromised the English position. The Anglo-Burgundian advance had been checked, but Charles proved incapable of exploiting his successes. The guerilla warfare manifesting itself in northern France lacked central direction and no support was given to his partisans. The real turning point came with the death of Bedford (15 September 1435) and the Franco-Burgundian *rapprochement* at the congress of Arras (concluded 21 September 1435).

What, then, was the importance of Joan of Arc? The story of the Maid (cf. pl. 77) has inspired such a vast corpus of literature, representing so many shades of interpretation, that it is difficult, perhaps impossible, for the historian to assess her contribution to the French recovery. He must risk seeming sacrilegious or bigotted according to his convictions and those of the reader and it remains difficult to comprehend fully the psychology of her times. Much of her life is known to us from the records of her two trials: the one by which the inquisitorial judges, on Bedford's orders, led her to the stake in 1431, and the other which Charles VII had carried out in 1456 to rehabilitate her. The former is the more valuable of the two in that it does not suffer from hindsight and (while bearing in mind that very little was said about her in the greater part of France and in English circles at the time) is our only really contemporary evidence. The procedure of the trial was the not unusual one of the Inquisition. It was conducted in absolute secrecy of investigation and testimony, about which Joan was left in ignorance. She had no advocate to defend her against repeated examination by fresh relays of interrogators. Threats and false promises were used to obtain an admission of guilt and the signature of a confession. Her recorded answers convey, with astounding clarity, the impression of a peasant girl of considerable intelligence and common sense, with a serene faith, a fanatical devotion to her king and an absolute confidence in the justice of her cause. From them we can perceive the fervour which she managed to instil into her comrades-in-arms; but that fervour scarcely went beyond the limited circle of those in close proximity to her. Beyond the region of the Loire she was comparatively unknown. Nor was the enemy any better informed of her epic: the English chroniclers hardly mention her and that Bedford did not bother to circulate the result of her trial throughout the territory recognizing the dual monarchy, suggests that she had not seriously weakened English morale.

Joan was only a girl of seventeen at the time of the relief of Orléans and, as she herself admitted, she had little military sense. Although she secured undoubted ascendancy over the troops, she did not lead them. Dunois, Alençon and Richmond were in command. Moreover, Orléans had been under siege for six months when she arrived on the scene and the situation on the English side was already deteriorating.

Fig. 23   Portrait of Henry VI (1422–61 and 1470–1) by an unknown artist. *London, National Portrait Gallery.* (51 × 43)

A shortage of men prevented a close blockade and supply difficulties had led to sickness and desertion. And yet the enigma remains: that an insignificant peasant girl from Domremy, a village in an area surrounded by territory in Burgundian control at the eastern extremities of the kingdom, could convince all those she approached of her mission and ultimately persuade the dauphin to allow her to play the decisive role in the relief of Orléans and lead him to his coronation at Reims. We might be inclined to think of Joan as mad, mentally deficient, visionary or even bogus. Her contemporaries simply wondered if she was sent by God or the Devil. Whether or not her 'voices' were genuine is immaterial. The fact remains that many people were prepared to believe that her mission was divine, either through conviction or convenience. Joan's powers were given substance by the credulity of her age, just as her ultimate martyrdom derived from the source which had previously been her strength.

More significant, in the long run, were the negotiations that were taking place between the Armagnacs and Philip the Good. Partial truces were concluded with the duke in 1421 and 1423 and the French offensive of 1429–30 had made him take heed. The death of his sister Anne in 1432 weakened the influence of Bedford, who had married her in 1423. The conclusion of an alliance between Charles and the emperor constituted a threat to Burgundy from the north and east. Between 1430 and 1433, Niccolò Albergati (cf. pl. 21), papal legate in France, was active in making truce overtures to either side. Then, in 1434, the council of Basle and Pope Eugenius IV recognized Charles as rightful king of France, thereby implicitly revoking the treaty of Troyes. Discussions for a general settlement with Burgundy began at Nevers early in 1435 and the *rapprochement* was achieved at a great international peace congress at Arras during the course of the autumn.

In the discussions that then took place, the question of sovereignty remained all important. The English were unable to renounce the French Crown, refused to hold territory in France by homage and preferred to defer discussions on a general settlement. Bedford was not present at the conference and it was not until after his death, and the departure of the English ambassadors, that Philip the Good agreed to recognize Charles VII as king of France. It was necessary for Duke Philip that the peace negotiations should break down before he renounced the treaty of Troyes and, to this end, Cardinal Albergati was empowered to absolve him from the oath he had sworn to its terms in 1420. Charles VII then made considerable concessions to Burgundy. Philip secured from him a grant of territories he had acquired from Bedford, the Somme towns against later repayment, relief from doing homage during his lifetime and an acknowledgement of responsibility for the murder of John the Fearless at Montereau. In addition, Charles abrogated his alliance with the emperor. The English position was immediately weakened. Paris was evacuated on the 13 April following and by 1444, when a truce was concluded at Tours, only Normandy and part of Maine remained to the dual monarchy in northern France.

Meanwhile, the political situation in England had steadily deteriorated. During Henry VI's minority (1422–37) a regency council took over the government of the realm under the protectorship of the late king's brother Humphrey, duke of Gloucester. A struggle for power had developed between Gloucester and his father's half-brother Cardinal Henry Beaufort (cf. pl. 63), and the council was divided into opposing factions. These divisions became more acute after 1435, with the break-up of the Burgundian alliance and the death of Bedford. The problem of the French territories of the Crown became the foremost political issue and, since no new regent was appointed to France, it was an issue that had to be solved in Westminster. A division over French policy thus aggravated the already dangerous divisions in council. Gloucester wanted war but Beaufort favoured peace. When Henry VI took over the direction of affairs in 1437 the effect was disastrous, for he was totally

86

unfitted to fulfil the contemporary tasks of kingship. He was a good man, pious and kindly and not a person to harbour animosities. He liked to please those in close contact with him. His endowment of Eton and King's College showed him to be a generous benefactor, but he lacked the craft and guile essential to meet the political situation of his day. Thus after 1437 temptation to seek the king's favour superseded any pretence of collective action from the council. Curial replaced conciliar government and during the remainder of his reign the king became subject to favourites and advisers, the most important of whom were Beaufort (until his retirement from active politics in 1443), thereafter the dukes of Suffolk and Somerset and the queen, who completely dominated Henry after their marriage in 1444. All these factions pursued a peace policy and, in consequence, an opposition group was formed among those lords of the council who no longer had any say in affairs; they took up the cause of war.

There were two main issues in the overtures for peace: the release of the duke of Orléans (a prisoner in England since his capture at Agincourt) and Henry's marriage to a French princess. In 1444 Suffolk was given charge of an embassy to arrange for Henry's betrothal to Margaret of Anjou, Charles VII's niece. That he expected stiff opposition to this is evident from the fact that he only agreed to take up the mission upon receipt of a guarantee from the council, including Gloucester, that he would not be held responsible for what might ensue. The drama of the late 1390s was being staged once again; but this time the acts were longer and the epilogue was to prove more tragic. In effect, Henry's marriage, like that of Richard II, was accompanied, not by peace, but the conclusion of a truce. Moreover, the French demanded, as part of the settlement, the cession of Maine where many of the frontier garrisons protecting Normandy were most firmly entrenched. Under pressure from Margaret, who was ambitious, active, intense and had no comprehension of English interests and affairs, Henry agreed. This went against Suffolk's whole policy of negotiating peace from a position of strength; but he was forced to accept it or face dismissal. Feeling against the cession of Maine ran high and it was increasingly coupled with distrust of the foreigner. Gloucester, like his namesake in the 1390s over the proposed cession of Calais and the surrender of Brest, whipped up the xenophobia. On his death in 1446 Richard of York took over the opposition and, up to 1448, the English captains in Maine refused to hand over the fortresses under their command. But it was of no avail. In the following year, the truce of Tours broke down and Charles VII's armies invaded and rapidly reoccupied Normandy. In Guyenne he met with stiffer opposition for the Gascons, only too aware of their economic and political interests and the relatively light taxation they had to bear, remained loyal to the English Crown. Although Bordeaux was captured in 1451, a pro-English rising allowed a relieving force to be sent out to the duchy under the veteran soldier John Talbot, earl of Shrewsbury (cf. pl. 92). But with his defeat and death in battle at Castillon (situated on the Dordogne, some thirty miles up stream from Bordeaux) on 17 July 1453, three centuries of connection with the English Crown were brought to a close. Guyenne, as it turned out, had been irretrievably lost. Only Calais and the Channel Islands remained of the Plantagenet dominions in France.

Charles VII's achievement had been stupendous; but it had come in fits and starts. He had failed to follow through the 1429–30 offensive and had not made the most of his great diplomatic victory of 1435. But the truce of 1444 allowed him to undertake extensive financial and military reorganization, similar to that carried out by his grandfather in the years after Brétigny. The reconquest of Normandy and the submission of Guyenne were achieved through an expanding machinery of taxation, the credit of the great merchant financier Jacques Coeur, and the creation of a standing army (cf. below, pp. 137-8). They were also made possible by the

39. The castle of Fougères, Brittany.

ever-increasing insolvency of the Lancastrian monarchy, as well as by the rapidly growing political discord in England; both of which made it impossible to implement a concerted war policy. Talbot's defeat at Castillon was followed within a month by the first signs of madness in Henry VI and on 13 October Margaret of Anjou gave birth to a son, Edward. These three events combined to destroy peace in England. Weak government had already led to a break-down of law and order in the provinces and during the following years regional rivalries between the magnates, and a struggle for control of central government, were intensified by the loss of the English territories in France and resulted in the outbreak of civil war.

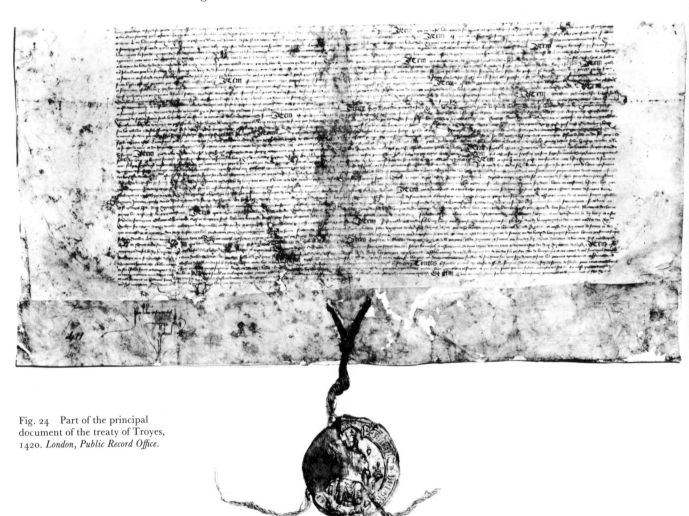

Fig. 24   Part of the principal document of the treaty of Troyes, 1420. *London, Public Record Office.*

40. The funeral achievements of the Black Prince, Canterbury Cathedral.

41. Helm of the Black Prince, Canterbury Cathedral.

40

41

The armies

3

From the outset of the conflict, both English and French armies were composed of paid companies of troops serving under professional commanders; they bore little resemblance to the feudal levy of former days. Such differences as existed between the military organization of the two countries were in part determined by the different ends they were intended to achieve, in part by the different social and administrative framework into which they had to be fitted; and they were often more documentary than real. Not the least significant factor is that throughout the period the war was fought on the continent, mainly in France, not in England. As a result, much of the English war effort in the fourteenth century was directed to the raising of short term expeditionary forces for raids of plunder and devastation, of *chevauchées* as they were known, while the Valois monarchy was faced with the exigencies of national defence, of resisting foreign invasion and maintaining military frontiers within the kingdom. Although this was also true of the English territories in France, it was not until the 1380s, and more especially with occupation of Normandy in the fifteenth century, that the nature of the English war effort changed. It is therefore essential to distinguish, on the one hand, between field and garrison forces and, on the other hand, between armies commanded by the king and those in which command was delegated. On the English side the first division was in a sense between expeditionary and occupation forces, in so far as the troops serving in Guyenne in the fourteenth century and Normandy in the fifteenth century can be referred to in these terms.

In both kingdoms the feudal contingents, drawn from the nobility, and traditionally forming the cavalry, obliged to do forty days' service upon receipt of a royal summons, had never been sufficient to meet the king's needs. Both the number of troops raised and the period and form of service were inadequate, so that the thirteenth century saw the gradual substitution of paid for unpaid service. Philip Augustus seems to have been the first king to pay the feudal host in France, Richard I in England, and their successors followed suit. The two generations which preceded the outbreak of the war in 1337 saw the widespread and general acceptance of the principle of payment for military service. Edward I appears to have been the first English king to offer pay systematically to all ranks of the army except the very highest and in France, by the reign of Philip VI, rates of pay were of sufficient long-standing to have become customary.

In the English armies pay had been guaranteed by contracts, both oral and written, at least from the time of Edward I, and during the early years of the war the drawing up of formal indentures (cf. fig. 26) to which the king was party became normal practice for the great expeditionary forces sent to France under military commanders who were granted extensive powers. The indenture of war was a particular form of contract in which a captain settled with the king or another leader the conditions upon which the specified military service was to be performed and remunerated. It stated the strength and rank of the forces to be raised, provided for musters to be taken both before and on the conclusion of campaigns, specified the period and place of service to be performed and set forth the rates of pay. Provision was usually made for the latter to be quarterly in advance, with agreement

42. The White Hart, from the Wilton Diptych; late fourteenth century. *Reproduced by courtesy of the Trustees of the National Gallery, London.* (46 × 29).

93

that service could be abandoned if the pay in question fell more than a quarter in arrears. Bonuses, or *regards* as they were known, were often made to encourage a captain to take up a command, to be kept by him for his costs in retaining and preparing troops if no campaign materialized. Transport costs for the shipment of men and horses to France were met by the king and compensation granted for horses killed on active service. Arrangements were made for the disposal of prisoners, for the division of ransoms and booty, and for the protection of the captain's estates in England through the appointment of attorneys to act in his name whilst he was absent abroad. The military advantages of this system of recruitment soon became obvious. Indentures were almost always short-term. They made even the greatest of magnates directly dependent on the king or his appointed representative, while safeguarding all captains against serious loss and offering a chance of profit. They substituted discipline and a proper subordination of commands for the unruly individualism of the feudal musters and allowed men to be chosen as commanders by reason of their ability, as well as by reason of their tenure of land.

In France much the same purpose was achieved by *lettres de retenue* concluded between the king and his military commanders which, while different in form from the English indentures of war, had much the same effect: they guaranteed to the king the services of a given number of men of a given rank for a given period of time in a given place, and to the captain the pay of himself and his men at agreed rates. It is clear from the accounts of the treasurers-of-wars that it was customary for advances to be made on the soldiers' pay and for compensation to be made for horses lost on active service. That the Crown often defaulted on these conditions was not, as we shall see, unique to the French. The *lettre de retenue* offered no more of an absolute guarantee than did the indenture of war, or *vice versa*. An English commander secured the forces he had contracted with the king to provide by means of sub-contracts with other men and his French counterpart concluded *lettres de retenue* with other captains to secure the service of an agreed number of troops. In both countries the king often did some of the sub-contracting for his principal commanders and, whereas a nucleus of a captain's forces were recruited in England from his permanent retainers, in France they were often his *alliés*. Upon their conclusion, copies of indentures or *lettres de retenue* were sent to the appropriate financial officers—in England the Exchequer officials, in France the treasurers-of-wars—instructing them to pay the prescribed wages after musters had been taken.

When the king was in command of his forces the arrangements made were somewhat different, for the armies in question were usually a good deal larger and the system of recruitment had to be extended. To secure more men the king could do a variety of things. He could offer money fiefs—annual pensions or rents in the form of fiefs, for which homage was to be done—to foreign princes or much lesser personages, as Edward III did in Gascony and the Low Countries during the early years of the war, or he might call on his tenants-in-chief (in France the *ban de l'ost*) to do military service with their contingents. In England the feudal host was called out for the last time in 1327 and only once thereafter, in 1385, was the feudal summons used to mobilize an army; but in France it continued to be used as a means of recruitment during periods of imminent peril, or when a large-scale enterprise was being undertaken. Apart from the feudal contingents, all able-bodied men between the ages of 18 and 60 (in France the *arrière-ban*) were liable to military service, but this was so impracticable that in England a principle of selection was applied, and in France, where the obligation technically remained, service was usually commuted.

In England the method of selection most commonly employed was that of the commission of array, whereby commissioners appointed by the Crown surveyed all the able-bodied men in each hundred, township and liberty within the shire, selecting the best of them to serve at the king's wages. The commissioners themselves

Fig. 25   Troops disembarking for France; detail from a drawing in the *Life and Acts of Richard Beauchamp, earl of Warwick,* by John Rous, *c.* 1485. *London, British Museum Cotton Ms Julius E IV Art VI, fo. 25.*

43. Detail from the tomb of Richard Beauchamp, earl of Warwick (d. 1439), Beauchamp Chapel, St Mary's, Warwick.

44. Richard II being presented by his patron saints, King Edmund, Edward the Confessor and John the Baptist, to the Virgin and Child; panel from the Wilton Diptych; late fourteenth century.
Reproduced by courtesy of the Trustees of the National Gallery, London. (46 × 29).

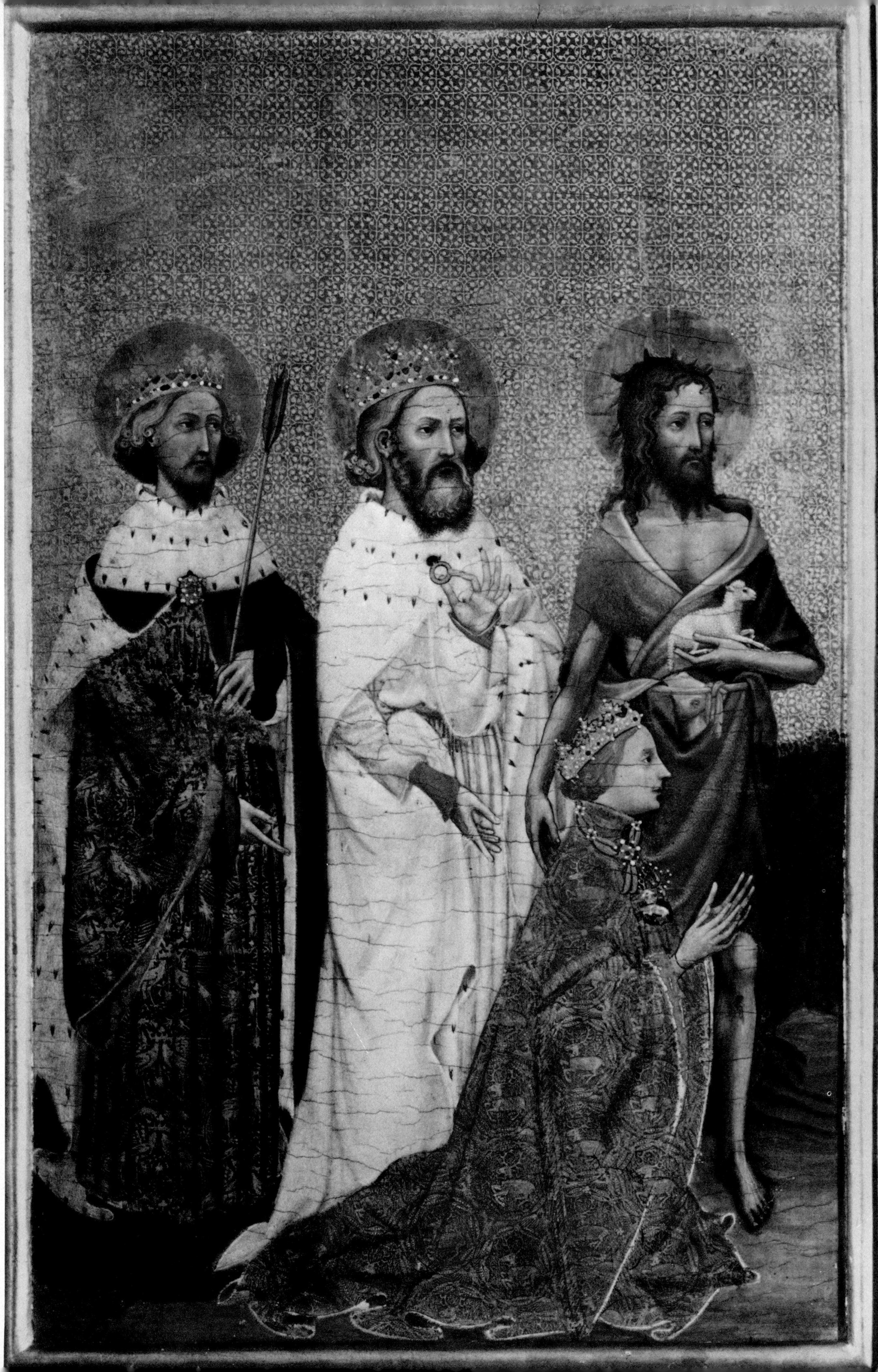

45

Fig. 26   An indenture of war concluded between Edward III and the earl of Warwick; Westminster 24 February 1372. *London, Public Record Office.*

were normally men of the knightly class, sometimes members of the king's household, sometimes prominent retainers of the leaders of the expeditions, who sought out men to make up their contingents. They were experienced staff officers who knew what they were looking for and may be presumed to have chosen well. Their efforts were assisted by proclamations issued at the beginning of each campaign, offering inducements to all and sundry to serve in the wars. Pardons for criminal offences, the prospect of good wages and of a share in the incidental profits of war attracted many to active service. The troops so raised were technically conscripts and compulsion may have had to be applied for service in Scotland; but there was no lack of volunteers for the campaigns in France, with their infinitely more attractive prospects of material reward. The vast majority of Frenchmen were freed from service in the *arrière-ban* by payment of an *impôt* and, with the development of royal taxation during the

99

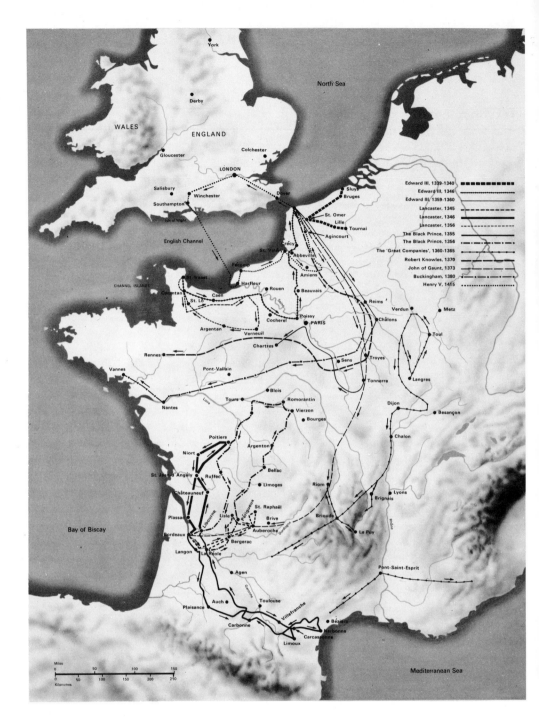

VIII   France during the Hundred Years War; the principal campaigns.

period, the words *arrière-ban* came to acquire a different meaning. Until around the middle of the fourteenth century they signified, at least theoretically, a *levée en masse*, but by the fifteenth century they seem to have denoted only the assembly of those 'tenants-in-chief, sub-tenants and other nobles practising arms'. Apart from these rights, the king could require towns to provide and equip a given quota of men, or transport facilities in the way of carts; but this service also came increasingly to be commuted for a sum negotiated with the king, or for an annual *impôt*.

However raised, the French forces were organized into *batailles* and *bannières*, *routes* or *compagnies*, which denoted both military and administrative units. The classic division of fourteenth-century French and English armies was into three battles, destined to engage the enemy successively and not, as in the sixteenth century, simultaneously. To these were not infrequently added two wings, sometimes of mounted troops, sometimes of archers or crossbowmen, which made tactics at once more complex and mobile. On the French side, these battles were not merely temporary groupings, formed to meet the immediate needs of an imminent combat, but also groupings of troops in existence from the beginning of each campaign and placed under the command or *gouvernement* of the king, the constable and marshals, a prince of the blood or other territorial prince. Sometimes, the troops arrived at the assembly point already formed into battles which corresponded to geographical or feudal groupings, a majority of the men being the tenants or sub-tenants of the leader of the battle. But sometimes they arrived in smaller numbers, to be assigned to one or several battles of a much more composite origin by the constable and marshals. The battles in which troops found themselves at the beginning of a campaign were, however, not necessarily those in which they found themselves during an engagement with the enemy—they were often too numerous for that. To 'order the battles' before a combat, which was the job of the constable and marshals and of which the chroniclers frequently speak, involved not only the designation of the van and the rearguard, the decision as to whether to fight mounted or dismounted, and the assignment of each battle to a particular part of the battle-field, but also their regrouping into more relevant and balanced units.

Fig. 27 A *hauberk. Tower of London, the Armoury.*

Within each battle the combatants were grouped around banners and pennons, which varied in number according to the strength of the forces raised, and which designated groupings under knights banneret or knights bachelor. A banneret was chosen from the body of knights by reason of his military skill and ability to sustain the expenses consequent upon the conversion of the knight's pennon into a rectangular banner. He must be able, in short, to dispose of a relatively large number of men-at-arms by reason of his wealth or his repute. In France, at the beginning of the war, the men serving under his command sometimes came from the same region and might be his tenants or sub-tenants, but just as often they were not. Already during the early years of the war it was not uncommon for a man-at-arms to leave his banner for that of another (a practice officially forbidden in 1351), and while the texts of the period sometimes refer to the troops serving with a banneret as his *hommes* (as synonymous with vassals), they more frequently refer to them as his *gens* or *compagnons*.

Thus in two essentials, English and French military obligation had already taken different directions by the outbreak of the Hundred Years War. Only once after 1327 did the king of England resort to a feudal summons as a means of recruitment and, unlike the king of France, his right to a general levy had long given way to the principle of selection as practised in commissions of array. During the course of the fourteenth century more striking divergencies were to emerge.

In France, military reforms were promulgated from time to time in royal *ordonnances*, of which the principal were published by John II in 1351 and 1363, by Charles V in 1373 and 1374, and by Charles VII in 1439, 1445 and 1448. Prior to 1351 not all men-at-arms were grouped under bannerets, particularly in the battles of the marshals, which included a high proportion of independent troops. It was one of the principal objectives of the *ordonnance* of that year to regroup these scattered elements into more viable military units and to increase the number of troops available by increasing the rates of pay. In future, all men-at-arms were to be organized in *routes, bannières* or *compagnies* (the words were used interchangeably to denote the same groupings) of between twenty-five and eighty combatants, and they were to be placed firmly under the command of *seigneurs, chevetainnes* or bannerets. Troops arriving at the assembly point in groups of less than twenty-five were to be provided by the constable, marshals, master of the crossbowmen or other war leader with a *maistre* or *chevetainne* who might be a simple knight with a pennoncel bearing his arms. The reform seems to have partially succeeded, for during the next few years the size of the companies recruited appears to have increased. Moreover, although the rates of pay temporarily fell to their previous level, the captain of each *hostel* or *compaignie* was to receive for each group of twenty-five men-at-arms, in addition to his pay, an indemnity of 100 *livres tournois* a month for his *état*. This was a significant innovation: in 1340 only the great lords in charge of a battle and the captains of royal garrisons, *establies*, had enjoyed such payments.

The *ordonnances* of 1363 and 1373, which saw the first attempts to set up a standing army, and those of 1445 and 1448, from which it achieved permanency, will be dealt with subsequently (below, pp. 134-8). That of 1374 put the strength of companies up to a compulsory figure of a hundred and made arrangements for them to be placed firmly under the control of supreme commanders (lieutenants and other war leaders), from whom, or from the king, they must have a commission. While the figure of a hundred was not strictly adhered to, companies were subsequently retained for service with a fixed number of men-at-arms: 20, 30, 50, 100, 200 and sometimes more. Moreover, the captains were not always bannerets or knights bachelor; they might equally be esquires and it was not unknown for an esquire to command a company which included knights. But while these innovations in French military organization brought about significant changes in the command of the forces, they did not involve a radical change in the social complex of the army. For although the system of recruitment was different, it nevertheless operated in the same social *milieu*. As in the English armies of the period, it was invariably the same men who were enlisted through new military and political structures.

The troops raised in any of these ways were either men-at-arms or infantry. The former group was made up of all heavily-armed mounted men, whether knights banneret, knights bachelor, or esquires. The latter was principally composed of archers, crossbowmen and foot-sergeants; though it occasionally included other troops: hobelars, pikemen, spearmen. In the English armies, however, the foot-archers were rapidly (though not wholly) replaced by horse-archers, who were particularly important in the *chevauchées* of the fourteenth century, when they contributed substantially to the victories of Edward III and his lieutenants. From an early date, it became common for most companies to be composed of an equal number of men-at-arms and mounted archers, organized together under the command of the contracting captains of the expeditionary forces. In France, on the other hand, the archers (who for the most part were not mounted) and the crossbowmen (who were always foot-soldiers), were formed into separate companies under constables and, together with the other infantry, were ultimately responsible to the master of the crossbowmen. Moreover, throughout the fourteenth century, the crossbowmen—of whom the most skilled were Genoese mercenaries—remained foremost among the infantry, whereas in the English armies they were hardly employed at all.

The second half of the fourteenth century and the early years of the fifteenth century, which saw continual experiments in methods of protecting the combatants, was a period of rapid evolution. In the early years of the war, the man-at-arms commonly wore a *hauberk* (a coat of mail, made by riveting or soldering together small rings of iron or steel) (cf. fig. 27), and a *jaque, gambeson* or *cotte gamboisée* (a quilted tunic made up of several thicknesses of material, or leather; frequently stuffed with cotton or silk flock). On his head he wore a great cylindrical helm, often surmounted with his crest, though this was coming to be superseded on the field of battle by the more mobile *bascinet*, or burnished helmet, which he closed with a *vizor* (cf. pls. 41, 48). His arms, shoulders and legs were protected by metal plates, and his

Fig. 28 A *brigandine*. Paris, *Musée de l'Armée*.

47. A roll of arms: the Carlisle Roll, 1334. *Cambridge, Fitzwilliam Museum Ms 324, fo. 117b.*

48. North Italian bascinet, *c.* 1380. *The Armoury, Tower of London.*

49. Armour of a cavalryman and horse of Charles VII's *compagnies d'ordonnance.* The cavalryman's armour was made in Milan. *Musée de l'Armée, Paris.*

50. Detail of gauntlets and sword from the tomb of a knight and his wife, 1391, Elford, Staffordshire.

51. A fireplace and doorway in the house of Jacques Coeur, Bourges.

Cjonſ Wa
ryn de Baſ
ſingborgh ꝗ

Poʒt Jeronue de veer ꝗ de gules de
ʒij petes ꝗ

Cjoſ
John
Duyn ꝗ

Poʒt dor one   vn griffon de gule
one vn baſtoun dalur ꝗ

Cjonſ
Geles de
Baſſigboʒgh

poʒt cella one vn   label dalur ꝗ

Cjonſ
Terry de
lynchefed ꝗ

poʒt dor one denx barres de gules maſſy
dargent one vn creſaunt dargēt en qua

Cjonſ
Williā de
Euphoʒd ꝗ

poʒt de gules one vn fretel en
greice deruyne ꝗ

Cjonſ
harry
hillory ꝗ

poʒt de ſable croi   flee dargent one tri
fluredeliz dargent ꝗ

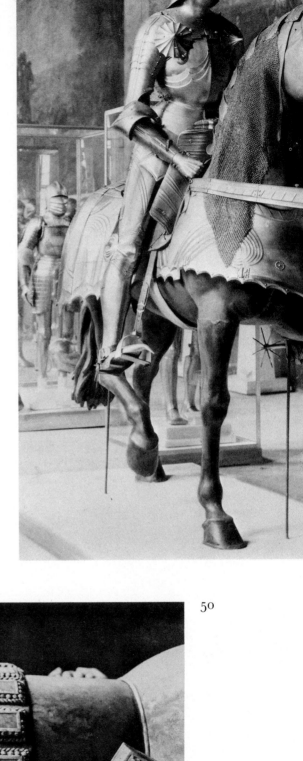

hands by gauntlets (cf. pls. 40, 50). Up to about 1350 he also wore a long surcoat known as a *cyclas*, and a transverse sword belt (cf. fig. 33). The disappearance of the latter garment occurred with the increasing use of metal plates of varying thickness and dimensions, which were worn over the *hauberk*. These were held in place by a tight-fitting surcoat or *jupon*, made up of one or several thicknesses of material, and and surmounted by a *baldric*, or horizontal belt, across the hips (cf. fig. 32). The development of this heavier type of armour led to the disappearance (between 1345 and 1375) of the shield, which had become superfluous, the armorial bearings being transferred to the *jupon* (cf. pl. 40). By the beginning of the fifteenth century these plates were large enough to cover the front and back of the trunk in two pieces, held together with straps, and from then onwards it became the fashion to leave them bare. This was plate armour, as opposed to the *brigandine*, which was made up of pieces of diverse forms, sometimes overlapping one another like fish scales, and of necessity fastened to material (cf. fig. 28). By 1450 the combatant was completely protected by armour of plate and mail. The development had reached its apogee. The most advanced centres of production were in Germany and Italy, at Nuremberg, Augsburg, Innsbruck, Brescia and, above all, Milan (cf. pl. 48). It was from there that most French and English armour was imported. By 1427 Milan had become such an important centre of production that it could supply the armour for 4,000 cavalry and 2,000 infantry from its warehouses within a few days. As early as 1398 the earl of Derby imported Milanese armour and Richard Beauchamp, earl of Warwick (d. 1439), had travelled to Italy, and clearly bought his armour there (cf. pls. 31, 43).

The great *destriers* and other war-horses of the combatants, the best of which might cost well over £100, were also protected with armour, known as *bards*. Usually, only the head was covered with metal plates, chain or boiled hide being used to protect the rump and flanks (cf. pl. 49). But from around 1400 it became increasingly common to suppress all protection for the horses, in part because the knights more frequently dismounted before battle, and probably also to achieve lightness for the cavalry charge. The weight of the armour of the man-at-arms, on the other hand, progressively increased, and had practically doubled by 1450. For whereas his *hauberk* did not weigh more than 33 lb. and his arms continued to weigh about 11 lb., complete plate armour weighed about 55 lb., and the *bascinet* and *vizor* (cf. fig. 29) about 11 lb. While this allowed him to mount and dismount without assistance, if he fought on foot he was reduced to semi-immobility.

The equipment of the foot-soldier (cf. pl. 24) was considerably lighter. His *brigandine* would weigh about 22 lb. and his *sallet* or helmet about 5 to 8 lb. (cf. fig. 25), which together with 17 lb. for his clothes and arms, amounted to little more than 45 lb. During the Anglo-French wars of the fourteenth and fifteenth centuries, however, the foot-soldiers were not very mobile, since their tactics mostly consisted of using their bows or crossbows from behind a fixed protection which broke the cavalry charge: hedges, tree-trunks, waggons, stakes driven into the ground, or large body shields known as *pavises* or *targes*. Moreover, they were encumbered by the variety of their arms since, together with their bow or crossbow, they also carried a sword or dagger, and sometimes an axe or a *halberd* (a combined spear and battle axe) (cf. fig. 31). Nor were they trained to manoeuvre together. The man-at-arms was always mounted (cf. pl. 70), but he sometimes dismounted to fight. His most important weapon was a lance of ten to twelve feet in length, made of wood, but terminating in a metal spearhead or *glaive*. He also carried a sword, a dagger (often a *misericord*, used for slipping between the plates of armour or through the *vizor*), and frequently a truncheon (cf. fig. 31) or an axe. The foot-soldiers, especially the Flemings, sometimes carried a pike of around six feet in length, terminating in a large and heavy spearhead, which they used to jab their victims to death. But the

Fig. 29 A *bascinet* with a *vizor*. Paris, Musée de l'Armée.

Fig. 30 A *helmet*; fifteenth century. Glasgow, Art Gallery and Museum.

52. Hunting scene; *Livre de la Chasse de Gaston Fébus. Paris, Bibliothèque Nationale Ms français 616, fo. 87.*

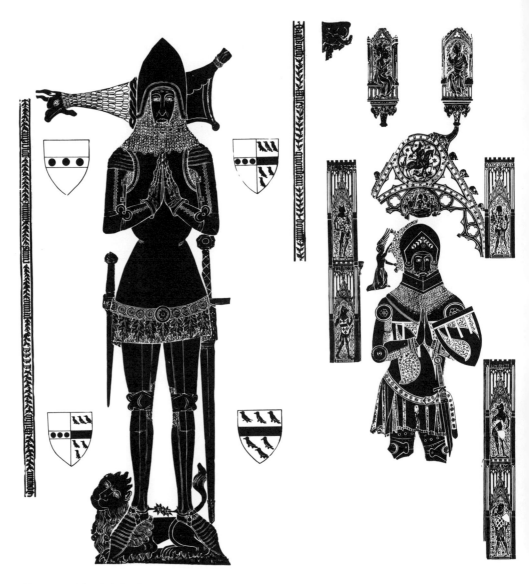

Fig. 32 *Left* Sir Nicholas Dagworth from a brass (1401) at Blickling, Norfolk. Note the horizontal sword belt across the hips. *London, Victoria and Albert Museum.*

Fig. 33 *Right* Sir Hugh Hastings from a brass (1347) at Elsing, Norfolk. Note the transverse sword belt. *London, Victoria and Albert Museum.*

Fig. 31 *Above left* Two *halberds—right* A truncheon. *Paris, Musée de l'Armée.*

favourite arms of the medieval infantrymen were the bow and crossbow.

The Welsh longbow was also the characteristic weapon of the English mounted archers, who first appeared in the Scottish campaigns of 1334–5. The value of the horse-archer lay in his ability to move quickly and dismount to shoot. He could not, of course, shoot from the saddle, since a solid foundation was needed for the pull. Generations of practice, at the town and village butts, in the conservation of energy and the correct use of weight and strength went to produce the skilled archer, who stood sideways to the enemy, so that—unlike the crossbowman—his acts of aiming and loading were practically one and both eye and hand were brought into play. It has been calculated that a good longbowman could shoot ten or twelve arrows a minute as against the crossbowman's two; and it was this rapid hail of arrows hurtling around the ears of an advancing enemy or, as at Crécy, maddening his horses, which made the longbows so deadly a weapon. By the mid-fourteenth century, the great six-foot bows of yew, maple, or oak, were capable of penetrating chain mail; their range was about 275 yards, although above 165 yards they were much less effective.

There were other limits to the effectiveness of the longbow. It was essentially a defensive weapon for use against advancing enemy cavalry, and the archers were to some extent dependent on a suitable terrain. If the enemy failed to advance, or the site of battle was ill-chosen, there was little they could do.

Although the French also employed the longbow, they preferred the crossbow—Italian or otherwise—which looks more efficient (cf. back endpaper), and had in fact a range superior to that of the longbow by 75 to 100 yards. It projected shorter

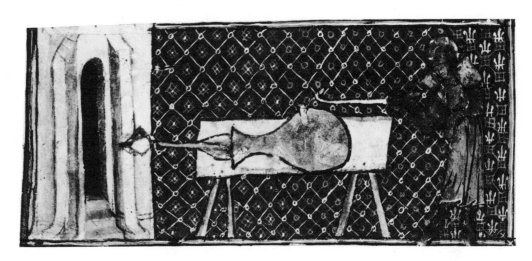

Fig. 34 A fifteenth-century
veuglaire. Paris, Musée de l'Armée.

Fig. 35   The earliest known representation of a cannon; from the Millemette ms.
Oxford, Christ Church Ms 92, fo. 7ov.

and heavier missiles—frequently known as *garrots* or *carreaux*, *dondaines* or *semi-dondaines*, and *viretons*—some of which were incendiaries. But it was a heavy instrument—it weighed between 15 and 18 lb.—and was difficult and slow to load. To secure the necessary tension, a hook attached to the crossbowman's belt had to be passed round the bow-string, while the bow itself had to be held firmly to the ground by means of a stirrup in which the operator placed his foot. The string could then be passed behind a notch which held it until the moment of firing. But other methods of loading were also used: jacks, screws, pulleys and goat's feet. Unlike the longbow, which could be operated by any man sufficiently sound in body and eye, and who was prepared to put in steady practice, the crossbow was essentially a weapon for technicians. Behind town walls, much heavier instruments were used: *espringales,* which projected heavy lead balls, and cannon.

Artillery, in the modern sense of the word was known and used in western Europe from the beginning of the fourteenth century and, while it did not supplant the bow and the crossbow, it was eventually to make obsolete the old war-machines imitated from antiquity. Henceforward, it played an important role, first in the defence of and then in attacks on military strongholds and in maritime warfare, where each ship was thought of as a floating castle. Firearms were used at the battle of Sluys and in the defence of Quesnoi and Tournai in 1340 and by Edward III to protect the approaches to Calais during the siege of 1346. These early guns were probably quite small, projecting quarrels as in the Millemette MS (cf. fig. 35), or lead pellets. Their effect was primarily psychological; but in the decade following the peace of Brétigny and, in particular, with the renewal of the war in the 1370s and 1380s, a new breakthrough was made in the production and use of cannon. Prior to 1370 they were nearly all made of toughened copper or brass (*cuprum*), and weighed about 20 to 40 lb. Thereafter, some were made of a hard yellow alloy closely resembling brass (*latten*); but as the century advanced wrought, then cast iron pieces became the most common, and they progressively increased in size. For the siege of Saint-Sauveur-le-Vicomte in 1375, the French had guns capable of firing 100-pound stone balls, 'in order that they might more diligently and continually fire upon and damage the said place of Saint-Sauveur', and at least one of these cannon weighed over a ton. The English probably did not have such heavy guns as this; although some six- to seven-hundredweight pieces were produced. For the defence of Cherbourg in 1379, the captain, Sir John de Arundel, had ten guns, 'seven of the said ten guns casting large stones 24 inches in circumference, and the remaining three casting large stones 15 inches in circumference'; but the average weight of the English heavy gun in the 1380s and 1390s was 380 lb. Such guns as these, employed in strategic fortresses, together with financial considerations and the French refusal to risk a battle in the field, probably contributed to the change in English military strategy after 1380, when the last great *chevauchée* of the century took place.

By around 1400 there were sufficient numbers of cannon for them to be divided into categories according to their thickness and length. The largest projected stone balls, and the smallest lead pellets. By order of decreasing size they were known as *bombardes* (which often weighed over 10,000 lb.), *veuglaires* or *fowlers* (which were up to eight feet long and ranged from 300 to 10,000 lb.), *crapaudaux* or *crapaudins* (which were four to eight feet long), *serpentins* and *couleuvrines*. The English do not appear to have possessed *bombardes* as early as this, but two which they used for the siege of Mont Saint-Michel in 1423 have survived. One of these weighs $5\frac{1}{2}$ tons, has a 19-inch calibre, and was capable of firing 300-pound stone balls. Mons Meg, which was probably made at Mons around 1460, is a foot longer, but of about the same weight and capacity (cf. fig. 36). Apart from these, a large variety of other guns were made during the fourteenth century: mortars, multiple fire guns or *ribaudequins*, and a variety of *handgonnes*. Perhaps the most amazing contraption produced in England during the 1380s was a seven-hundredweight, eleven-barrelled *ribaudequin*, built by William Woodward, a London founder, which had one great barrel for shooting stone balls, and ten surrounding ones for quarrels or lead pellets.

Large guns like the *bombardes* and *veuglaires* clearly played an important part in the sieges of such places as they could be transported to by river or by sea, and when the time factor was not a primary concern. They were used to good effect at Harfleur in 1415 and on many occasions thereafter: in particular by Jean Bureau for the French at Meaux in 1439, Pontoise in 1441, and Caen in 1450. But it was not until the second half of the fifteenth century that artillery began to play a significant part on the battlefield. Bringing a large cannon up on a four-wheeled waggon and assembling it on the spot was a cumbersome and slow business. The vital breakthrough was not made until the development of more advanced gun-carriages in the 1470s, with trunnions permitting speedy elevation of the gun-barrel. In the later years of the fifteenth century the French royal artillery was the most formidable in western Europe, as the intervention in Italy in 1494 was to show. Although the cannon under Bureau played a decisive role at Castillon in 1435, this was due to the French formation—the entrenched artillery camp—rather than to more advanced guns. On this occasion, the commander of the Anglo-Gascon forces, the veteran eighty-six-year-old Talbot, acted courageously but impetuously and on false intelligence. He dismounted his troops in traditional fashion and stormed the French positions. But the French formation was very different from that which he had known during the formative years of his military career and English tactics no longer held good. The gallant earl was thrown to the ground by a culverin shot and then met his death from either the blow of an axe or a hail of arrows from the French archers. Castillon marked a new departure in the art of war, to which the technological advances of the 1470s and 1480s gave deeper meaning. In that sense, the last battle of the Hundred Years War was the first in which artillery played a significant role.

Fig. 36 Mons Meg, a *bombarde* made c. 1460. *Edinburgh Castle.*

53. Hammerbeam roof in the Great Hall of Richard II, Palace of Westminster, 1394–1401.

54. June—The royal palace and the Sainte Chapelle, from *Les Très Riches Heures du duc de Berri*, by Jean and Pol de Limbourg. *Musée de Chantilly.* (17 × 15.3).

55. October—The Louvre, from *Les Très Riches Heures du duc de Berri*, by Jean and Pol de Limbourg. *Musée de Chantilly.* (17 × 15.3).

These developments in the production and use of cannon in their turn brought about a revolution in military architecture. The most advanced fourteenth-century fortresses were built with high walls, which were surmounted by machicolated galleries with one and sometimes two walks, from which bowmen or crossbowmen could shoot, protected by crenellations in the form of battlements, cruciform loops, or both. Projecting towers, taller than the walls, but organically connected with them, were built at intervals, so that an attacking party armed with rams or ladders could be shot at from the flanks. The height of the walls was determined by the need to prevent scaling, and to allow missiles to be dropped vertically from the machicolations on to the heads of the assailants. The second walk, where it existed, also gave cover to the first and could be used to keep an attacking party at a distance. All of these features were present in the castle of Pierrefonds, built by Louis of Orléans in the years after 1390 as one of a group of fortresses—Vez, La Ferté-Milon, Montepilloy and Crépy were the others—to protect his *apanage*; many of them are still apparent at Fougères, situated on the border between Normandy and Brittany, much of which dates from the same period (cf. pl. 39). Such defences were admirably suited to meet the traditional forms of attack, since the main role of siege engines was to hurl incendiary materials over the walls and, like the early mortars, they were not so accurate that they could land repeated blows on the same place. But the gun provided a hard-hitting long-range horizontal blow and, as the fifteenth century wore on, an increasingly accurate one.

There was no provision for cannon at Pierrefonds but, already in the later fourteenth century, coastal and frontier fortifications were being adapted to the use of artillery. To begin with these changes were slight, since guns were principally employed for defensive purposes against assault parties rather than as long-range deterrents. Gun towers were therefore built on the model of the old round or pentagonal towers, but they were thicker and provided with loops for hand-guns and small cannon. As early as the invasion scares of the late 1370s and 1380s, fortifications built to guard the south coast of England were equipped with six to twelve-inch gun ports—at Cooling, Canterbury, Bodiam (cf. pl. 36), Saltwood, Carisbrooke, Winchester; and probably also at Queenborough, Dover, Porchester, Southampton and Corfe. Together with the coastal fortresses at Calais, Cherbourg and Brest in France, and Roxburgh and Berwick on the Scottish border, they were well stocked with guns and ammunition. During the same period the French made similar provisions for their garrisons on the Picardy and Flemish frontiers. But more major changes were not long in coming. Walls were made thicker, sometimes lower, and were scarped to deflect cannon-balls. The castle of Rambures, built some fifteen years after that of Pierrefonds, had four large angle-towers connected by scarped walls in addition to gun-ports, and the *enceinte* of Mont Saint-Michel (1426–45) was also adapted to meet the challenge of gunpowder. Gradually, however, it was realized that heavy guns could be used to break up the besiegers' concentrations and dismount their artillery; but since they could not be used inside towers, because they were too smoky and the loops restricted their angle of fire, they were placed on top of them. Some fortresses, like that of Queenborough on the Isle of Sheppey, built for Edward III in the years following the treaty of Brétigny, could not be adapted to the new techniques; for as the commissioners who condemned it to demolition in 1650 commented, 'beinge built in the tyme of bowes and arrowes, . . . noe plattforme can be erected thereon for the plantinge of cannon'. But other fortresses were transformed by more or less makeshift means. By the end of the fifteenth century, in both France and Italy, walls and towers had become thicker and lower, they were scarped, and protected by wide platforms. The bringing together of these diverse elements gave birth to the modern bastion, which is an aggressive rather than a defensive form, a solid platform rather than a tower, maintaining the tower's

Fig. 37 Troops scaling the walls of a town; from a late fourteenth-century manuscript. *London, British Museum Ms 20C VII, fo. 19.*

56. The Beaufort Chantry, *c.* 1447, Winchester Cathedral.

function of providing cover to the adjacent part of the fortifications, but thrust forward to obtain as wide a field of fire as possible. It appeared early in France, but late in England, and was most precocious in Italy from the middle years of the *quattrocento,* and particularly from the time of the French invasion.

Arms, armour and artillery, and all kinds of equipment needed for the prosecution of war, were manufactured on an almost industrial scale by royal order and deposited in arsenals at the Tower of London, the Louvre, Caen during the English occupation of Normandy in the fifteenth century, and the *clos des gallées* near Rouen, where the necessary equipment for the French maritime expeditions was kept. In France, from the time of Charles V, all this military equipment was administered by special departments under a *général maitre et visiteur de son artillerie* at the Louvre, and a *garde de son clos des gallées, armeures et artilleries pour le fait de la mer* at Rouen. They received regular funds from the treasurers-of-wars, even during peace and truce; but in wartime the treasurers and the *receveur-général des aides* met all the expenses of the artillery. In fourteenth-century England, on the other hand, the keeper of the king's privy wardrobe was responsible for the administration of the armaments in the Tower. Although this sphere of the wardrobe's activities secured financial and administrative autonomy in the 1360s, and by 1369 a sub-department for gunnery under a *clericum pro officio gunnorum* had been created, nevertheless it was not until 1414 that a distinct Ordnance department was set up under a clerk (subsequently known as master) of the king's ordnance. The first holder of this office, Nicholas Merbury, was responsible for the administration of the English artillery during the Agincourt campaign; but during the conquest of Normandy Caen became the principal English artillery depôt and, after 1422, along with the arsenals at Rouen and the Louvre, was run by a 'master of the king's ordnance in France and Normandy', who was usually an Englishman. Since, during the 1420s and 1430s, most of the military effort was concentrated in central France, there was not much activity at the Tower and consequently little is heard of the English officer prior to the appointment of Gilbert Par in 1437. Specialist gunners, on the other hand, are to be found in the principal fortresses from a much earlier date and, already in the 1370s, master-gunners were appointed to the coastal forts; these were not administrative officers, but military engineers specializing in gunnery. Some of them were, however, quite local appointments and here, as in other fields, English military administration was much less centralized than that of France.

In both England and France the supreme command of the military forces was invested in the king and the constable, marshals and lieutenants-general appointed by him; but the powers and functions attached to these offices varied considerably from one country to the other. Until the beginning of the fourteenth century it had been customary for the king personally to direct military operations, and it was in this way that the early campaigns of the fourteenth century were fought. But the permanence of the Anglo-French conflict, the widely scattered provinces in which hostilities took place, the English occupation of different regions of France, all necessitated delegation of the royal command and a steady growth in the powers and privileges of the royal commanders.

When the king personally directed military operations, the constable and marshals shared command of the army with him. The constable of France was at the height of his glory during this period and he secured powers almost equal to those of the king in military affairs. His office was greatly enhanced by the Anglo-French wars, and by the undoubted ability of some of its occupants: the brothers-in-arms Bertrand du Guesclin (1370–80), Olivier de Clisson (1380–92) and Louis de Sancerre (1397–1403), and perhaps also of Arthur de Richemont (1425–58), the genius behind the military reforms of Charles VII (cf. pls. 25, 26). It was not until the time of Louis XI that the office began its rapid decline. The constable of

57. Looting a house; late fourteenth century. *London, British Museum Royal Ms 20 C VII, fo. 41v.* (10 × 17.8).

58. Assassination of John the Fearless, duke of Burgundy, in 1419; Monstrelet's Chronicle. *Paris, Bibliothèque de l'Arsenal Ms 5084, fo. 1.* (20 × 21.5).

57

58

Our aumener en
perpetuele memoi   se de faire et accomplir la
                      cronique. En faisant laquelle

Messire Phelippe de commines ss dangenton
hystorien

Saint-Pol (1465–75) was executed for betraying the king, and thenceforth, particularly after the treason of the constable of Bourbon (1490–1527), the office was held in extreme distrust, remaining vacant for many years until it was permanently suppressed by Louis XII in 1627.

According to Guillaume le Tur, president of the *parlement de Paris* after the fall of the city to the French in 1436, the constable's office was, by the time of Charles VII, 'the principal and first office of France in honours and prerogatives, coming before that of the chancellor and all others'. Implicit in it were the powers of a lieutenant-general, which the constable could exercise in the absence of the king (to make treaties and other agreements, grant pardons, etc.), and which normally required a special commission. Already in Clisson's time his office entitled him to a place in the *conseil privé,* where military policy was worked out and in the direction of which nothing could be done without his consent. He was entitled to a room at court wherever the king might be. He assisted at the king's coronation, when he carried the Saint Ampoule, and a crime against him was considered *lèse-majesté.* In war time he had supreme command of the armed forces: he decided on how the troops should be deployed, ordered all battles, *chevauchées* and garrisons, and assigned to each person his rank and place. During military engagements he was in the van of the host, with the marshals in his battle. The banner of his office was carried after that of the king and, if the king was absent at the taking of a town or fortress, the constable's banner was the first to be unfurled as a symbol of possession. Only the battle cries of the king and constable could be given when the king was present in the host. He was responsible for sending out all messengers and spies. If he chose to take men out of the host to *chevaucher* without a bodyguard he could do so whenever he pleased, and to this end he had the first choice of horses in the host after the king, and could take ten men-at-arms from all save the royal battle. If his forces were in garrison they were not obliged to do watch unless he commanded it.

He enjoyed extensive financial benefits from his office. The king met all his costs during war time, including that of replacing his horses and those of his companions. During sieges and battles he enjoyed double pay. He was entitled to the equivalent of a day's pay from all the troops on the king's payroll or all those who received some other form of remuneration for their service, and from garrison troops the equivalent of a day's pay for each garrison in which they served. He had fifty *livres tournois* a day when conducting a simple *chevauchée* and a hundred when armed for battle or assault. On these occasions he was entitled to all the booty taken by him and the men of his *hôtel,* save the gold and prisoners which went to the king. When a fortress was taken by force, or surrendered, he was entitled to a share in the spoils, except gold and prisoners, which went to the king, and the artillery, which went to the master of the crossbowmen.

The military powers of the marshals were much less extensive, although their position was frequently exalted by additional commissions as lieutenants-general. They had command of part of the army under the constable and they also had disciplinary and administrative functions. Their principal task was the supervision and management of the muster and review of the troops. They were responsible for the prior arrangement of the camps, the maintenance of the good administration of the combat units and the protection of the civil population from the excesses and depredations of the soldiers. In the more strictly military sphere their powers were greatest in secondary operations: they conducted the government of the army wherever they happened to be and when the constable was absent. In armies commanded by the king and constable, and when they were in garrison, on the other hand, they could not undertake any military enterprise without the constable's consent, nor could they *chevaucher,* order battles, or issue banishments or proclamations in the host without his sanction. They received 2,000 *livres tournois* a year

59. Pen-drawing of Philip of Commynes, lord of Argentan, historian, by an anonymous artist. *Paris, Bibliothèque Nationale, Receuil d'Arras.*

pay for their office and, like the constable, they enjoyed a number of remunerative perquisites, although it was royal policy to try and cut these down.

In France, two other men shared high military office: the master of the crossbowmen who had supreme command of the infantry and artillery, and the keeper of the Oriflamme. The Oriflamme, which was the banner of Saint-Denis and the first banner of the host, was entrusted only to knights of proved ability, like Geoffrey de Charny and Arnoul d'Audrehem, and its bearer, who was appointed for life, had to swear an oath to face death before he would surrender it.

The constable and marshal of England enjoyed much less extensive powers and privileges. This was already the case at the beginning of the fourteenth century, but it became increasingly so as the years wore on. The rapid extension of the powers of the constable of France owed not a little to the weakness of the French monarchy. Charles V, although a great statesman, had a delicate constitution and was no soldier. Charles VI was only a boy when he came to the throne and, quite apart from other factors, his subsequent madness ruled out any possibility of his taking an active part in military affairs. After 1422 the position in France was chaotic and for long Charles VII was not the man to put it right. In these conditions, with the enemy almost continually in the land, it is hardly surprising that the office of constable went from strength to strength. England, on the other hand, was blessed in Edward III and Henry V with her two greatest warrior kings, and after 1422 had Bedford as regent of France. That the war was fought in France not only prevented the creation of a standing army at home, but it also made unnecessary the development in England of an extensive machinery of muster and review and wide judicial powers such as those which had brought the marshals of France into eminence. Moreover, the conquest of Normandy and the settlement of Troyes made the Lancastrian monarchy heir to French offices and traditions. In Normandy and the *pais de conquête*, English military administration experienced considerable French influence, while in other regions of France recognizing Henry VI it was almost entirely French. After 1422 Henry VI appointed marshals of France in an Anglo-Burgundian state. The true parallels to Richemont as constable (1425–58) and La Fayette as one of the marshals (1421–64) of France for Charles VII, are not Bedford as constable (1403–35) and Mowbray as marshal of England, but Humphrey Stafford, first duke of Buckingham, as constable (1430) and John Talbot, earl of Shrewsbury, as marshal (1435–53) of France for Henry VI.

By the beginning of the fourteenth century and up to 1373 the office of constable of England was hereditary in the family of Bohun and for a considerable part of the period under review (1385–98 and 1410–76) that of Earl Marshal was hereditary in the family of Mowbray. All the holders of either office were recruited from the great noble houses and many of them served as lieutenants-general in France. But although they could boast some notable soldiers, none of them were of relatively humble origins like the constables of France Robert de Fiennes (1356–70) and Du Guesclin (1370–80), or the marshals of France, many of whom came from the lesser nobility. Moreover, in France it had been royal policy not to grant the office of marshal for life, in order to keep it out of the hands of powerful families and to prevent it from becoming hereditary, as had tended to happen during the thirteenth century; and in any case the marshals themselves did not regard the office as a final goal, but as a step up the ladder to becoming keeper of the Oriflamme (as witness the marshals Mile de Noyers and Arnoul d'Audrehem) and constable of France (like Louis de Sancerre).

In the frontier and occupied territories the military forces were placed under the command of governors, lieutenants and captains-general with virtually viceregal powers who exercised jurisdiction over extensive provinces. They had overriding military authority, with powers to recruit troops into the king's pay and assemble

60. Philip the Good, duke of Burgundy (1419–67), and his son Charles the Rash (1467–77); anonymous pen-drawing. *Paris, Bibliothèque National, Receuil d'Arras.*

Phlˢ dⁱᵗ le bᵒⁿ Dᵘᵉ de bourgōgⁿᵉ

Charleˢ Dᵘᵉ de bourgōgⁿᵉ filz de
Phlˢ et dᵗ le temeraire
occis en 1477

and command his armies. They could garrison towns, castles and fortresses, appoint and dismiss the captains in charge of them and make all the necessary provisions for their defence. They had overriding judicial authority, with powers to appoint and dismiss local officials at their discretion. They could receive individuals and communities into the king's allegiance, take their homage, confirm their liberties, privileges and franchises, bestow new ones, grant pardons and reward them with lands and pensions. Conversely, they could confiscate the lands of those who deserted the king's allegiance and employ such properties as they thought best. They could issue safe-conducts, take fines and ransoms, and conclude alliances and agreements with important personages, or local truces with the enemy. To assist them in this work they were advised by councils made up of their chiefs of staff, local officials and royal officers who accompanied them for that purpose. They were also accompanied by secretaries and notaries who drafted their letters and, on the French side, these were drawn up and sealed as those of the king, and had equal authority.

The French lieutenants had other, more extensive powers. Within their circumscriptions all other officers were subordinate to them. They could pardon all civil and criminal offences, including *lèse-majesté*; they could grant respites or pardons for not paying debts to nobles; sometimes they even had powers of ennoblement. In the financial sphere all their expenses were met by the king. They could treat with local inhabitants on subsidies and expend all forms of royal revenue on the war or to reward the deserving. Upon their orders, the treasurers-of-wars, their deputies and all other royal treasurers and receivers, paid the expenses ordered by them with the sole provision that they should furnish accounts at the *Chambre des Comptes* in Paris. In the military sphere the right to have castles and fortresses razed to the ground was not extraordinary: it formed part of their military powers and could be exercised by inferior officers. Beneath them, in a more or less steady hierarchy of command, were seneschals, *baillis*, captains of towns and castellans, whose powers varied according to the importance of their commands. But the conditions were seldom identical in any two regions at once and it would be hazardous to generalize further about the nature of military command during the course of more than a hundred years of conflict.

The territories occupied by English or allied troops changed a good deal during the course of the war (cf. maps IV-VII). In Guyenne, forces had to be maintained throughout the period. A considerable part of the duchy of Brittany was occupied for twenty years after Edward III's intervention (1342–62) and a number of garrisons remained there after the return of John IV. Garrison forces were permanently installed at Calais after its capture in 1347 and for a while in Normandy (1356–61). After the battle of Poitiers, allied forces occupied isolated towns and castles in the Loire provinces, in Picardy, Champagne, Burgundy and elsewhere in France, if only briefly, and often for their own profit as much as that of the Crown. Under Edward III, the occupation of Calais, the Breton ports, and a number of strategically vital fortresses in the bay of Bourgneuf and at the mouth of the river Charente, guaranteed communications with Gascony and made it possible to keep supply lines open for allied forces operating in the interior. The occupation of Saint-Sauveur-le-Vicomte (1356–75) and Bécherel (1362–74) provided a useful foothold in Normandy and Brittany after the treaty of Brétigny. But in the later fourteenth century most of the occupation forces were concentrated in a string of fortresses down the French Atlantic seaboard: at Calais, Cherbourg (1378–94), Castle Cornet and Mont Orgueil in the Channel Islands, Brest (1378–97), Bordeaux and Bayonne. These, together with improved coastal defences in England, were intended to give the king control of the Channel and ensure that the war would continue to be fought in France. The policy was clearly outlined in parliament by Sir Richard Scrope in 1378 and it doubtless owed something to the costs of mounting large scale expeditions

Fig. 38 Sir Edward Dallingridge, lieutenant of the earl of Arundel, captain of Brest (1388–9) from a brass at Fletching, Sussex. *London, Victoria and Albert Museum.*

61. The Wheel of Senses; early fourteenth-century wall-painting of a king in Longthorpe Tower, Northamptonshire.

and of occupying extensive territories. It may also have been occasioned by developments in the construction and use of cannon in the 1370s and 1380s. After 1420, however, the English war effort was overwhelmingly directed toward the occupation of French territories and the piecemeal expansion of frontiers in accordance with the treaty of Troyes. Calais and the other seaboard fortresses were no longer as important as they had been during the long years of truce that had set in during the 1380s and the great expeditions of the fourteenth century had finally been abandoned as an instrument of war policy.

The extent of the English occupation in each of these regions varied enormously from one time to another according to the fortunes of war, financial capacity, and the dictates of government. Aquitaine was at its greatest during the 1360s, when the duchy was elevated to a principality for the Black Prince, and it was several times reduced to a narrow maritime strip, without any deep hinterland, running from the estuary of the river Gironde to the Pyrenees, and largely dependent upon the two bastions of English rule in the south: Bordeaux and Bayonne. Between 1380 and 1413 the principal frontier zone (essentially a frontier in depth) lay between the rivers Charente and Dordogne. In Brittany, after 1343 and throughout the greater part of the occupation, the territories under allied control were for the most part situated in the Breton speaking south and west. They included almost the whole of Léon and Cornouaille with their ports of Conquet and Brest, and the southern coast as far as the mouth of the Vilaine with the ports of Quimperlé, Hennebont and Vannes (cf. map IV). Most of upper Brittany, which was French speaking, supported Charles of Blois; but English garrisons were established at Bécherel, Ploërmel, Fougerai and Chateaublanc, which tended to form the frontier regions with the French, who brought in re-enforcements by way of Rennes and Nantes. At Calais (cf. pl. 72) the competence of the military administration extended over a much greater area than the town and castle. Apart from the garrison in the town, there was another under a separate command in the castle, and yet others in the fortresses which one by one came to be taken by the English around Calais: some thirteen places by 1371 (cf. map VI). To begin with, some of these appear to have formed separate units, but from an early date the captain of Calais became the officer responsible for the royal government throughout the march of Calais and, in the fifteenth century, he was invariably styled 'lieutenant of Calais and its march'. Similarly at Brest during the '80s and '90s, the jurisdiction of the captain seems at first to have been limited to the town and castellany, but eventually it was extended to the whole of western Finistère, together with the off-shore islands, where the captains also acted as lieutenants. At Saint-Sauveur and Cherbourg, English control extended throughout the greater part of the north-west Cotentin peninsula and it was sufficiently extensive in the early 1370s to merit the appointment of a lieutenant at Saint-Sauveur. In the fifteenth century, when the occupation of northern France was at its maximum, the frontier between Anglo-Burgundian and dauphinist control ran roughly from the Breton frontier above Craon, between Maine and Anjou-Touraine, through the county of Vendôme to Orléans, and thence down the Loire to Raonne (cf. map VII). But almost throughout the period there were dauphinist enclaves well inside Anglo-Burgundian territory and *vice-versa*. After the break-up of the Anglo-Burgundian alliance at Arras, the frontiers were brought into the Ile-de-France and eastern Normandy and once again around Calais in Artois. Only in Maine did the southern frontier remain for a while intact.

In Aquitaine, Brittany, Normandy and the other regions held by English and allied forces in the fourteenth century, the troops were placed under the command of a lieutenant-general. Lieutenants were also appointed to the whole of France, usually for the purpose of prosecuting war outside a provincial base, and the lieutenants in Aquitaine usually had powers to act in Languedoc. At Calais,

Fig. 39 Effigy of John Holland, earl of Huntingdon, lieutenant-general of Aquitaine (1439–41), Chapel of St Peter de Vincula, the Tower of London.

Cherbourg, Brest and the other coastal fortresses, the troops were responsible to a captain with less extensive powers and a more limited jurisdiction. But the military administration was alike in no two regions or coastal forts. In Aquitaine there were already well established offices and institutions operating under the aegis of the government at Westminster and a substantial section of the population favoured the English cause. Lieutenants were only appointed during periods of military threat, and when an expeditionary force was sent out to the duchy. At other times the seneschal of Aquitaine was in charge of military affairs. In Normandy, on the other hand, the English position very largely depended upon Navarrese interests and support. In Brittany, the military personnel was almost entirely English, but the administration had to be superimposed upon native civil institutions. The lieutenants who were occasionally appointed in Picardy had to work with and through the English administration under the captain of Calais. During the fifteenth century, lieutenants continued to be appointed to Aquitaine, Normandy and France as a whole; but the position and powers of the lieutenants in the northern circumscriptions were transformed by the changed political circumstances following the treaty of Troyes and the deaths of both Henry V and Charles VI in 1422. During Bedford's regency (1422–35) the lieutenants (of whom Salisbury, Warwick and Suffolk were the most prominent) were appointed to smaller circumscriptions and had less extensive powers, and they were also appointed by Bedford in his capacity as regent of France. Bedford's successors to the government of France—the duke of York (1436–7 and 1440–7), the earl of Warwick (1437–9) and the duke of Somerset (1447–50)—were primarily governors, although they also bore the title of lieutenant-general.

The majority of the English lieutenants were men of royal or noble birth. Four of Edward III's sons held the office; three of them (the Black Prince (cf. pl. 30), Edmund Langley and Thomas of Woodstock) on one occasion and John of Gaunt on no less than eight. Two members of the higher nobility were pre-eminent among the lieutenants of his reign: Henry of Lancaster, who served on six separate occasions, and William de Bohun, earl of Northampton, who was twice lieutenant in Brittany. Two of Gaunt's sons held the lieutenancy of Aquitaine (John Beaufort in 1398 and Thomas Beaufort in 1413), and three of his grandsons served in that capacity there or in France and Normandy. Edmund Langley's son, Edward, held the lieutenancy of Aquitaine in 1401, and his grandson, Richard duke of York, was twice lieutenant-general and governor of France and Normandy. Henry V's brother, Clarence, served as lieutenant in Aquitaine and subsequently in Normandy, and prominent among the nobility were Thomas Montagu, earl of Salisbury; Richard Beauchamp, earl of Warwick (cf. fig. 40); William de la Pole, earl of Suffolk; Edmund Mortimer, earl of March; and John Talbot, earl of Shrewsbury.

There were, however, some exceptions to the requirements of noble birth and ability could sometimes make up for the deficiencies of breeding. This is particularly true of the lieutenants in Brittany during the fourteenth century, who for the most part came from non-noble families, and included the famous captains Sir Thomas Dagworth and Sir Walter Bentley, and the less well-known John Hardreshull (cf. pl. 27) and John Avenel. After the treaty of Brétigny, Sir John Chandos acted as Edward III's lieutenant in Normandy and France, though more in a diplomatic capacity for the execution of the treaty than anything else—an employ which he carried out sufficiently impartially to bring him friends in both camps. But the most exceptional appointment of all was that of Sir Robert Knowles, Alan Buxhill, Thomas Grandison and Thomas Bourchier to a joint-lieutenancy for France in 1370, an experiment not to be repeated. After the disaster of Knowles's expedition in that year, the office was never again granted to a person who was not a member of the higher nobility. The appointments of the fifteenth century were without exception

Fig. 40 The installation of Richard Beauchamp, earl of Warwick as lieutenant and governor-general of France and Normandy; *Life and Acts of Richard Beauchamp, earl of Warwick*, by John Rous, *c.* 1485. *London, British Museum Cotton Ms Julius E IV Art VI, fo. 26.* (22.8 × 16.2)

aristocratic.

This emphasis upon aristocratic background is evident in other appointments of the late fourteenth and fifteenth centuries. Up to the 1380s the captains of the coastal fortresses were almost without exception recruited from men of knightly background who had proved themselves in the wars. Thereafter, especially at Calais, they were drawn from the higher nobility, and exercised their commands through lieutenants whom they appointed in their place. In Aquitaine, on the other hand, the office of seneschal continued to be held by men recruited from the gentry and during the years of the principality there were also opportunities to serve as sub-seneschals. But the war brought a fundamental change in the governing personnel of the duchy. Throughout the thirteenth century the office of seneschal had been held by loyal Gascons; after 1337 it was, with only one exception, granted to Englishmen. Even the mayors of Bordeaux during the period came to be appointed in Westminster and were nearly all English. Like the seneschals, they were first and foremost soldiers. In the appointments to high office in France during the period, something like a 'foreign service' began to emerge. Many became almost professional captains and lieutenants and, while the greatest offices were filled by members of the higher nobility, there were soldiers like the Cheshire knight Sir Hugh Calveley, who saw service in France and Spain, who in the years between 1375 and 1393 was successively captain of Calais, Brest and Cherbourg, and warden of the Channel Islands; or the Essex family of Swynburne which produced two mayors of Bordeaux (cf. fig. 41), one of whom was also captain of Guines and Hammes in the march of Calais.

The circumscriptions of the French lieutenants and captains-general fluctuated a great deal during the course of the war according to the extent of English and Burgundian infiltration, the activities of the free companies and princely resistance, which made them necessary. Languedoc and Gascony was one of the first and most important commands in that Anglo-Gascon forces were continually present on the frontiers of Guyenne and, being a long way from Paris, it was necessary to grant the lieutenants more extensive powers than those in regions nearer to the Ile-de-France. As the English frontier in Aquitaine was pushed northwards after 1346, lieutenants were appointed to a circumscription ultimately comprising the entire region between the rivers Loire and Dordogne. With the arrival of the Black Prince in Gascony in 1355, these two circumscriptions were temporarily united to form a command for the king's son John, count of Poitiers, subsequently duke of Berry. Appointments were also made for Normandy and the frontiers with Brittany, to Picardy and the surrounding counties to meet the English hold at Calais and in Flanders and even, as the menace of the free companies necessitated, to the central regions of the kingdom. As the war spread from province to province, there were few places in France that had not seen this supreme representative of the royal authority.

The most important French lieutenants, like their English counterparts, were men of royal or noble birth. All of John II's sons held the office. Much the most successful of them was his second son, Louis of Anjou, who held the lieutenancy of Languedoc and Guyenne for sixteen years (1364–80) together with four others in different parts of the kingdom. Doubtless he owed much of his achievement to the abilities of his generals—the constable Du Guesclin, the marshal De Sancerre, and the future constable Olivier de Clisson; but Anjou was a lieutenant of outstanding ability whose undoubted claim to fame is the reconquest of Aquitaine. The king's third son John, duke of Berry, who succeeded his brother as lieutenant of Languedoc and Guyenne (1380–9) was much less competent. He only secured the office after fighting the count of Foix for it and had to be dismissed for gross abuse of his powers. First made lieutenant at the age of fifteen in the largest circumscription ever—the whole of France south of the river Loire (1356 and 1358), he was subsequently lieutenant in Languedoc (1357–61), recovered the lieutenancy of Guyenne for a

Fig. 41 Sir Robert Swynburne and Sir Thomas Swynburne, mayors of Bordeaux (1325 and 1405–12) from a brass formerly in Little Horkesley Church, Essex. *London, Victoria and Albert Museum.*

62. Knight charging the beasts, from one of seven tapestries of the *Apocalypse,* woven in Paris by Nicolas Bataille, 1373–80. *Castle of Angers.*

62

63

64

short time in 1392 and held it again, together with that of Languedoc, for a further thirteen years (1401–11 and 1413–6). To these circumscriptions must be added the lieutenancy of Mâconnais and Lyonnais (1359), together with the provinces of Normandy, Anjou, Maine, Touraine, Auvergne, Berry and Bourbonnais (1369). His powerful commission for the government of Languedoc and Guyenne in 1380 also included the provinces of Auvergne, Berry and Poitou, which he held as an *apanage*. He thus wielded enormous power which he was able to use to his own advantage. In a similar way the counts of Armagnac and Foix were able to use the office of lieutenant of Languedoc to build up their position in the south.

It was probably for this reason that the kings of France preferred to promote the constables and marshals to many of the lieutenancies. Most of the constables of the fourteenth century served as lieutenants on one or more occasions and, as we have seen, by the time of Charles VII their office automatically entitled them to a lieutenant's powers. But particularly noteworthy in this respect were the marshals Guy de Nesle (1348–52), Arnoul d'Audrehem (1351–68), Jean de Clermont (1352–6), the elder and the younger Boucicaut (1356–68 and 1391–1421), Moutain de Blainville (1368–91) and Louis de Sancerre (1368–97), who were almost professional lieutenants, succeeding from one circumscription to another during the course of their active military careers. With the exception of Sancerre these men were drawn from the lesser nobility and, like another active lieutenant, Amaury de Craon, who had held eight lieutenancies in the years between 1351 and 1369, had meagre fief holdings. During the fifteenth century, however, the marshals were no longer so eminent as lieutenants and, as with English appointments, there was an increasingly aristocratic candidature. The days of Nesle, Clermont and Audrehem were over; but during the fourteenth century these men had enjoyed a position unparalleled among English lieutenants. Avenel, Bentley and Dagworth had by comparison enjoyed but brief terms of office in Brittany.

The prominence of men from the lower nobility among the high command of the French forces during the fourteenth century, was a major weakness in French military administration. For the offices which these men held gave them extensive powers, which were sometimes abused, and they were frequently resented by the traditional aristocratic leaders in a society deeply divided in itself. Froissart was astounded at the favour shown to Du Guesclin, who could hardly read and write. Reporting the king's intimation of his wish to bestow the office of constable upon the Breton knight, he tells us how the latter repeatedly excused himself:

'Right dear sir and noble king, I may not nor dare not withsay your noble pleasure: howbeit sir, it is of truth that I am but a poor man and too low of blood to come to the office of constable of France, the which is so great and so noble an office. For it is convenient that he that will exercise and acquit himself well in that office must command as well and rather the great men than the small personages. And, sir, behold here my lords your brethren, your nephews and your cousins, who hath charge of many men of war in your host and journeys. Sir, how durst I then be so bold as to command them? Certainly, sir, envy is so great that I ought to fear it. Therefore, sir, I require your grace, pardon me, and give this office to some other that would gladlier have it than I, and that may better execute the office.'

63. Effigy of Cardinal Beaufort (d. 1449) in his Chantry at Winchester Cathedral.

64. Effigy of Richard Beauchamp, earl of Warwick (d. 1439), Beauchamp Chapel, St Mary's, Warwick.

When he entered the king's service, on the eve of Charles V's accession, he was no more than a captain of *routiers*, fond of pillage and raids, but surpassing his fellows (with the exception, perhaps, of Arnaud de Cervole) by the iron authority and strict discipline he imposed on his mercenaries. And yet this man of dubious background and uncouth appearance—his tomb at Saint-Denis is a striking portrayal of his big head, his square shoulders, his broad, flat nose, his mouth on which only the smile seems human (cf. pl. 25)—was within six years to be elevated to the most powerful royal office in France. It is hardly surprising that on his death Louis of Anjou wished to keep the office vacant, finding the powers attached to it too wide, and that the dukes of Burgundy and Berry were opposed to Charles V's preference for another, though more socially acceptable Breton, Olivier de Clisson.

Among these supreme officers divisions were not infrequent. The dispute between the marshals Clermont and Audrehem in the preliminary council of war at the battle of Poitiers contributed heavily to the French disaster on that occasion. So also the less famous quarrel between Du Guesclin and the French treasurer-of-wars Jean le Mercier—a man of unknown origins who had also come to a position of great power—contributed to the failure of the siege of Cherbourg in 1378, thus allowing that strategically vital fortress to remain in enemy hands for the next sixteen years. And elsewhere there was a lack of a sense of public service at the top. Robert de Fiennes, Du Guesclin's predecessor as constable (1356–70), was able to avoid rendering accounts for the wages received by the troops of his *hôtel* during his entire tenure of that office. We have already noted that Berry, Armagnac and Foix were able to use their powers as lieutenants in Languedoc for their own aggrandizement.

For the upkeep of the troops established in these widely scattered territories and under the command of one or other of these officers, a considerable machinery of military finance had to be evolved. The number of troops employed by the Crown, although small by today's standards, was enormous for the time, and immensely costly. While the English expeditionary forces served on campaigns of short duration and were relatively small in size, seldom exceeding 6,000 men, the length of the period during which hostilities took place and the inability to conclude a peace meant that they were frequently employed and, above all, that the frontier garrisons, which were often as many as 5,000 strong, had to be maintained even during time of truce (cf. maps IV, V, VI). The strength of the French forces, both field and garrison, was frequently a good deal greater, and their financing was the responsibility of two treasurers-of-wars, whose offices were well established and their functions defined as early as 1318. They were both receivers and paymasters. They received money from treasurers and receivers of all kinds of taxes (*gabelles, aides, tailles* and special war subsidies) accountable at the *Chambre des Comptes,* to which they in turn were responsible. The king or his captains and lieutenants informed them of the troops which they recruited, they paid their wages upon receipt of a warrant from the marshals of France attesting that the troops had been mustered before them, and they received acquittances from the troops for the sums they had paid. These warrants and acquittances served to verify their accounts.

To provide for the many theatres of war in which the troops were employed, the treasurers-of-wars were assigned to specific regions and expeditions, and both they and the marshals of France appointed deputies to accompany the field forces under the command of the lieutenants and captains-general and tour the frontier garrisons within their circumscriptions. Occasionally, special paymasters with independent funds were also appointed. Only after the troops had been mustered by the marshal or his deputies did the treasurer or his clerks pay them. The operation of muster and review had both a financial and a military purpose: it was intended to verify the strength of each company and to ensure that the horses and equipment of the troops were as they should be. The frequency of these musters was very irregular, but an effort was made to see that they were held fortnightly (*ordonnance* of 1351), and then, when this proved impossible, monthly (*ordonnance* of 1374). On these occasions, muster rolls were drawn up stating the names and military standing of the men reviewed, the dates of their retention, and the number of days on which they had served. A description and valuation of each horse of the men-at-arms was also included, for the purpose of reimbursement in case of loss. In such an eventuality, the owner handed over the skin to secure the appropriate

65. The vaulting in Henry IV's Chapel, Canterbury Cathedral.

65

66

indemnity and, to prevent fraud, it was necessary for the colour and markings of each horse to be entered on the muster rolls. Prior to 1374 each captain received the pay of his entire company, but from that date, doubtless to prevent him from embezzling the entire funds, each company was divided for financial purposes into smaller units known as *chambres* (usually of ten men-at-arms), the leader of each of which received the pay of its members. The captain himself only received the pay of his personal retinue or *hôtel*, and his *état*.

It was inevitable that such a complex, highly centralized and all-pervading machinery of military finance should have been open to constant abuse. Among the many charges levelled against the French forces after their defeat in 1356, the anonymous author of the *Complainte sur la bataille de Poitiers* included one on the covetousness of the captains:

'When they muster before the marshals,
They borrow boys, arms and horses from each other,
Counting their valets and pages for men-at-arms,
So taking the wages of four persons from the king for one.'

The *ordonnances* of 1351 and 1374 amply bear him out. From them we learn that not only the captains and their troops were defrauding the king, but the mustering officers and paymasters were also at fault. The latter paid wages in kind out of army stocks, accepted bribes from the captains, and withheld wages. Defaults at musters were ignored by the marshals and their deputies. By making inspection more rigorous, the *ordonnance* of 1351 sought to prevent the captains from drawing pay for non-existent members and the men from serving with inadequate, borrowed or stolen arms and horses. Musters might be taken anywhere and at short notice. Horses were to be branded on their flank with a mark common to each company, their markings were to be carefully noted in the muster rolls and they were only to be accepted for service if above prescribed values (30 *livres tournois* for those of men-at-arms and 20 for those of valets). To keep a check on the captains, the leader of each battle as well as the captains' subordinates within their companies were to inform the constable, the marshals, or their deputies, of any men absent from service or who were inadequately armed or mounted between musters. Captains were to do likewise, and they were to take an oath to their superiors not to draw unwarranted wages. In 1374 more elaborate precautions were taken to see that men unfit for service were not recruited or paid, that those accepted for service did not leave their companies between musters, and that the captains did not defraud the men of their wages. Paymasters and mustering officers committing offences were to be reported to their superiors and removed from office. But it is clear that many of these malpractices remained.

Nevertheless, the vast policies which this machinery of military finance supported in all parts of the realm and beyond its boundaries should make us chary of concluding that the system itself was a failure. Not until the occupation of Normandy in the fifteenth century was England able to produce anything like it. In part, this was due to the absence of centralization in the Plantagenet administration in France; but it was also due to the short-term expeditionary nature of much of the English war effort in the fourteenth century, and in part to the inability of the Crown to finance large sections of the occupation forces during the same period. Up to 1380 the instrument of English military success was the expeditionary force, recruited by contract and almost always short-term. It cost much less than military occupation, required no elaborate machinery of muster and review, and was relatively easy to control. It was the ideal instrument of war for conducting raids of plunder or *chevauchées*.

It was not, however, until the occupation of Normandy in the fifteenth century

66. Detail of 'The Boar Hunt' from the Devonshire Hunting Tapestries (Tournai, 1425–50). *London, Victoria and Albert Museum.*

133

that a comprehensive machinery of muster and review was developed to meet occupation needs. Such provisions depended upon the existence of a centralized financial administration upon which all garrison forces relied for their pay. In the fourteenth century this was patently lacking not only in Normandy and Brittany, but also on the frontiers of Guyenne, where the troops were obliged to live off the country they occupied (cf. below, ch. 4). But in fifteenth-century Normandy, the creation of a sound financial administration based on Caen (to 1422) then Rouen (1422–49/50), coupled with the relative strength of the English financial position in the duchy (cf. above, p. 83) made it possible for the contract system to be combined with a regular machinery of muster and review. Indentures were drawn up annually between the captains of the garrisons and the king or regent and, about the same time, warrants were sent to the treasurer-general of Normandy authorizing payment of wages as detailed in the indentures. After verifying the indentures and other relevant records, the treasurer instructed the receiver-general of the duchy to pay the garrisons in accordance with the warrants. Commissions of array were issued quarterly, providing for musters to be taken. As an added check on the reliability of the musters, the captains only received pay for their garrison forces after the muster rolls had been checked against *contrerolles* drawn up by a controller, resident in each garrison and responsible to the financial officers and not the captain. All ransoms and booty taken from the enemy also had to be reported to him, in order that a check could be kept on that part of the profits due to the captain and the king. This prevented the troops from becoming financially independent—as happened in Brittany in the fourteenth century—and so preserved intact the authority of the superior officers.

In 1439 by act of the English parliament it was declared that any soldier who had been mustered and received pay, and who departed from the garrison in which he owed service, without first having secured the permission of his captain, was to be regarded as a felon. What had previously been a violation of contract had come to be recognized as an evasion of public duty and a crime against the king. Such an attitude of mind was a step towards a more modern conception of an army.

In France, that goal was reached by the creation of a permanent force, first brought into being in the years of peace which followed the peace of Brétigny in an attempt to get rid of the free companies to which the country was prey. With that immediate end in view, in the spring of 1362 John II proposed to Edward III that they should together raise and finance a force of 1,000 archers and 500 men-at-arms. In December 1363, after this scheme had not surprisingly failed, John put the matter to a meeting of the Estates of Languedoïl, and the conclusions which were reached there were embodied in a royal *ordonnance* which gave France her first standing field army. It provided for the maintenance of a permanent force of 6,000 combatants, to be chosen by the *élus* of each diocese on the advice of nobles and men-at-arms, and paid for out of the proceeds of a subsidy on wine and a special hearth-tax (*fouage*) to be raised in every parish. The troops selected for service were to receive a commission and they were to be ready for service upon the command of the king or of his captains-general. Comprehensive musters were to be held regularly and deficiencies in the quota of troops to be raised in each diocese, whether they occurred through death or bodily incapacity, were immediately to be made good. In practice, the money raised only sufficed for the maintenance of 1,500 men; but with the renewal of the war in 1369 a number of new taxes were introduced, the *fouage* increased and the selection of troops entrusted to specially appointed captains in each diocese. The result was that between 1370 and 1380 the strength of the field army averaged about 3,000 men, although it was still intended that it should stand at 6,000. As well as this permanent force of mounted men, a standing force of crossbowmen was brought into being—800 according to an *ordonnance* of 1373—placed under the command of a captain-general, as opposed to the master of the crossbowmen who

traditionally had supreme command of the infantry.

The setting up of these permanent forces was without doubt an important innovation and it may have contributed substantially to the achievement of Charles V after 1369. For the most part, however, the permanence of the forces remained somewhat theoretical. Military and financial pressures produced constant changes in the strength of each company; wages were often in arrears or remained unpaid and, whilst the personnel of some companies was relatively stable, that of others changed with alarming rapidity. After Buckingham's expedition in 1380, and with the constant renewal of truces in subsequent years, the standing army was allowed to die out. Such permanent forces as remained were installed in the garrisons of the frontier fortresses, while others came to operate on their own account, swelling the ranks of the *routiers*, who were again a major problem in the last two decades of the fourteenth century (cf. below, ch. 4).

It was not until the reign of Charles VII that a standing field army was finally established in France. While his *ordonnance* of 1439 added little to the *ordonnance* of 1374, that of 1445, which must be seen in the context of the truce of Tours concluded in the previous year, marked a real turning point. As in 1363, the principal purpose of the legislation of that year was to rid France of the free companies or *Écorcheurs* by employing the more trustworthy and capable of them in a permanent force, and leading the others out of the country, on this occasion, against the Swiss. In order to prevent unwanted troops from supporting themselves off the countryside, a scheme was arranged with the English to transform the arbitrary ransoming of the frontier districts into a regularized system of taxation under royal control. The *ordonnance* itself provided for a permanent force of fifteen companies of cavalry, each composed of 100 lances, in each lance a group of six men: a man-at-arms, a *coutillier* (so called because of the infantry dagger, *coustille*, which he carried), a page, two archers, and a *valet de guerre* or, in some companies, a third archer. In 1446 the scheme was extended to Languedoc with another five companies, making a total force of 12,000 men, of whom 2,000 were men-at-arms and 4,000 were mounted archers. Under Louis XI this was increased to 2,636 lances, in all some 15,816 men. These *gens d'ordonnance du roi* (cf. pl. 49) as they were known, were recruited by the constable from existing companies, other troops being technically disbanded and sent back to their native *pays*. For the infantry, the Crown resorted to the old device of encouraging a local militia of archers. This was embodied in the *ordonnance* of 1448 which provided for an archer to be raised in each parish, and subsequently from each group of fifty hearths. He was paid during war, but was exempt from taxes during peace. In this way a total force was recruited which rose, at least on paper, from about 8,000 under Charles VII to about 16,000 under Louis XI. But as a fighting force the *francs-archers*, as they were known, rapidly became obsolete. They could only be utilized in defensive actions, which were not frequent after 1453. Increasingly the Crown came to rely on the Swiss infantry, which could be employed in an offensive against groups of cavalry. After the 1480s the *francs-archers* were therefore gradually abandoned as a weapon of war, although they remained popular as a fiscally exempt group.

These innovations were not, of course, made at the expense of more traditional forms of military organization: garrisons, on the one hand, large armies assembled for a short campaign, when the nobles of the realm combatted under customary banners and pennons, on the other. But the standing army brought into being in the 1440s was maintained long after the internal threat from the companies and the external threat from England had in fact subsided; for in 1453 no peace treaty was made with England, and contemporaries were not in a position to know that the Hundred Years War was over. Nevertheless, not all of them were pleased by the changes that had been brought about. In a celebrated passage in his *History of*

137

Charles VII, the Norman ecclesiastic Thomas Basin voiced his criticisms of them. Writing shortly before 1475, he comments: 'Since time immemorial the kingdom of France furnished a permanent and ordinary army of spectacular proportions: that is the nobility of the realm. Each time that he required their service the king drew from his nobility an army of more than 50,000 cavalry, without counting the incalculable number of foot-soldiers which he could raise in case of necessity. The welfare of the State does not seem to necessitate that, in addition to this ordinary army, for which the people contribute taxes and customary services, another mercenary army should be recruited and that it should be paid and maintained at customary wages even in peace time and when war is not imminent.' It was the burden of taxation which the standing army necessitated that to Basin seemed a mark of servitude: 'And thus the realm of France', he writes, 'once the land of nobility and liberty, under pretext of the necessity of maintaining this army in the king's pay, has been precipitated into this abyss of servitude, of tribute and exactions, to the extent that the entire population has by public acknowledgement become taxable at the king's will by his treasurers, called *généraux des finances*, and also by their deputies, and are effectively taxed (*taillés*) in the most inhuman fashion, nobody daring to speak out against it. For in the eyes of these satellites of tyranny, there is more danger in questioning this matter than in denying the faith, and he who, in one manner or another, dares to say a word to the contrary, is accused of the crime of *lèse-majesté* and is speedily punished.'

That Charles VII succeeded where Charles V had failed was in the main due to the strength of the Crown's financial position in the mid-fifteenth century. The extraordinary taxes, introduced in the later years of John II's reign, but abandoned or appropriated under Charles VI, were reintroduced or made effective again in the 1430s and 1440s. With the expulsion of the English, the French financial administration reached into almost every household in France. Under Charles VI this had been impossible, the position of the monarchy and princely ambitions being what they were. Had a monarch of Charles V's capacity inherited the throne in 1380, the position might well have been different. There is no parallel in English military organization during the period to the establishment of this standing field army. That the war was not fought in England, and that the land frontiers were in France, made it unnecessary for the king to create a standing army at home. His need for men on a permanent basis was for the most part restricted to the garrisons which were essential for the defence of the territories which, by conquest, treaty or inheritance, he had come to occupy in France. But elsewhere in Europe, save in the Empire and Venice, the French example was soon imitated.

Technological developments, which made military equipment more expensive, stimulated change. At the beginning of the fourteenth century, the equipment of a foot-soldier in France cost 40s. *tournois*, which represented between 30 and 40 days pay (at 1s. to 1s. 3d. a day). By 1460 the equipment of a *franc-archer* amounted to 15 *livres tournois* and, since his wages were 100s. *tournois* a month, his equipment cost him three months pay. Thus, when in 1466 Louis XI decided to increase the number of *francs-archers* from 8,000 to 16,000, he was demanding an extra war effort of 120,000 *livres*—twice the ordinary revenues of the Crown in the period. During the 150 years or so after 1300 the price of a soldier's armour increased from 6 *livres* to 30 *livres*, although his wages only went up from five to ten shillings a day; thus, whereas in 1300 the armour of a man-at-arms represented 24 days' wages, around 1450 it represented two months'. The use of cannon, the repairs necessary after each campaign, the construction of gun carriages, the manufacture of powder and amunition, were also very costly and the number of guns produced rapidly increased in the second half of the fifteenth century. Between 1440 and 1490 the expenses of the French royal artillery multiplied by five, from 10,000 to 50,000 *livres* a year.

These rising costs had profound social consequences. During the first half of the fourteenth century the forces recruited for the king's wars were provided by his tenants-in-chief or his sub-tenants, and they were made up of knights and esquires. This distinction was above all social, but it also had a military significance: the knight had a more complete and modern armour, he possessed more horses, and more expensive ones, than did the esquire. But from around 1450, when they were called up in the *ban* or *arrière-ban*, these same fief holders only played a secondary role: nine out of ten of them served as *coutilliers*, *vougiers* and archers, using reputedly non-noble arms. They now only supplemented the professionals who outclassed them, were better equipped and in the king's pay. Technical progress had favoured the wealthy and princes who could raise large sums of money were in a position to consolidate their authority. Wherever financial resources were inadequate—as in the late medieval empire—unity was not realized. Tactical changes also stimulated this social change. Until the close of the Middle Ages the man-at-arms, invariably a nobleman, fought on horseback bearing the noble arms of lance and sword. He monopolized military prestige: to fight in the ranks of the heavy cavalry was itself a means to social advancement; to bear arms in the service of a prince or king tended to be considered as denoting nobility. Foot-soldiers, even if better equipped, armed and paid, were regarded as supplementary. It was much better to be an anonymous man-at-arms in a mounted company than a captain of a body of infantry. But in the years between 1470 and 1480, the successes of the Swiss infantry, who manoeuvred *en masse* in balanced formations, proved a decisive stimulus to change. The nobleman had lost his monopoly.

The establishment of standing armies across Europe thus had many consequences. It gave birth to a new social and professional group alongside the nobility. It contributed to the duration of war, which became at once more intelligent, more complex and more cruel. It modified the character of international relations: there was nothing easier for the king of France than to invade a foreign province unexpectedly and occupy it with troops which he had constantly at hand. In case of a foreign invasion his reactions were speedier and more efficient. If his troops were defeated in combat, it was not necessarily disastrous, for he could still call out the nobles and towns to make up his numbers. But above all else, the standing army assured his authority in his realm. It enabled him to suppress rebellion quickly and was at once the symbol and the guarantee of his power. Born in the disorders and convulsions of the Hundred Years War, it became perhaps the most efficient instrument of absolute monarchy.

Chivalry, war and society

4

Warfare during the period was cloaked in, and to some extent modified by, the prevailing code of chivalry. This was in essence a doctrine of knightly service to the community and of equality between knights. It emphasized the virtues of military prowess, personal honour and *courtoisie*—of considerate manners towards other members of the chivalrous class—and was what differentiated them from their social inferiors. While its origins belong to an earlier age, and although by the fourteenth century the hard realities of the contemporary scene cut across the old ideals, chivalric notions still coloured the literature and to some extent affected the practical affairs of the times. To the men who set the tone of chivalrous society in the Later Middle Ages, imitation of the great men of the past—the heroes of Antiquity, the knights of King Arthur's court and Charlemagne's paladins—was the way to glory, and they were cast in that image by the chroniclers of the period, among whom Jean Froissart (d. *c.* 1404), Enguerrand de Monstrelet (d. 1453), Jean de Wavrin (d. *c.* 1474), Georges Chastelain (d. 1475), and Olivier de la Marche (d. 1502) were the leading exponents of the chivalric point of view. These writers concentrated their attention upon the wars and tournaments of the times, drawing their information from the men whose actions they were describing, and from pursuivants, heralds and kings-at-arms, who were sometimes themselves historians, like Chandos herald, Berry herald, and the king-at-arms of the Golden Fleece, Lefèvre de Saint-Remy.

In the prologue to his chronicles (the different recensions of which cover the period from about 1326 to 1400), Froissart tells us that he had undertaken their writing 'to the intent that the honourable and noble adventures of feats of arms, done and achieved by the wars of France and England, should notably be enregistered and put in perpetual memory', and that he had got his information from 'valiant men, knights and esquires who have taken part in them, and from several kings-at-arms and their marshals, who by right are and should be just inquirers into and narrators of such matters'. Monstrelet (who thought of himself as Froissart's continuator, and who covered the period 1400-44) was of the same opinion: 'I have been informed', he tells us, 'on every point in these chronicles, from the first book to the last, from kings-at-arms, heralds and pursuivants of several lords and countries who, by their right and office, should be just and diligent inquirers, well informed and honest narrators'.

Heralds rapidly increased in number in the Later Middle Ages and they were, in fact, in a unique position to secure information. They enjoyed immunity from war on the grounds that they belonged to an international order, to which they owed allegiance as well as to their own masters. Their coats of arms were therefore sufficient safe-conducts for them in all places and they could not be treated as subjects of the enemy and thus taken prisoner. According to Nicholas Upton (who had seen service in northern France during the 1420s, and whose treatise *De Studio Militari* was written some time before 1446), heralds-at-arms were chosen from pursuivants of at least seven years' standing, who were in turn chosen from horsemen with three years' experience in riding. They were 'to honowre chyvalry and to desyre to be present in all actes off warre, . . . to shewe ffeythefully and trewly bysnes

69. View of Paris; detail from a retable formerly in the chapel of the Parlement de Paris; Flemish school (1455–60). *Louvre, Paris.*

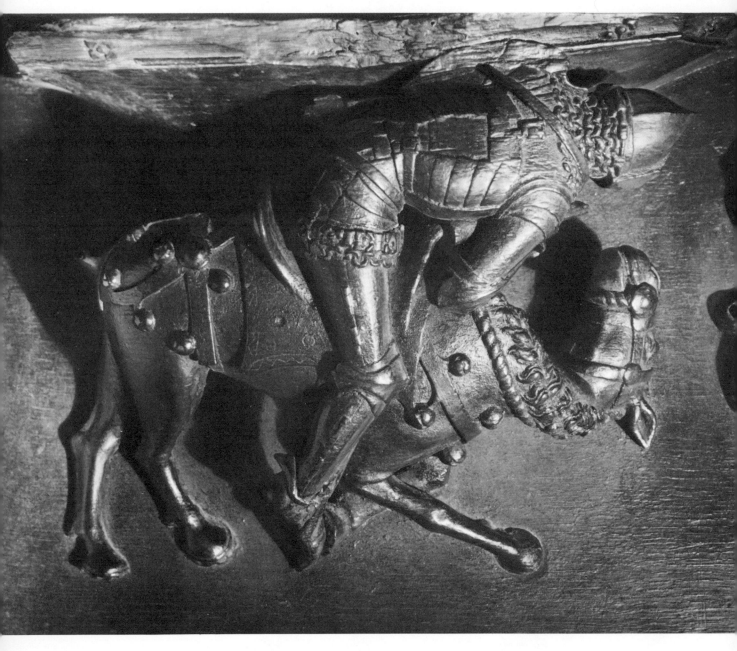

70

betwene enemyse, and to favoure no party in soche actes of batell or fyghtyng whyche ys had bytwene ij noble men'. A fifteenth-century manual written for the use of heralds records their by then well-established functions on the field of battle: they were to identify the gonfalons of the enemy in order to inform their masters or whatever knights or noblemen requested information of them; they were to record the names of those dubbed and to be as close to the scene of action as possible in order 'to see the most valiant of either side assemble and combat and to take note of the blazons'. When the rout came, they were to notice who fled the field and to count and identify the most important among the dead. It is not difficult to understand why Froissart recorded so many scenes of 'the fresh, shining armour, the banners waving in the wind, the companies in good order, riding a soft pace', or of famous knights like Sir John Chandos, 'with his banner before him and his company about him, with his coat-of-arms on him, great and large, beaten with his arms'; nor is it difficult to understand where he got his information from. The aspects of war which the heralds recorded were those which were likely to appeal to the chivalrous school of historians, who were primarily writing for a nobility who wished to secure honourable mention in their works.

Attempts were also made to inaugurate a sort of cult of those contemporaries who showed to perfection the virtues of chivalry and these were embodied in a number of laudatory biographies, of which those of the Black Prince by the herald of Sir John Chandos, of the constable Du Guesclin by Cuvelier, of the second marshal Boucicaut and of Jacques de Lalaing are among the more noteworthy. 'This frank prince of whom I tell you', wrote Chandos herald of the victor of Poitiers, 'from the day that he was born thought only of loyalty, of free courage and of gentleness, and endowed was he with prowess'. He wished to spend all his days 'upholding justice and integrity', and was 'so preux, so hardy and so valiant, so courteous and so wise'. According to Cuvelier, in a work which has been described as the last of the *chansons de geste,* Du Guesclin was the most honourable knight since Roland and his deeds compared with those of Alexander, Arthur, Pippin, Godfrey de Bouillon and Saladin. Eustache Deschamps went further and added him to the list of the Nine Worthies, the symbol of pagan and Christian chivalry. The Burgundian *bon chevalier,* Jacques de Lalaing, whose knight errantry is described in another *livre des faits,* was, we are told, fair as Paris, pious as Aeneas, wise as Ulysses and passionate as Hector, yet *courtois, débonnaire* and even humble towards his opponents. As for the younger Boucicaut, the eulogistic biography published in his lifetime tells us that besides accomplishing imperishable feats of arms, he was so devout that he daily rose early and prayed for three hours, heard two masses, and always wore black on Fridays. On Sundays and feast days he made pilgrimages on foot, discoursed on holy matters, had some saint's life read out to him, or some story of 'the valiant dead—Roman or other'. He lived soberly, spoke little—and then only of God and the saints, or of chivalry and virtue. He even persuaded his servants to refrain from swearing! The hard lives of these soldiers and statesmen are hidden beneath the appearance of ideal heroism. The real men did not, of course, resemble these portraits. They were no more free from violence and avarice than the rest of chivalrous society; but the literary models and the high allusions to a pure and noble life were those which contemporaries accepted.

The ideals of courage, honour and fidelity were not wholly relegated to literature. They found expression in tournaments, orders of chivalry, devices and knightly vows, even though these increasingly came to be harnessed to the dynastic ambitions of kings and princes. The tournament was no longer the murderous *mêlée* of two bodies of armed knights, a gathering in the open for the trial of horses and arms, which it had been in the Early Middle Ages. Fought in the lists (an area enclosed by palisades; cf. fig. 44), late medieval tournaments were governed by elaborate formal regulations and were less of a danger to public order. A series of single combats, or joustings

Fig. 42 The death of Bertrand du Guesclin. *Paris, Bibliothèque Nationale Ms français 6465, fo. 458.*

70. Wooden misericord, *c.* 1380, Lincoln Cathedral.

(cf. pl. 94), replaced the mock battles of an earlier age and were made the occasion of much fantastic pageantry. They afforded an opportunity for the demonstration of individual prowess, for hazardous encounters and the winning of knightly reputations. Such displays needed large resources—not least because of the elaborate armour that was worn. It was natural, therefore, that their main patrons were great princes—Edward III, John II, Philip the Good and Charles the Rash—and that

Fig. 43 *Left* A joust; *Life and Acts of Richard Beauchamp, earl of Warwick,* by John Rous, *c.* 1485. *London, British Museum Cotton Ms Julius E IV Art VI, fo. 15v.* (19.5 × 16.2)

Fig. 44 *Right* A tourney; *Life and Acts of Richard Beauchamp, earl of Warwick,* by John Rous, *c.* 1485. *London, British Museum Cotton Ms Julius E IV Art VI, fo. 11v.* (18.3 × 16.5)

the most sumptuous examples of this kind of chivalric activity occurred when they met in connection with diplomacy or marriage, or to celebrate a victory.

So too, the various orders of chivalry founded in the century or so after 1348, while directly inspired by ideals of loyalty, prowess and honour, were also intended to serve the interests of their founders. There was a profusion of such orders in the Later Middle Ages. Edward III's Order of the Garter (1348), King John's Order of the Star (1351), and Philip the Good's Order of the Golden Fleece (1430) are among the most famous; but in France the great feudatories also had their own orders and devices—the Breton Order of the Ermine (1382), the Orléanist Porcupine (1396), the Golden Shield and Prisoner's Chain (1414–5) of the dukes of Bourbon, the Dragon of the count of Foix (*c.* 1414), the Crescent of René of Anjou (1448)—and even less important noblemen had their own orders, like the Green Shield of the White Lady of the second marshal Boucicaut, and the Golden Apple (1394), a fraternity of knights of the Auvergne and Bourbonnais who sported the device *la plus belle me doit avoir.* The royal and princely orders were more formally constituted than the others, but each had its own foundation statutes purporting to record the aims and wishes of its founders. They also varied greatly in the number of members admitted and in their duration. While the Order of the Garter prospered from the outstanding victories of Edward III and his generals, and has lived on to this day, the Order of the Star (cf. pl. 37) rapidly sank into oblivion with the defeats and capture of its founder.

The ends which these foundations claimed to serve were religious devotion, the protection of ladies of the upper classes and war to the death. They had the triple character of an honorific distinction, a society of mutual help and a brotherhood dedicated to the application of the chivalrous ideals. Louis de Bourbon summoned the knights of the Golden Shield to accompany him 'wherever we can find and achieve honour by deed of chivalry', and his son made similar demands of the members of the Prisoner's Chain. The Order of the Golden Fleece was inaugurated by Philip the Good 'from the great love we bear to the noble order of chivalry, whose honour and prosperity are our only concern . . . and for the furtherance of virtue and good manners'. Its rules were conceived in a truly ecclesiastic spirit; many are concerned with mass and obsequies and, as in the Order of the Garter, the knights were seated in choir-stalls like canons. But a deeper political purpose lay behind the statutes of some of the orders. The foundation of the Garter may well have been connected with Edward III's pretensions to the French throne. While its membership was restricted, it was not limited to England, and among the early companions were some useful allies in France. Moreover, its patron Saint George was the universal patron of chivalry and the blue and gold robes of its companions were in the colours of the arms of France. Similarly, the Order of the Star was intended to bind the French nobility more closely to the Valois monarchy and its knights were required to withdraw from every other order. The fact that membership of an order often constituted a sacred and exclusive tie in itself had political repercussions. Philip the Good declined the honour of the Garter, in spite of the insistence of the duke of Bedford, for fear of tying himself too closely to England. Charles the Rash, on accepting it, was accused by Louis XI of having broken the peace of Péronne, which forbade alliance with England without the king's consent.

If the Golden Fleece eclipsed all other orders, it was because the dukes of Burgundy placed at its disposal the resources of their enormous wealth. In their view, the order was to serve not only as a symbol of their power; it could also be used to tie together the scattered dominions of the Burgundian state. For them, as for other French feudatories, orders and devices, along with *alliances*, offices and pensions, could be used to bind their members more closely to their policies and persons (cf. above, p. 37), and it has recently been demonstrated how the foundation of the Golden Fleece must be seen in the wider context of Philip the Good's policy for the nobility of his lands. The Breton Ermine, with its apparently large and eclectic membership, fulfilled a similar purpose, and it is significant that its inauguration coincided with Duke John IV's return from exile in England to a divided duchy, and with the beginnings of that policy of neutrality in Anglo-French relations which he had come to regard as essential if he was to secure the undivided allegiance of his people. But the most striking example of the foundation of a chivalric order as an instrument of policy is that of the Porcupine, intended to strengthen the Orléanist cause, and which threatened Burgundy with its spines.

The essence of the conception of an order of chivalry is to be found in its knightly vows. Every order presupposes vows, but the chivalrous vow also existed outside the orders, under an individual and occasional form. Du Guesclin was reputed to have uttered such vows frequently: not to eat until he had effected an encounter with the English; not to undress until he had taken Montcontour. In *Le Voeu du Héron,* a poem of the fourteenth century describing the feasts given at the court of Edward III at the moment when Robert of Artois is reputed to have urged the king to declare war on Philip VI, the earl of Salisbury is said to have kept one eye closed until he had

145

accomplished some deed of bravery in France. Froissart tells us that he actually saw English knights who had covered one eye with a piece of cloth, which they had pledged themselves not to remove until they had done some such deed. But it is difficult to believe that such things were taken seriously. Like so much of the knightly code, their importance is belied by the serious business of war reported in military despatches, by chroniclers not consumed by the chivalrous point of view and by the very scale and complexity of military organization during the period. Even Froissart

Fig. 45   Letter obligatory of Edward, prince of Wales, by which he promises to pay 25,000 gold florins to Jean de Grailly, captal of Buch, and others for the purchase of Jacques de Bourbon, count of Ponthieu and La Marche, taken prisoner at the battle of Poitiers; Bordeaux, 12 February 1357. *London, Public Record Office.*

himself records endless treasons and cruelties, looting, pillaging and ransoming, without seeming to be aware of the contradiction between his general conceptions and the contents of his narrative.

How much influence, then, did chivalrous ideals have on the conduct of the Anglo-French wars? Undoubtedly such conceptions lured men into service and could be harnessed to the ambitions of princes. Tournaments were eagerly sought out and actively indulged in, even though they were becoming decorative and expensive. Vows and devices and perilous adventures were enjoyed not only by young gentlemen but also by their seniors, and on many occasions the gentry appear to have treated the war as a kind of joust. During the long periods of truce, unemployed soldiers went on crusades to Prussia and Lithuania to join the Teutonic Knights in their struggle against the heathen Slavs, or to fight the Moors in Spain and North Africa. Like Chaucer's Gentle Knight, the house of Lancaster has a fine record in that respect—though one which has its diplomatic background. In 1396 the duke of Burgundy launched and financed a crusade against the Turks in Bulgaria —even if it was intended to bring him renown in western Europe as much as it was to defend Christendom. Both Edward III and Henry V offered to settle their quarrels with the house of Valois by challenging their opponents to a duel 'to prevent Christian bloodshed and the destruction of the people'; but it should be noted that these challenges, like other duels which were not infrequently proposed between princes, never came to anything.

Similar proposals were sometimes made for combats between small teams

71. Detail of 'Falconry' from the Devonshire Hunting Tapestries (Tournai, 1425–50). *London, Victoria and Albert Museum.*

representative of the protagonists, and these occasionally took place—like the famous Combat of the Thirty at Ploërmel in Brittany between the French of Beaumanoir and a company of thirty men, English, Bretons and Germans, under a certain Bamborough. 'And let us right there try ourselves and do so much that people will speak of it in future times in halls, in palaces, in public places and elsewhere throughout the world', Froissart makes the English captain exclaim before battle is joined; but he also adds that 'some held it a prowess and some held it a shame and great overbearing'. Such challenges were in the tradition which saw warfare as a series of equal engagements conducted in such a manner as to show the prowess of the individual knightly participants. A head-on clash was thought to be the most impartial trial and during the siege of Calais William of Hainault suggested that a truce of three days should be declared so that a bridge could be built to enable the English and French armies to meet in battle. Needless to add, his advice was not taken. In so far as it affected warfare then, the chivalrous outlook detracted from the efficient conduct of war; its emphasis was on the manner of the accomplishment rather than on the thing accomplished, on glory rather than on 'results'. We have seen that the English successes in the three great actions of Crécy, Poitiers and Agincourt, were in no small measure due to their use of a non-noble weapon, the longbow, in well-chosen defensive positions, against the chivalrous mode of attack, the cavalry charge. The use of dismounted men-at-arms, the increasing importance and use of cannon, the growing costs of military equipment, and the eventual superiority of the infantryman in military tactics, destroyed the military monopoly of the knightly class and made nonsense of chivalrous notions (cf. above, ch. 3). Moreover the *chevauchée*, by its very nature, was anti-chivalrous (cf. below, p. 152).

The fact that many went to war to seek financial gain was in itself contradictory to the knightly ideals. Ransoms and booty were indeed the very stuff of war. The late medieval soldier rarely fought solely for the sake of king and honour, or to achieve glory, let alone immortality. He fought for himself, knowing full well that war, and especially successful war, could be highly profitable. 'Do you not know that I live by war and that peace would be my undoing', Sir John Hawkwood, the English *condottiere* who rose to fame in Italy, is said to have remarked. The possibilities of plunder were thoroughly demonstrated not only by his career, but by those of Knowles, Chandos, Calveley and Fastolf. The whole of military society was imbued with the desire for profit-making and elaborate rules were established to ensure fair profit-sharing. In the English armies, arrangements for the division of the spoils of war were usually entered into the military indentures and the expeditions of the fourteenth century, which were often jointly financed by the king and the contracting captains, were thus something in the way of joint-stock enterprises. By the end of Edward III's reign, it was customary for soldiers to pay a third of their profits to their immediate superiors, who themselves paid a third of these thirds—a ninth of the original—to the king, together with a third of their own profits; though some captains took as much as a half. Both English and French companies had their own *butiners*, appointed to supervise the division of the booty (*butin*) taken on a successful *chevauchée*, and, as we have seen (above, p. 134) in the fifteenth century the English garrisons in northern France each had a resident controller, who recorded the takings of the captain and his men, so ensuring that the king secured his thirds. All ranks of the army, from the king to the humblest soldiers, thus had an opportunity for sharing in the material benefits of war and some knights and esquires associated together as brothers-in-arms for mutual help and assistance, profit-sharing and common liability for the payment of ransoms in the eventuality of capture by the enemy.

The profits of war were of two principal kinds: ransoms extracted from prisoners, and booty taken from churches, houses and the bodies of the dead—and living—during the course of battle (cf. pl. 57). Ransoms were the most valuable form of

72. A sixteenth-century view of Calais. *London, British Museum Cotton Ms Augustus I, ii, fo. 70.* (83 × 160).

73. Rouen in 1525; drawing by Jacques Lelieur. *Rouen, Bibliothèque Municipale.* (143 × 65).

plunder, for all men had their price. The sums demanded from the most important prisoners were enormous: the ransoms of King John of France and of David II of Scotland were fixed at £500,000 and 100,000 marks (£66,666 13s. 4d.) respectively and in both cases a substantial proportion was paid. Such figures as these were of course exceptional, but ransoms running into four figures were not uncommonly demanded for important noblemen. For obvious political reasons, the king normally reserved the most notable prisoners to himself, the captor being paid an indemnity in compensation. Sir Thomas Dagworth was paid 25,000 gold *écus* for the capture of Charles of Blois at La Roche-Derrien (cf. pl. 10). Fourteen of the noble captives taken at Poitiers were bought from their captors by the Black Prince on behalf of the king for £66,000, and subsequently shipped from Bordeaux to Plymouth along with King John, in order to secure the maximum terms from the French. Similarly after Agincourt, although many of the surviving prisoners were sold at Calais for greater or lesser sums, the more notable were taken back to England. Sometimes, too, a prisoner not classed among the most important might finish up in the hands of the king, having changed hands not merely once but several times—for ransoms were marketable commodities.

But for the majority of the troops the principal source of financial gain was loot. According to Froissart, Lancaster's army returned from its raid into Poitou in 1346 'so laden with riches that they made no account of cloths unless they were of gold or silver, or trimmed with furs', and Walsingham tells us that there was scarcely a woman in the land who was not decked out in some of the spoils of Caen, Calais, or other towns abroad. Though a few commanders made efforts to spare the churches, pillaging was accepted as the soldiers' right. From the Black Prince who robbed King John of his jewels, down to the common soldiers who found in Normandy such abundance of booty that good furred gowns were despised, all threw themselves with zest into the business of plundering the French, which to the majority of the soldiers was the most powerful inducement to service in the wars. Yet chance was perfidious and it has too often been assumed by English historians that the traffic in ransoms and booty was a one-way affair. Even the most famous of English captains—among them Knowles, Calveley, Percy and Felton—spent periods of their lives in the hands of the enemy, disbursing part of their ill-gotten gains to buy back their freedom; and in the business of plundering enemy territory the French had nothing to learn from the English, even though their activities in that direction took place in France. It was not the certainty of profit that lured men to service in the war, but the chance, often no more than one in a hundred, of hitting the jack-pot.

Alongside the splendour of the court, knightly exploits and noble deeds of arms, must thus be set the search for profit, the devastation wrought through prolonged warfare and the bitterness and suffering which it engendered. 'In his day,' wrote Thomas Basin of the reign of Charles VII, 'as well through the effect of continual wars, civil and foreign, as through the negligence and idleness of those who conducted business or commanded under his orders, as through lack of military order and discipline and the greed and slackness of the men-at-arms, the said kingdom was reduced to such a state of devastation, that from the Loire to the Seine the peasants had been slain or put to flight. Most of the fields for long remained, over the years, not only uncultivated but without men enough to till them, except for a few odd pieces of land where it was impossible to extend the little that could be cultivated away from the cities, towns and castles owing to the frequent forays of the robbers. We ourselves have seen the vast plains of Champagne, of Beauce, of Brie, of the Gâtinais, Chartres, Dreux, Maine and Perche, of the Vexin (French as well as Norman), the Beauvaisis, the Pays de Caux, from the Seine as far as Amiens and Abbeville, the countryside round Senlis, Soissons and Valois right to Laon and beyond towards Hainault absolutely deserted, uncultivated, abandoned, empty of inhabitants, covered with scrub and brambles; indeed in most of the more thickly wooded districts dense forests were growing up. And, in a great many places it was feared that the marks of this devastation would long endure and remain visible unless divine providence kept better watch over the things of this world.'

Basin probably exaggerated the state of affairs, however true in its essentials, and some recent historical works have tended to play down the destruction of war in the economic conjuncture of the Late Middle Ages. It was only one source of affliction, terrible because of its combination with others: sickness, bad harvests, famine, plague, monetary instability and all the other troubles and difficulties to which Late Medieval society was susceptible. Neither was the devastation of war spread equally throughout the land, but concentrated in certain areas: in the paths of the great campaigns and *chevauchées*, the frontier regions and the districts around the castles and fortresses occupied by the *routiers* and free companies (cf. maps IV ff). Nor was the war permanent; it was limited in time as well as in place. Long periods of truce, financial difficulties and hard winters, limited the frequency of campaigns, even if they did not prevent the continuance of border warfare and illicit raiding. Moreover, the theatres of military activity changed a great deal over the course of the century; few regions were involved throughout. It has been calculated that the Bordelais was hardly affected for more than twenty-three years throughout the entire war and even during these years the destruction was intermittent, either because of the oncoming of winter, suspensions of arms, or because the armies were conducted into neighbouring provinces. The devastation of the *routiers* was unknown there until the arrival of André de Ribes in 1432 and Rodrigo de Villandrando six years later. At the other side of the kingdom, across the Massif Central in Velay, the region lying to the west of the Loire and around Le Puy suffered greatly at the hands of the companies which occupied fortresses in Auvergne and Gevaudan, while across the river the central and eastern provinces were hardly touched by the war. In the region around Paris during the fourteenth century the worst calamities were limited to a few terrible years: 1348–9 because of the Black Death; 1358–60 as a result of the *Jacquerie*, civil and foreign war. The fifteenth century, on the other hand, saw the worst thirty years in the history of the region: social difficulties, the conflicts of Armagnac and Burgundian, war against the English, foreign occupation, endless epidemics. The disasters of these years have been recorded for all time in the journal of an anonymous burgess of Paris who lived through them and who set them down in a style, if somewhat heavy, nevertheless personal, human, incredibly moving. But Paris in the early decades of the fifteenth century was no more typical of the rest of France than anywhere else. To imagine a hundred years of destruction and suffering would certainly be wrong. Some places were worse hit than others and for longer than others, and in war, as in all human activity, there were good men as well as bad, and that could occasionally make a difference. Basin himself tells us that 'the Bessin and the Cotentin and Lower Normandy which, under the sway of the English, were far enough away from the enemy's defence line, less easily and less often exposed to the robber raids, remained a little better cultivated and populated' than the rest of northern France, 'though often borne down by great poverty', and he makes it clear that this was in part due to the duke of Bedford, who he says 'was courageous, humane and just; he was very fond of the French lords who obeyed him and he took care to reward them according to their merits. As long as he lived Normans and Frenchmen in this part of the kingdom had a great affection for him'. The tragedy was that there were few men of Bedford's stature.

And yet, however we may minimize the effects of war on Late Medieval French society, in the literature of the times, in chronicles, treatises, epistles, poems and songs, as in legal, financial and other records of government, both central and local, war is the principal source of all the misery and suffering of the period, more so even

Fig. 46 A group of men-at-arms; *Grandes Chroniques. Paris, Bibliothèque Nationale Ms français 2813, fo. 399b.*

than the recurrence of plague and famine. Taken together, these records present a picture of physical destruction so enormous that it defies all attempts to catalogue it; it is the mass of evidence, of burning villages and deserted dwellings, of murder and rapine, of refugees along the roads of the war-stricken districts, that is so staggering. War was not only destructive, it was vicious, bitter and cruel. Perhaps its worst effects are to be found in the mentality of the times, in the violent contrasts of life, in the fears and excitability of a people suffering from a *malaise* created by violence and brutality.

It was rural society, and in particular the peasantry, which suffered most from the war, both from the major campaigns of the period and from the static but continuous garrison warfare that interspersed them. Whilst there was relative security within the walled towns, the open country—the *plat pays* as it was known—was defenceless against the incursions of the troops. Churches, houses, and the movable goods found inside them; crops, animals, vines, fruit trees, beasts and instruments of labour, the peasants themselves; all were easy prey. The only possible defence, providing always that there was sufficient warning, was to take refuge in a neighbouring fortress or walled town, with such movable goods as could be transported there. Charles V gave instructions that this should be done as a matter of policy; but, of necessity, everyone could not be accommodated and much had to be left behind. Some took refuge in caves; and many underground workings, sometimes quite elaborate, attached to fortified churches, castles and private houses, or of a simpler kind in the open country, date from this period. Others, like the prior of Brailet in the diocese of Sens, took to the woods, where they built themselves huts. 'But the English learned of this and they resolutely sought out these hiding places, searching numerous woods and putting many men to death there. Some they killed, others they captured, still others escaped', he wrote to a friend, and he concluded his letter: 'Written . . . in the year 1359, behind my grange, because it is not safe anywhere else. Did you ever see trouble like mine, you who dwell safe in cities and castles? Adieu. Hugues'.

The great *chevauchées* of the fourteenth century were carried out by relatively small forces that could move quickly. They struck deep into enemy territory, picking off small places that could be carried by assault, but by-passing centres of real resistance and returning to base before an effective intercepting force could be brought up. They were designed to destroy the enemy resources by devastating the countryside, burning the defenceless villages, small townships and the suburbs of walled towns. Sieges were to be avoided as costly in time, men and money; engagement with the enemy was, whenever possible, to be avoided for the consequences it might have. The troops invariably had to live off the country they passed through; often they were not paid and pillage was their main concern. When they had taken what they wanted and could carry away with them, they set fire to the rest. Personal and national advantage went hand in hand. For those left behind in the hamlets and villages there was little hope.

'On Monday, the eve of Saint-Matthew', wrote Edward III (cf. pl. 6) to his son and the council in London of the Thiérache campaign of 1339, 'we left Valenciennes, and the same day the troops began burning in Cambrésis and they burnt there throughout the following week, so that the country is clean laid waste, as of corn, cattle and other goods . . . The Saturday following we came to Marcoing, which lies between Cambrai and France, and the men began burning within France the same day; and we heard that the said lord Philip (of Valois) was drawing near to us at Péronne, on his march to Noyon . . . So we proceeded each day, our men together burning and destroying the country for twelve or fourteen leagues around.' The English chronicler, Geoffrey le Baker, tells us that during the course of the five weeks campaigning the Cambrésis, Vermandois and Thiérache were devastated; only

74. Drawing of a knight, attributed to Pisanello. *Paris, Louvre Codex Vallardi 2617.*

75. Drawing of a horse's head, attributed to Pisanello. *Paris, Louvre Codex Vallardi 2360.*

75

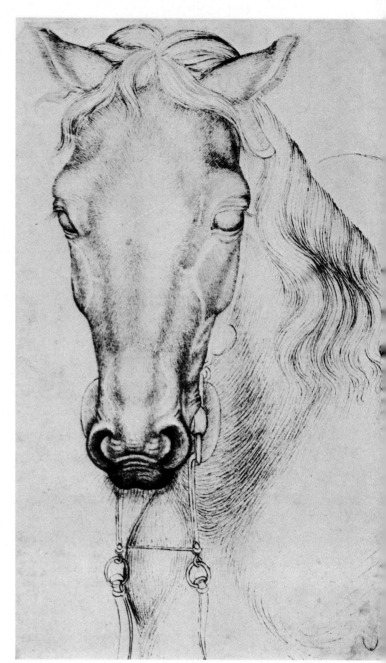

74

Il ce tampx es
toit entrattiez
de mariage la

walled towns, churches and castles were spared; the inhabitants fled before the destruction. Other chroniclers tell the same story. 'The Cambrésis was badly devastated', wrote the Liègeois Jean le Bel. 'All the hamlets were burning', adds Jean le Clerc of Antwerp. Knighton, the chronicle of Lanercost and Hemingburgh all agree with them on the destructiveness of the military operations.

These accounts are amply borne out by the record of a charitable mission to the devastated regions of Cambrésis, Vermandois and Thiérache, organized by Pope Benedict XII through the agency of Bertrand Carit on the conclusion of the campaign. Carit distributed money to the worst afflicted, specifying their state and condition, and distinguishing between those who had suffered from the enemy invasion and those whose condition arose from other causes. His account is therefore particularly valuable for measuring the effects of the year's campaigning. In the four dioceses of Laon, Reims, Noyon and Cambrai, 174 parishes were devastated by the invasion. Many monasteries, hospitals and parish churches had suffered; but much the worst affected were the defenceless rural habitations which were burned, looted and laid waste (*combuste, depredate, vastate*). Not only had whole villages gone up in flames, but such movables as could not be carried off were taken away and burned (*et bona populi apportata et combusta*). The recipients of alms included nobles and clerics, but almost all of the beneficiaries were artisans and labourers. The record states the condition of these people: old people, widowed and infirm, others with children and orphans in their charge; and it sometimes states the extent of their loss. Some of the refugees who, in trying to escape, had been run to ground at Saint-Quentin, were utterly destitute, some to the last extremity. Altogether, Carit was responsible for distributing assistance to some 7,879 victims. He could do nothing for the dead.

The Thiérache campaign was, however, hardly worse than others. 'We took our road', wrote the Black Prince (cf. pl. 30) in a despatch describing his first campaign in Aquitaine in the autumn of 1355, 'through the land of Toulouse, where many goodly towns and strongholds were burnt and destroyed, for the land was rich and plenteous'. At Carcassonne (cf. pl. 32) the castle was too strong to be taken, but a whole day was spent 'for burning of the said city, so that it was clean destroyed'. Sir John Wengfeld, the prince's steward, wrote in a similar vein. 'And know for certain that, since this war began against the king of France, there was never such loss nor such destruction as hath been in this raid', and there was no doubt in his mind as to the utility of the damage done. 'For', he continues, 'the lands and the good towns which are destroyed in this raid found for the king of France each year more to maintain his war than half of the kingdom . . . as I could show you by good records which were found in divers towns in the houses of receivers', and he goes on to enumerate the details.

It is possible that the English military operations became progressively more destructive. In describing Edward III's great campaign of 1346, Baker mentions firing nine times, but uses the same word (*comburo*); in narrating the Black Prince's first campaign in the south in 1355 he makes seventeen allusions to the practice, but contrives to use a dozen different phrases (burnt, went up in flames, burnt to ashes, etc.) to describe it. And although the king's last campaign in the winter of 1359–60 was notable for its peaceful progress to Reims for his would-be coronation, and for the immense baggage train that accompanied him, nevertheless, when his fantastic plan failed, and after he and his troops had recuperated in Burgundy, they proceeded to Paris 'burning, killing and destroying everything around them'. Jean de Venette, a peasant boy from a village outside Compiègne, who rose sufficiently in the world to become prior of the Carmelite convent in Paris and head of the order's French province, has left a terrible account of Edward's investment of the capital during Easter 1360, as he himself saw it:

76. Marriage of the duchess of Berry. *London, British Museum Harley 4380, fo. 11.* (12.9 × 19.4).

'In A.D. 1360, Edward, King of England, his eldest son, the Prince of Wales, and the Duke of Lancaster left Burgundy for France. They passed through the Nivernais and burned and wasted the whole district. At length, at Eastertide they reached Châtres and Montlhéry, within six leagues of Paris . . . Everyone fled in terror and took refuge in Paris or elsewhere. The residents of the three faubourgs of Paris, Saint-Germain-des-Prés, Nôtre-Dame-des-Champs, and Saint-Marceau left their houses empty and came into the city. On Holy Saturday the famous butchery of Saint-Marceau was moved to the Place Maubert near the Carmelite friars, and the butchery of Saint-Germain was also moved within the walls . . . On Good Friday and Holy Saturday the English set fire to Montlhéry in the bourg and to Longjumeau and to many other towns round about. The smoke and flames rising from the towns to the heavens were visible at Paris in innumerable places. Thither a great part of the rural population had fled. It was lamentable to see men, women, and children desolate. On Easter Day, I myself saw priests of ten country parishes communicating their people and keeping Easter in various chapels or any spot they could find in the monastery of the Carmelite friars at Paris. On the following day, the nobles and burgesses of Paris ordered the faubourgs of Saint-Germain, Nôtre-Dame-des-Champs, and Saint-Marceau to be burned. Permission was given, so it is said, to everyone to carry off anything he could from the houses: wood, iron, tiles, or any other materials; and go openly and pillage. There were found many to do this, who ran swiftly to execute the edict. Then you might have seen some rejoicing over their gains and others groaning and moaning over their losses.'

With the renewal of the war in 1369, the French took the initiative. During the early 1370s much of Aquitaine was recovered, naval raids were mounted on the south coast of England and the threat of invasion was very real (cf. above, p. 70). English military policy during these years was therefore that of an offensive defensive. The three great *chevauchées* of the decade—of Sir Robert Knowles in 1370, John of Gaunt in 1373, and the earl of Buckingham in 1380—were designed to keep the French engaged on the continent and so prevent a naval invasion and to devastate the countryside and destroy the enemy's resources to as great an extent as possible. They were all mounted in the summer, before the harvest was gathered in, and they all proceeded through Picardy, Vermandois and Champagne to within the region of Troyes, following much the same route as Edward III's forces in 1359–60 (cf. map VIII). Owing to the financial embarrassment of the Crown, the troops were not paid by the Exchequer, but were to be paid out of the proceeds of ransoms and booty taken during the course of military operations. Special receivers and pay-masters, responsible to the Exchequer, were appointed for that purpose. The campaigns that resulted were little more than legalized brigandage, resembling the activities of the free companies more than they resembled anything else. The men recruited for service included some of the most hardened criminals and riff-raff of England and the campaign of 1370 was led by a man who was little more than a *routier* made respectable. They were undoubtedly the worst raids of the century, and they were intended to be.

They were not, of course, the only ones. Nor were Edward III's armies alone in spreading destruction. The devastation caused by the free companies was probably a good deal worse, that of the French forces probably not much less. In the fifteenth century, however, the character of the war changed and, after the Agincourt campaign (which repeated faithfully the strategy of the Crécy-Calais expedition), the *chevauchée* ceased to be the principal mode of warfare. Beginning with the conquest of Normandy after 1417, and implicit in the treaty of Troyes, was the systematic occupation of French territories in the name of the dual monarchy. The strategy of the war was therefore one of sieges, of the piecemeal extension of frontiers and the occupation of dauphinist territories to the south. Edward III had tried something similar in Brittany during the fourteenth century, but had been unable to accomplish the occupation of the entire duchy owing to financial weakness and the inability

77. Joan of Arc at the siege of Orléans. *Paris, Bibliothèque Nationale Ms français 2679, fo. 66.*

78. Portrait of Edward IV (1461–83). *Windsor Castle; reproduced by Gracious Permission of Her Majesty the Queen.* (68 × 47.9).

79. Portrait of Richard III (1483–5). *Windsor Castle; reproduced by Gracious Permission of Her Majesty the Queen.* (57 × 35.4).

80. Naval battle off La Rochelle (1372); Froissart's Chronicles. *Paris, Bibliothèque Nationale, Ms français 2643, fo. 393.* (31.2 × 42.5).

81. Edward III taking Caen (1346); Froissart's Chronicles. *Paris, Bibliothèque Nationale Ms français 2643, fo. 157v.* (32 × 43.3).

77

Tem apres q̄
les cappitaines
des anglops
dessusdits auec
ques leurs gẽs
eurent par lespace de sept mop

I toft que les agsou   furent ce premier io tonant
furent duant les   lançant efcarmouchit et

Il ce io e leuerent   Si approuchierent la groffe

82

83

De uiuis Regibus.   De mortuis Regibus.

Primus rex uiuus.   Primus rex mortuus.

Compaynouns vez cco ke ico uoy ·   Ly premier mort dist damoysel ·
A py ke ico ne me deuoy ·   Ne ubliez pas pur sel oysel ·
De grant pour le quoer me tremble ·   Ne pur uos robes a orfiris ·
Vez la treis mors ensemble ·   Qe no ne tieignez bien les leys
um il siunt hidous et diuers ·   Qe ihu crist ad ordine ·
Purriz et mangez des uers ·   De sa seinte uolunte ·

Secundus rex uiuus.   Secundus rex mortuus.

E secunde dist ico ay enuie ·   Signours dist li secund mort ·
Compaynoun de amendr ma uie ·   Certe est ke la mort ·
trop ay fet de mes uoluntez ·   Nous ad fet tiels cum nous sumus ·
Et mon quoer est entalentez ·   no purrez come nous sumus ·
De fere tant ke malme acorde ·   Nut seez ia si pur ne si fin ·
A l dieu rei de misericorde ·   Ore puruez no deuant la fin ·

Tertius rex uiuus.   Tertius mortuus.

Ly tierz uif ki destreint ses meins   E tierz mort dit sachez ·
Dist p quei fut fet hõme hunteis ·   Ieo su de mon lynnage chief ·
ur ky deit receuere tiele peine ·   Princes rys et conustables ·
A ceo fust folie trop aperte ·   Beals et riches royanz mes tables ·
ceste folie ne fist unkes dieu ·   Ore su si hidous et si nuz ·
Si counte ioye et si grãtz deduitz ·   De moy uer ne deigne nuls ·

to adapt the organization of expeditionary forces to occupation needs. Under Henry V and Bedford much was accomplished in this direction and up to the 1430s it seemed as if there would be eventual if only gradual success. But in 1435 the strategy of Henry V was called into question. Sir John Fastolf, one of the most experienced of the war captains, advised that the policy of conquest and consolidation by the maintenance of garrisons had become too expensive. He advocated a return to the scorched earth policy of the great *chevauchées* of the previous century, a policy of terror and destruction:

'. . . First, it seemeth . . . that the king should do lay no sieges nor make no conquest out of Normandy . . .; for the sieges hath greatly hindered his conquest in time passed, and destroyed his people, and wasted and consumed innumerable good of his finances, both in England, and in France, and of Normandy. For there may no king conquer a great realm by continual sieges . . . Wherefore, . . . it is thought right expedient, for the speed and the advancement of the king's conquest and destroying of his enemies, to ordain two notable chieftains, discreet and of one accord, having either of them seven hundred and fifty spears of well chosen men, and . . . that they begin to oostay [i.e. *chevauchée*] from the first day of June continually until the first day of November, . . . brenning and destroying all the lands as they pass, both house, corn, vines, and all trees that bearen fruit for man's sustenance, and all bestaile [i.e. livestock] that may not be driven, to be destroyed . . . Item, it is thought . . . that this war should be continued forth still puissantly three year day at least, to th'intent to drive th'enemies thereby to an extreme famine . . .'

Fastolf's advice was not, however, taken and the occupation of towns, castles and fortresses, which the extension of frontiers by either side involved, continued to be the chief characteristic of the war. This was fundamental for the civilian population, for, dreadful as the effects of the *chevauchées* undoubtedly were, the most affected parts of France were probably the frontier districts (cf. maps IV, V, VI) where the garrisons of the opposing parties had settled, often out of the surveillance of central government, and difficult for the lieutenants of the region to control. There were no hard frontiers during the great campaigns of the fourteenth century but, during periods of truce, and in the conditions of fifteenth century warfare, there were carefully delineated ones. Most of the *chevauchées* of the fourteenth century and the major siege operations of the fifteenth century were short lived. They were often, if not always, concluded by the on-coming of winter, or because of the exorbitant cost of keeping a large military force in the king's pay for any length of time. But the static garrison warfare on the frontiers was prolonged and the troops had to support themselves from exactions on the countryside surrounding their headquarters. Behind the front, the country could be more peaceably governed; but in the regions where the rival obediences made contact and there was a mingling of powers and jurisdictions, central control was slight, violence and destruction the most prevalent. As Froissart says of the confines of Poitou and Saintonge in 1371, 'the towns and castles were so intermingled the one with the other, the one English, the other French, who continually raided and pillaged each other without sparing'. It was in these regions that fortunes could most persistently be made and lost, rather than in the great battles, which were infrequent, and when the chances were one in a hundred.

The situation in the frontier districts was aggravated by the system of *rançons* and *appatis*, which provided for the upkeep of garrisons from charges levied in enemy territory. This method of financing the troops was already operative in Brittany in the 1340s and 1350s and rapidly spread throughout France after the battle of Poitiers, when independent Anglo-Navarrese forces came to occupy towns and castles all over the country. A varying number of parishes were tied to a fortress and were obliged to pay a fixed levy to the receiver of the garrison, who kept a schedule of ransoms due from each parish. Payments were usually made quarterly,

82. Fifteenth-century battle scene. *Paris, Bibliothèque Nationale Ms français 2691, fo. 38.* (27.3 × 38.5).

83. Fifteenth-century battle scene. *Paris, Bibliothèque Nationale Ms français 2691, fo. 197.* (28.2 × 38).

84. *Danse Macabre. London, British Museum Arundel Ms 83, fo. 127.* (11.6 × 18.8).

85. Portrait of the Emperor Sigismund of Luxemburg (1410–37), attributed to Pisanello. *Vienna, Kunsthistorisches Museum.* (64 × 49).

86. John, duke of Bedford, kneeling before St George. *London, British Museum Add. Ms 18850, fo. 256b.* (14.9 × 9.7).

partly in money and partly in kind, and a receipt (*bihète, billet, bullette*) was issued to each household upon payment. Many of the smaller garrisons only collected revenues from a few parishes, but the more important establishments often controlled an entire region. In Brittany in the 1350s, as many as 220 parishes were ransomed to the garrisons of Bécherel and Ploërmel; Saint-Sauveur-le-Vicomte controlled 263 in 1371, and Brest 160 in 1384. The castle of Colet, situated to the south of the bay of Bourgneuf, was in control of 32 parishes in 1362 which stretched through the *pays de Retz*, along the southern side of the Loire estuary below Nantes and almost to the Angevin frontier. At Mont-Saint-Michel in the 1420s and 1430s the French garrison levied ransoms from 34 parishes situated on the Norman mainland, and that at Châteaudun from parishes some sixty miles north along the Norman frontier.

As a method of upkeep, the system could be very brutal and it was particularly open to abuses by isolated garrisons operating on their own account. During the course of 1381, the *jurats* of Bergerac in Périgord paid more than double the receipts of the town for that year in *patis, suffertes* and *rançons* demanded by the captains of five different garrisons as protection money. To raise the cash to pay these, each citizen was required to purchase from the authorities a safe-conduct for half a franc and a *billet* for six shillings sterling; both presumably provided by the captains of the garrisons in question. But in previous years, Sir William Scrope, captain of Fronsac and subsequently seneschal of Aquitaine, had been issuing these to individual citizens at 17s. 6d. each.

Even where an element of central control was present, the oppression was often dreadful. Much depended upon the arbitrariness of the levies, the manner in which they were collected (whether or not they were in the hands of the civil authorities, for instance), and the extent to which prompt payment was demanded and exceptions made for hard cases. In Maine during the 1430s and 1440s the levy was probably little different from the *taille* collected from those in the king's obedience. The collection was centralized on the three fortresses of Le Mans, Saint-Suzanne and Mayenne, and it was carried out by native *collecteurs* appointed in parish assemblies, who paid what was due from their parishes to the receiver of the county and his officers in each town. This was very different from the situation in Brittany in the 1350s, where only a part of the ransoms were centrally collected, and where the parishes ransomed to Vannes, Ploërmel and Bécherel were divided into circuits, each with a collector, who was appointed by the receiver of the duchy and responsible to the military authorities (captain and receiver) in each garrison. But above all else, the real issue for the people paying was the amount demanded. In Maine during the 1430s, although each parish was assessed at a flat rate of 17 *livres tournois*, this was a relatively small sum (less than £2 sterling), and there seems to have been little resistance to payment. Such abuses as did occur arose from the failure of captains to respect the regulations, some of whom, like William Oldhall at Fresnay in 1431, seized provisions from those who had paid their *appatis* and had to be punished for their misdemeanours. The situation in Maine in the 1430s is yet another commentary on Bedford's clemency. It was very different in Normandy and Brittany in the fourteenth century. The average assessment for each parish ransomed to Saint-Sauveur-le-Vicomte in 1371 was £13 13s. 4d. (82 francs), and for those ransomed to Brest in 1384 it was £37 10s. 0d. Much of this money was going into the pockets of the captains and receivers of the garrisons, and their abuses, as those of William Lord Latimer at Bécherel in the 1360s, were notorious. But it was in Brittany during the 1350s, in the parishes ransomed to Vannes, Bécherel and Ploërmel, that the recorded situation was the worst. Here the assessment averaged about £58 sterling a parish, a rate which provoked widespread rebellion and harsh repression, in spite of which £10,785 (an average of £41 a parish) was collected in the financial year running from 29 September 1359.

87. Portrait of Philip the Good, duke of Burgundy (1419–67), after van der Weyden. *Louvre, Paris.*

Dfin que vous
sachies la rai
se pour quoy
nea quel tiltre
les guerres de france et.
dangleterre encommencerent
premierement se le vous diray
et racompteray en brief.
Verite est que le bon roy edou
ard de carnarenam sadis roy
dangleterre et pere du noble roy
edonard de windesoze comme
Il aeste dit ou sixiesme et derrai
liure du premier volume de ces
te œuure presente eult espouse
ysabel de france fille du beau
roy philippe qui en son viuant
estoit vne des belles dames du

Mieu Valle.

Surviving letters of the king's lieutenant in Brittany, many of which describe the situation in the duchy during the course of that year, make depressing reading. Ransoms could not be raised in many parishes because they were 'so poor and weak'. Some were 'poor and abandoned' as a result of excessive demands and *extorcions* perpetrated by the receivers and other officials to whom the ransoms had been farmed out, and many were *rebelles*. Of the parishes ransomed to Ploërmel, 29 which had not kept up with their quarterly payments 'were often destroyed by fire and otherwise as appertains' by the lieutenant of the duchy and the captain of Ploërmel, but still refused to pay. In 83 parishes ransomed to Bécherel, those who left their homes to avoid the collectors returned to find their houses destroyed.

The situation in Brittany in the fourteenth century was not, however, untypical. The truces of the 1380s and 1390s give an appalling picture of the frontier districts, especially in Guyenne. The levying of *rançons* and *patiz* was so unremitting upon the country folk that they met demands for payment with armed resistance or fled the ransom districts, taking what possessions they could with them. Villages, parishes, even entire ransom districts had been deserted. Captains met failure to pay within the required terms with reprisals of death and the confiscation or burning of the properties of the debtors. In these conditions, the truces were constantly being violated, and prevention of their infringement became one of the principal problems facing their negotiators. Nor were these abuses perpetrated by English troops alone. Jean Juvénal des Ursins, bishop of Beauvais, has left a dismal picture of the activities of dauphinist forces in his diocese in the 1430s. In an epistle written for a meeting of the Estates at Blois in 1433, he described the violence and destruction that was then current in these words:

'I do not mean to say that the said crimes are committed by the enemies alone, for they have also been committed by some of those who claim to be the king's liege men, who under pretext of *appatis* and otherwise have seized men, women and little children, without regard as to age or sex; ravished wives and daughters, seized husbands and fathers, killed husbands and fathers in the presence of their wives and daughters, seized nursing mothers, thereby leaving little children to die for want of nourishment; seized priests, monks and lay brothers, and put them in thieves' chains and other instruments of torture called *singes*, and beat them whilst they were there, by which some were mutilated, others driven mad; levied *appatis* in the villages to such an extent that a poor village owed *appatis* to eight or ten places, and if one did not pay they went and set fire to the villages and churches, and when the poor men were taken and they could not pay, they have sometimes been smothered whilst in chains and thrown into the river, and there remained there neither draught-horse nor other beast.'

Part of the problem was that, from the point of view of the troops exacting them, ransoms levied on the countryside could be treated as ordinary spoils of war, and it was as such that they were regarded by the *routiers* or free companies, over whom it was virtually impossible to exercise control. The developments in the recruitment and organization of the royal armies during the fourteenth century had brought into existence companies of professional soldiers, unfettered by feudal loyalties or tenurial bonds, who relied on employment by the Crown or some other prince for their livelihood. During periods of truce and military inactivity, when the Crown was unable to pay them and they found themselves unemployed, they supported themselves by living off the countryside, operating on their own account and for their own profit—though invariably claiming to be in the service of a patron (like the counts of Foix and Armagnac, the duke of Brittany, or the king of Navarre). Grouped in *routes* under the leadership of experienced captains, the companies seldom exceeded a few hundred men; but some of them were well-knit, with a strict hierarchy of command and a considerable degree of organization. They were staffed with constables, secretaries and treasurers, had *butiners* to divide up their

88. A siege; Wavrin's Chronicles. *Paris, Bibliothèque Nationale Ms français 87, fo. 1.*

169

booty, and some of them—like Arnaud de Cervole's *bandes blanches*—had their own uniform. The *grandes compagnies* of the 1360s were grouped in *routes* according to nationality (the English leaders, for instance, called themselves *capitaines et chevetaines des gens des routes des engleis des granz compaignies*), but, although they were sometimes referred to as the *grant compaignie* or *magna societas*, there was no such thing as a single great company with a common organization and an acknowledged leader. Each *route* maintained its distinct unity under its own captain, none of whom had supreme authority.

They were a motley lot. Among them were to be found a few English and Germans, plenty of Bretons, Spaniards and, above all, Gascons. Of the more famous captains, Seguin de Badefol (d. 1365) and Arnaud de Cervole, known as the Arch-priest (d. 1366), came from the banks of the Dordogne in Périgord. Geoffrey Tête-Noir and Bertrand de Garlanx were Bretons. Mérigot Marchès (d. 1391) came from Limousin, Rodrigo de Villandrando (d. 1457/8) from Castile, and François de la Surienne (d. 1462) from Aragon. They have often been described as 'obscure adventurers' and 'men of low birth'; but many of them were scions of noble families—the *petite-noblesse*—some of whom had gone down in the world or had been hit by the economic regression of the times and who, through truce or failure to secure royal employment, took to the highways. Neither Seguin de Badefol, Mérigot Marchès, Rodrigo de Villandrando, John Cresswell, David Holgrave nor Robert Knowles were of low birth. Their backgrounds were as respectable as those of other soldiers who secured commands in the royal armies.

Their method of operating was to take two or three well-fortified castles by surprise and use them as a base from which to terrorize a district: they demanded ransoms from individuals and whole parishes, requisitioned victuals, cut roads, controlled bridges (cf. pl. 22), and sold safe-conducts at extortionate prices. When they had extracted all they could from one district, they let themselves be bought out by the local community and moved on to another. If they stayed long enough, their exactions took on the form of an ugly protection racket. 'Dear lords and good friends', wrote Jean de Seignal, captain of Bannes for Perducat d'Albret, to the governors and consuls of Bérgerac on 12 March 1380, 'I make known to you that, as soon as you have read this letter, you will come and *appatisser* yourselves at Bannes, for you are nearer to Bridoire, Issigeac and Bannes than you are to any other English place. Otherwise, beware of us, because if you do not come we will do all the damage to you that we are able to do. And reply to this. May God have you in his keeping.' The records of the frontier towns contain many such letters from other men. The most successful *routier* captains were able to gain an ascendancy over other captains in an extensive region, making them their lieutenants, and taking a share of their profits. Froissart has rendered accounts of some of the more notorious of them in his inimitable way: of Mérigot Marchès, of whom it was said that the *appatis* of the country he held under his subjection were well worth 20,000 florins; of Geoffrey Tête-Noir, who was able to dominate lower Limousin and Quercy from his castle of Ventadour and who was said to have put the country to ransom for more than thirty leagues around him; and of the bascot of Mauléon who claimed to have held more than twenty-seven towns and castles in the marches of Nivernais in the 1360s and who boasted that 'there was neither knight, esquire, nor rich man who dared come out of his house unless he paid *appatis* to us'.

The *routiers* were particularly menacing when they banded together for large-scale operations, like the *grandes compagnies* formed on the conclusion of peace at Brétigny, which descended the valleys of the Saône and the Rhône, seized Pont-Saint-Esprit and held the pope to ransom, or the *Tard-Venus* or 'Latecomers'—their picturesque name indicates that they were operating on ground already exploited by others—who in the following years threatened Lyons. In the decade after the treaty of Arras (1435–44), when hostilities between French and Burgundian troops north of the Loire were brought to an end, and the garrisons in Champagne were disbanded, the whole of that county, Burgundy, Alsace and Lorraine were prey to the appalling activities of the *Écorcheurs* or 'Skinners'—so called because they pillaged districts already fleeced over and over again and robbed the unlucky people of their shirts and sometimes even of their skins. The *routiers* were active in most parts of France (and also in Spain and Italy), but concentrated in those areas which had suffered least from the great campaigns and thus offered the richest pillage: the Central Plateau and Languedoc (cf. map VIII). The large fortunes they are said to have amassed have, however, almost certainly been exaggerated. The story about Sir John Harleston and his companions drinking the profits of their ravages in Champagne in 1375 out of a hundred chalices stolen from the churches is a good one, but as unlikely as the 100,000 francs Mérigot Marchès was said to have possessed at the time of his death, or the 60,000 offered as his ransom. Many of the *routier* captains came to a sticky end. Seguin de Badefol was poisoned at the instigation of Charles of Navarre, the Archpriest was assassinated by his own troops, Petit-Meschin and Perrin de Savoie were drowned in the Garonne at Toulouse by order of Louis of Anjou, and Mérigot Marchès was decapitated in Paris. Those who did well for themselves—the Archpriest, Calveley, Knowles, Du Guesclin, Villandrando and Gressart—owed their success to royal and ducal employ, and to rich marriages, more than to anything else. For the Crown found it impossible to avoid giving the more able of them advancement, either because of their command over men, or because of the strategically vital places they controlled.

Fig. 47 A battle scene; from the early fifteenth-century manuscript of the Poems of Christine de Pisan. *London, British Museum Harley Ms 4431, part i, fo. 110.* (12.2 × 7.8)

From the point of view of those paying *appatis*, they implied purchase of immunity from war, and hence their name *abstinences* or *souffrances de guerre*. The problem was to make the arrangements as inclusive as possible—not always an easy matter. All too often it was impossible to satisfy the demands of separate companies operating on their own account and an indication of a situation which must have been common is given by Jean Juvénal in an epistle written for a meeting of the Estates at Orléans in 1444. After commenting on the continual pillaging of the troops and the suffering of the people, he continues '. . .: Therefore, the poor people of all estates, thinking to improve their lot, decided to pay *appatis* to the nearest garrison; but soon all the other garrisons, also wishing to have *patis*, began to raid the villages; and since the poor people were unable to pay, they have left their homes so frequently that the country has become completely uninhabited, and only one person remains out of a hundred, which is a pitiful thing'.

Appatis were not the only tribute paid in the frontier territories. Captains could also exact payments for safe-conducts, protections and permits of various kinds. In Maine in the 1430s these documents were issued under Bedford's seals, and the revenues accruing from their purchase were paid to the duke's receiver in the county. His accounts show that many parishes in English obedience found it necessary to take out *bulletes de ligeance* quarterly (one for each household, but usually purchased for the parish collectively) to protect them from the raiding parties. Abbeys and other religious communities were obliged to secure protections (*sauvegardes*) and *certifications* for the same purpose. The inhabitants were also obliged to pay to leave the county as well as to stay. They had to secure permits (*congés*) and safe-conducts to travel into enemy territory (*hors cette obéissance*), and even to go *en pays appatissé*, whether to see their relatives, as pilgrims to the well known shrines or to attend religious festivals, and even in connection with their work or trade. The sums demanded for these documents varied in each case according to the length of the visit and the standing of the traveller. Many *congés* were not valid for more than a month, and their average cost was 12s. 6d. sterling (4 *saluts*); but it was often a good deal more. The trouble with safe-conducts and protections was that, as with ransoms, *appatis* and other charges on the civilian population, they could be issued primarily for private profit on the part of the individual operator. As captain of Creil in 1359–60, the English knight John Fotheringhay is said to have made 100,000 francs on the sale of safe-conducts to travellers between Paris and Noyon, Paris and Compiègne; Compiègne, Soissons and Laon, and the neighbouring places. But such safe-conducts only bound the troops of the captains who issued them. In an area where the free companies were operating, and in the frontier districts, it might be necessary to obtain a whole series of safe-conducts from different captains. In 1358 a traveller from Valognes to Coutances needed three safe-conducts; one from the English at Saint-Sauveur, one from the Navarrese at Valognes, and one from the French at Saint-Lô. They constituted yet another burden on the civilian population.

All of these practices were illegal other than in 'just war' and even then they could technically only be employed by the official authorities. It has recently been shown how Late Medieval society acknowledged a legal code known as the law of arms. This was derived from ancient feudal practice and the law of nations, which had been evolved earlier by canon lawyers and civil lawyers from natural law. It laid down the precise obligations of a soldier in public and private warfare, according to which disputes relating to acts committed in war and battle might be settled. It governed alike the conduct of soldiers to one another and towards enemies, the discipline of armies, rules concerning rights in spoil, and armorial disputes. Although it lacked an international body for its enforcement, it was applied in the military courts as part of what was then understood to be the law of nations. Its real sanction was, however, a fear of acting not so much illegally as dishonourably, and it owed much to chivalric ideals and obligations. But although it did a great deal to ensure a humane standard of conduct for those in arms (gentlemen prisoners, for example, were usually treated well and allowed to go free on parole; and the practice of taking men for ransom helped to prevent unnecessary bloodshed in the field), it did little for non-combatants.

The precise nature of the conduct to be expected of the troops, both within the field armies and garrison forces, and in their relations with the civil population, was laid down in ordinances and other regulations which were issued by the kings and their military commanders. The responsibility for seeing that these were enforced among the English troops rested with the constable and marshal of England in the main field armies under the king's command and, by delegation from the commanders-in-chief, special constables and marshals were appointed to accompany the subsidiary forces. Within the English field armies judgement was executed by summary course, and did not come within the purview of the court of the constable and marshal (the High Court of Chivalry), which was primarily concerned with the settlement of international disputes coming under the law of arms. In the French forces, on the other hand, the constable and marshals, who each had a court at the *Table de Marbre* in Paris (so called because it sat around a marble table in one of the rooms of the royal palace in the Ile-de-la-Cité), exercised their jurisdiction through a lieutenant and *prévôt* respectively, and this central *prévôt* appointed subsidiary *prévôts* who served with the military commanders in the provinces and resided in the principal towns of the frontier districts. It was to these *prévôts* that complaints against the excesses of the soldiers and other matters affecting the civilian population were lodged and an appeal could be made from their decisions to the court of the central *prévôt* at the *Table de Marbre*, and even to the *parlement de Paris*. The arrangements for the regulation of the behaviour of the English occupation forces varied according to the region and period of the occupation. The captains of the garrison forces were responsible for matters affecting the internal discipline of their own garrisons; but in allied and occupied territories, disputes arising with the civil population were normally settled according to the custom of the country. In fifteenth-

89. Detail from the tapestry
La Justice de Trajan et d'Archambault
woven at Tournai (?), (1455–61).
Berne, Historisches Museum.

172

89

90

LOVIS·D·DÁNIOV·R·DE·NAPLE·SICILE·&

century Normandy, and to some extent in Maine, the responsibility for implementing this was placed in the hands of the civil authorities—of the local *baillis* who, although invariably English, normally exercised their judicial functions through their lieutenants, who were French (cf. above, p. 83). The organization of local supplies and local labour for the army was entrusted to the *vicômtes* who were purely civilian officials and were almost without exception French. In Normandy after 1428, if a complaint was registered before a *bailli*, *vicômte*, or other officer of justice, the latter was obliged to enquire into the offence complained of and not until the matter had been dealt with could the captain of the troops involved secure his pay. The controllers of the garrisons kept a careful check on the takings of the troops and, at least under Bedford, were to certify that they had not been levied in other than enemy territory.

The limitations of these arrangements are obvious: they did not apply in enemy territory and were difficult to enforce in the frontier districts where the distinction between friend and foe was much less well defined than it was behind the front. They were therefore least effective where they were most needed. Moreover, on the French side, the jurisdiction of the *prévôts des maréchaux* (who were essentially military personnel, with troops of archers under their command to enforce their judgements) over the civil population often created more trouble than it eliminated. Exemption from their jurisdiction in all save strictly military matters was sought after as a privilege by towns in the frontier regions and already in 1355 and 1357 they were prohibited, in a general fashion, from encroaching upon ordinary justice. But in a war-ridden country, it was difficult to distinguish between ordinary justice and the extraordinary jurisdiction of the marshals in matters touching the civil population.

These arrangements applied only to the excesses of native or occupation forces. To deal with the excesses of the enemy during time of truce, special conservators were appointed to cope with infringements of their terms and to whom complaint could be made. Indeed, the various forms of extraordinary jurisdiction connected with the war were so numerous and bewildering that there were not infrequently conflicts between the constable and the marshals, the marshals and their *prévôts*, and even between the *prévôts* and conservators of the truces, over the trial of cases connected with the war. Those upon whom judgement was passed could appeal from the decisions of the provincial *prévôts* to the central *prévôt* and, in some cases, from the court of the marshals to that of the constable, and finally to the *parlement de Paris*. It is from the records of the latter body that much of our evidence must be drawn.

While these arrangements could do much to control the activities of royal troops, they were clearly of no avail for dealing with *routiers*, brigands, and other 'unofficial' soldiers. To deal with these, military forces were occasionally despatched by the Crown to the affected provinces; but more often than not it was left to individual towns to provide for their own defence, which usually meant paying protection money to the *routier* captains. Theoretically, it was forbidden for individual towns to trade with the enemy or pay *appatis* to him and it became a matter of royal policy to bring such payments under central control. During the truces of the 1380s and 1390s, the Estates of the affected regions were called together to raise the money required to purchase immunity from or the departure of the marauding troops. This was collected by special treasurers and handled by the lieutenants and captains-general, who were empowered to conclude general *patis* for an entire province, or by the conservators of the truces. In this way, some of the arbitrariness was taken out of the traffic and the money raised was like any other *taille*; but there were accompanying disadvantages. The administration of the monies was open to some of the worst kinds of peculation: the count of Armagnac even used such funds to enlist the *routier* captains for service in his wars against the count of Foix. The arrangements often had the effect of merely whetting the enemy's appetite: the more

90. Portrait of Louis II of Anjou (1377–1417), *c*. 1400. *Paris, Bibliothèque Nationale, Cabinet des Estampes.*

175

he was given, the more he asked for, and this the Estates of a region were in a better position to provide. It is hardly surprising that there were frequently refusals to pay and rebellions, and the records of towns which were represented in the provincial assemblies amply demonstrate the resistance which was aroused by this new form of taxation.

The dilemma of the civilian population need be underlined no further; the complaints of contemporaries everywhere abound. The tensions created by war— by foreign invasion, military occupation, the necessities of national and local defence, and the activities of brigands and *routiers*—deepened the divisions in an already hierarchic society and opened a great social wound. Firmly entrenched privileges, long held liberties and private interests, were everywhere being compromised. Royal intervention in seigniorial castles and towns, necessary in view of their strategic importance, was strongly resisted. Castles too difficult to defend, or not worth the effort, often had to be destroyed—a systematic policy after the *débâcle* of Poitiers. So also had the often considerable urban agglomerations outside town walls, which might give cover or access to the enemy. Strategically important buildings within had to be requisitioned for garrisons and other necessities of defence.

Exemptions from service were another source of trouble—of the nobility from war subsidies, because of the military service which they ostensibly performed, of clerics (though they were often engaged in the affairs of the world) and moneyers (a largish body). When taxes were voted in provincial assemblies, divisions arose over the proportions to be paid by the different estates and regions involved. There were also disputes over service itself—among commoners over the division of expenses in arming the levies (*arrière-ban*), among townsmen about who should decide whether service should be done in person or commuted, and among religious communities about which lands were subject to them for purposes of providing contingents or money in lieu of them. The fact that the war was for long fought on a private basis, in which the troops had private interests in prisoners and ransoms, and were able to treat the castles they took in war as private conquests secured by right of arms, set up tensions of many kinds. The line differentiating public and private interests was so finely drawn that the two were often in conflict, leading to the detriment of the former during periods of real crisis. Only by degrees were royal and national interests seen to be alike and then only at the expense of older forms of social organization and loyalties. But above all else was resistance to taxation. The permanence of war, and the fear of future wars, necessitated continual demands for 'extraordinary' war subsidies, which in due course became permanent *impôts* levied without much regard for consent (cf. above, p. 138). The vital period for the establishment of the *taille* and other extraordinary taxes appears to have been the decade which followed the battle of Poitiers and King John's capture and, although they were temporarily abandoned on Charles V's death, they were re-established in 1388. There was widespread resistance to taxation under Charles VI, especially in the 1380s and 1390s, in particular in the south and east, where the *routier* captains had settled in. For the inhabitants of these regions of the kingdom—in Saintonge, Angoumois, Périgord, Quercy, Rouergue, Auvergne, Velay, Gévaudan, Vivarais, Valentinois, and elsewhere—the multiplication of taxes was often crippling. In addition to royal *tailles, aides* and other *impôts*, money had to be collected to pay the local captains and garrison forces and to repair and defend castles and town walls. For long periods at a time protection money had to be paid to the *routiers*, or funds raised to buy them off. Altogether, these amounted to a great deal and must have added to the burdens of economic regression in the affected areas.

In these conditions of social unrest, one section of society came in for criticism more than any other: the soldiers, often associated in the minds of the peasantry with their own lords and the nobility in general. The records of towns affected by the activities of the soldiers make little or no distinction between those troops fighting for a cause and those fighting solely for their own profit. In the minds of contemporaries they were all *gens d'armes,* and there was often not much to choose between them. A fourteenth-century tract, *La complainte sur la bataille de Poitiers,* gives us a picture of the men-at-arms as its author saw them:

'. . . Feasting and carousing, vain glorious, dishonest of dress,
With gilded belts, a feather in their hats,
A large goat's beard—which is a vile fashion,
They stun you like lightning and tempest . . .'

and he makes a valuable comment upon the social *milieu* from which they were sometimes drawn:

'. . . They claim to be of noble parentage,
My God! From where do they get such false wishes.
What good deeds have they engaged in?
It is from their great pride that they are so convinced,
For each of them studies how to renounce God,
And each of them glorifies in perjuring himself . . .'

Fig. 48   Troops leaving a town to board ship; from the early fifteenth-century manuscript of the Poems of Christine de Pisan. *London, British Museum Harley Ms 4431, part i, fo. 125.* (12.5 × 8.1)

In so far as one can penetrate peasant mentality, it seems that first and foremost they blamed the noble class for not having fulfilled its social function, for having betrayed the implicit pact by which the peasantry should be defended. In their eyes, the war conducted by the nobles was a sport in which they were caught up, in which the soldiers were ransomed rather than killed, and the payment of which, in one way or another, fell on their shoulders.

'. . . When it was seen that our host could easily defeat
The host of the English, it was said: "If we go and kill them
Wars will come to an end, which will be the worse for us
Because we will lose our livelihood; it is better for us to flee".
So no blow was made of weapon or pike . . .'
'. . . They have made a pact with those of England:
"Don't kill each other, make the war last,
Feign being a prisoner; much can be gained there" . . .'

Sometimes they dreamed of a war which they would lead themselves, in the name of the king, and which would be without consideration:

'. . . If he is well counselled, he will not forget
To lead Jacques Bonhomme in his great company;
He will not flee from wars to save himself . . .'

Such dreams were dangerous. Jean Juvénal reminds us in his *Histoire de Charles VI* that Charles V's *ordonnance* of 1368, making it compulsory for the peasants to practice archery, had subsequently to be revoked because the peasants had become too adept, and 'if they had been brought together, they would have been more powerful than the princes and the nobles'. The *Jacquerie* had left too indelible a mark. Jean de Venette, that peasant boy made good, repeatedly recorded his own indignation at the failure of the ruling class to find a remedy to the plundering and dangers of the road. 'There was none', he wrote, 'to defend the people, nor to meet these dangers and perils. Rather did the burdens which bore so heavily upon them seem to please the lords and princes whose duty it was to oppose and remedy these evils with a strong hand . . . Furthermore, the friends whose duty it was to protect

177

our peasants and wayfarers were themselves, alas! all basely intent upon plundering and robbing indiscriminately as if they were foes.' And like a good preacher, he illustrated his point with the fable of the dog and the wolf. Probably Jean was giving expression to opinions widely held after the battle of Poitiers and reflecting the popular feeling of the time. Both his ideas and his words suggest such contemporary tracts as the *Tragicum argumentum de miserabili statu regni Francie*, and the *Complainte sur la bataille de Poitiers*, the views of which he seems to have shared. But in the

Fig. 49   A battle; from a late fourteenth-century manuscript. *London, British Museum Royal Ms 20C VII, fo. 20v.*

Tragicum argumentum, brother Francis Beaumont argued that, although the people threw all the blame on the nobles for the disaster, they were themselves as much to blame. For, whereas the nobles had neglected to learn discipline and the military art because they were devoted to pleasure and luxury, the people were torn with discord, 'their God is their belly', and they permitted their women to rule them. Even the clergy were at fault for being given over to vices and voluptuousness.

   In the hour of disaster, the emotions and feelings of at least one section of French society are voiced in these tracts. In 1422, when France was again torn by foreign invasion and civil war, they were summed up by Alain Chartier (a Norman from Bayeux who had studied at Paris) in his *Quadrilogue Invectif*, in which 'France', 'the people', 'the knight' and 'the clergy', expound their separate views on the causes of the then current situation. The people complain that the soldiers live off them, instead of defending them; that because they are badly ordered and disciplined they are able to conduct robbery and brigandage in the guise of war; and that they do all these things at the expense of the people. To this the knight replies that the people are too fond of a good life and that they grumble when they are asked to pay taxes to maintain the war. 'We cannot live off the wind', he says, 'and our revenues will not suffice to pay the costs of the war. If the prince does not receive from his people the wherewithal to pay us, and in serving the community we live off the goods we find, God will allow our consciences to be excused.' Chartier, as secretary to the

91. Henry VI crowned king of France in 1431; *Life and Acts of Richard Beauchamp, earl of Warwick*, by John Rous, *c.* 1485. *London, British Museum Cotton Ms Julius E IV Art. vi, fo. 24.* (19.7 × 16.6).

Here shewes howe kyng Henry was after crowned kyng of ffrannce at Saynt
Denys besydes parys. Of the which coronacion in ffrannce and also the said
Erle to haue the rule of his noble psone vnto he were of the age of xoj yeres
it was the will & ordenmce of almyghty god / as o blessed lady shewed by relacion
vnto Dam Emme Rawghton Reclusse at all halowes in Northgate strete of york
and she said that thorowe the Kynne of Englond, was no psone lorde ne other
like to hym in habilite of grace and true feithfulnesse. to vertuwsly norisshe & gouerne
his noble psone accordyng to his Rial astate. / Also she put grett comendacion by
the ordenmce of god of his grett benefytes in tyme to come of debout conuers to ye places

Syr clif ydwyse called Cliclyff // which in
passe of tyme shal growe to a place
of grett Worshipe. oon of ye
most re...med in englond

dauphin Charles, and subsequently much employed in diplomatic circles, was one of a group of propagandists and pamphleteers—his friend Jean Juvénal des Ursins was another—who sought to build up the French monarchy and give some semblance of unity to what he himself calls *la communité du peuple françois*. In so doing, they were putting new ideas into an old garb, and thus paving the way for Joan of Arc.

As the Anglo-French conflict became progressively more violent, the tenets of chivalry and the law of arms became increasingly strained, or were even ignored. In a semi-autobiographical work by Jean de Bueil (d. 1477), entitled *Le Jouvencel*, written half a century after *Le livre des faicts du mareschal Boucicaut*, chivalric sentiment is giving way to patriotism. De Bueil disapproves of single combats because 'In the first place, those who do it want to take away the good of others, that is to say, their honour, to procure themselves vain glory, which is of little value; and in doing this, he serves none, he spends his money; . . . in being thus occupied, he neglects his part in waging war, the service of his king and the public cause; and no one should expose his body, unless in meritorious works'. No other literary work of the fifteenth century gives so sober a picture as *Le Jouvencel* of the wars of the period; and in it the chivalric knight is merging into the soldier of modern times; the universal and religious ideal is becoming national and military:

'It is a joyous thing, is war . . . You love your comrade so in war. When you see that your quarrel is just and your blood is fighting well, tears rise to your eye. A great sweet feeling of loyalty and of pity fills your heart on seeing your friend so valiantly exposing his body to execute and accomplish the command of our Creator. And then you prepare to go and die or live with him, and for love not to abandon him. And out of that there arises such a delectation, that he who has not tasted it is not fit to say what a delight it is. Do you think that a man who does that fears death? Not at all; for he feels so strengthened, he is so elated, that he does not know where he is. Truly he is afraid of nothing.'

Jean de Bueil had fought under the banner of Joan of Arc, he held office as lieutenant-general in the frontier districts of Anjou and Maine in the late 1430s, he took part in the rising called the Praguerie and in the war 'du bien public'. His words have since been echoed by many a soldier.

92. Portrait of John VIth lord Talbot (d. 1453), Compton Wynyates, Tysoe.

Court patronage and the arts

Cultural development in France and England in the Later Middle Ages is inevitably overshadowed by the Italian Renaissance which, since it became the European Renaissance in the course of the sixteenth and seventeenth centuries, has tended to hide the rich and continuous contacts between England and France and Italy, and the impact of northern intellectual and artistic influences south of the Alps.

The development of humanist studies in Italy, and the rediscovery of classical attitudes which that involved, led to a new conception of the place of the artist in society and made his works a matter for intelligent discussion and worthy of record. As a result, the artist emerged in a new and more personal dimension while, in the North, where he tended still to be regarded as no more than a superior craftsman in a particular occupation, his life and works for the most part remain somewhat obscure. Moreover, already by the beginning of the fourteenth century, the cultural leadership which France had long enjoyed in western Europe was to all intents and purposes lost. Other countries were producing their own variations of the French Gothic style and were developing their own vernacular literatures. In Italy, the poetry and prose of Dante Alighieri (1265–1321), Francesco Petrarca (1304–74) and his friend and contemporary Giovanni Boccaccio (1313–75) assured the competence of Tuscan as the main literary language in a country where there was hitherto no written tradition in the vernacular, and which had previously shared the bond of Provençal with southern France. The interest which these writers showed in antiquity is also noticeable in the sculpture of Niccolò and Giovanni Pisano (*fl.* 1260–1314), and in the paintings of Giotto (1266–1337) which show a new solidity and care for reality. In England too, the vernacular developed significantly as a literary language in the writings of John Gower (*c.* 1330–1408), William Langland (*c.* 1332–1400) and Geoffrey Chaucer (*c.* 1340–1400); and it is from the 1330s, with the building of the south transept of Gloucester cathedral, that we may confidently perceive the development of the English 'perpendicular' architectural style. The name is derived from the vertical lines of the window tracery and of the panelling which covered both internal and external walls and accentuated the feeling of height; vaulting became more complex and ornate with the development of the fan-vault, which first appeared in the cloister of Gloucester Cathedral (*c.* 1370), and finally the pendant-vault, of which one of the finest examples is in Henry VII's chapel at Westminster (1503–19).

It would be wrong, however, to press these points of departure too far. France and England still had much in common apart from their political and military involvement. They both belonged to a predominantly northern, rural, chivalric world and, for all its subtle and growing differences, they shared a similar social structure which determined much of the literary and artistic production of the period. French or Anglo-Norman was demonstrably still a living vernacular in fourteenth-century England and recent work has pointed to its continuing use by all literate groups, not only by the nobles and gentry. Froissart was appreciated in England, as well as in France, and he owed a great deal to the patronage of the English royal court, almost nothing to the French. There was, moreover, an astonishing degree of interdependence of theme and inspiration. A large number of the works written in English were composed of translations from French or adaptations of French originals. Chaucer, for instance, translated the *Roman de la Rose* of Guillaume de Lorris and Jean de Meun, and he evidently knew Froissart and the works of his French contemporaries Guillaume de Machaut (*c.* 1300–71) and Eustace Deschamps (*c.* 1346–*c.* 1406). Even in the fifteenth century Thomas Malory (d. 1417) produced in his *Morte d'Arthur*, the 'noble hystores of . . . Kynge Arthur and of certeyn of his knyghtes . . . teken oute of certeyn bookes of Frensshe and reduced into English'. The advance of the fourteenth century was limited mainly to verse and just how inadequate the language was for serious prose can be seen in Chaucer's version of Boethius and in the laborious works of Reginald Pecock, bishop of Chichester (d. *c.* 1460). At the end of the fourteenth century and at the beginning of the fifteenth there was an astonishing homogeneity in European art which has been called 'international Gothic'; its elegant and delicate characteristics suggest aristocratic patronage, and it was in fact a courtly and highly cultivated manner.

The extraordinary prestige which Paris and the French royal court had secured as a centre of cultural activity during the course of the twelfth and the thirteenth centuries, and the extraordinary wealth and continuing patronage of the French royal house, remained a decisive factor throughout the greater part of the fourteenth and the early years of the fifteenth centuries. Thus, although many of the greatest artists who worked in France came from outside the boundaries of the kingdom, and in particular from Flanders and the Low Countries, down to around 1420 they were attracted to Paris and the royal and princely courts and thus contributed to the French cultural achievement. They included Charles V's painter Jean Bandol of Bruges, and André Beauneveu of Valenciennes, Jacques Coene, Jacquemart de Hesdin, and later the famous brothers Jean and Pol de Limbourg who illuminated manuscripts for John, duke of Berry. At Dijon, Philip the Bold employed, in addition to the great Claus Sluter of Haarlem in Holland and his collaborator Claus de Werve, Jean de Beaumetz, a native of Artois, Jean Malouel, who came from Gelderland, and Henri Bellechose from Brabant. It was on French soil and with French patronage that all these artists found an environment propitious for the development of their personal styles. Nor was France entirely lacking in native talent. She could still produce an excellent building in her own idiom, like the abbey church of Saint-Ouen at Rouen, the choir of which (built in 1319–39, possibly by Jean Camelin) in many ways served as a model for the last two centuries of French Gothic style. Her writers could still produce good vernacular prose which, under Italian influence, became increasingly rhetorical in style. And it was France, too, which in the 1360s produced the first known examples of the portrait, rightly regarded as the hall mark of patrons interested in the depiction of an actual world. It was not until after 1420, when Philip the Good was seeking a capital outside the direction of France and concentrated his court in the Low Countries, that the real break came. For although chroniclers and historians like Georges Chastellain, who came from Alost in modern Belgium, and Philip de Commynes, who was born near Lille, contributed to the development of French prose, the van Eyck brothers and Roger van der Weyden can hardly be described as contributing to French art in the way that André Beauneveu, the Limbourg brothers and Claus Sluter can.

France also benefited from the presence of the popes at Avignon (cf. pl. 2) which, although then outside the boundaries of the kingdom, was in many ways the intellectual capital of the fourteenth century, an early centre of humanism in which bishops, scholars, men and ideas from every part of Christendom and beyond came into contact, and which formed an important crossroads in the cultural contacts between North and South. It was there that many Greek works previously unknown in the West were translated and to be found, and that a number of Italian painters for a while lived and worked: Paulo and Duccio of Siena under Benedict XII

Fig. 50 The sceptre of Charles V.
Paris, Musée du Louvre.

(1334-42); Simone Martini, also a Sienese, and Matteo Giovanetti of Viterbo under Clement VI (1342-52). Of these four, Simone Martini (1284-1344) was the most influential and his presence at the papal court during the last four years of his life was decisive for the future of European painting. In the works which he executed there the influence of French Gothic art, and particularly illumination, mingled with the new Tuscan art and anticipated the effects of flamboyant Gothic in their extreme delicacy, while his figures foreshadowed much of the intimist and narrative painting of the late fourteenth and fifteenth centuries in northern Europe. The importance of Avignon was thus very real and, backed by the prestige of the papal court, the influence of these Italian painters spread to Provence and the rest of France, to Flanders, Catalonia and Bohemia.

Patronage came from many quarters apart from the papacy: from religious corporations and confraternities, from private individuals, and from civic authorities; but lay patronage was still largely aristocratic and, together with the social life of the upper crust of the nobility, it was being increasingly concentrated in the royal and princely courts. Almost from the beginning the Valois dynasty showed itself to be an interested patron of the arts. Both Philip VI and John II were keen bibliophiles and they promoted artists and writers in their service. But John also inherited much from his mother Jeanne de Bourgogne, who had enjoyed an education outstanding for ladies of her day. He showed himself very favourable to artists and men of letters and, although he was unable to attract Petrarch to his court, he nevertheless surrounded himself with some very remarkable men. They included, among others, the painters Jean Coste and Girart d'Orléans, Gace de la Bigne, and the poets and composers Philip de Vitry (1291-1361) and, for a while, Guillaume de Machaut (c. 1300-71), a native of Champagne. Girart d'Orléans, who became a close companion of the king, was responsible for the remarkable portrait of John (cf. pl. 5), a surviving leaf, it seems, of a polyptych which once also included portraits of Charles V, the emperor Charles IV, and Edward III of England. Philip de Vitry was a musical theorist of considerable standing and one of his treatises entitled *Ars Nova* was not only instrumental in shaping the musical idiom of France for the next two generations, but also brought him international repute and influence by spreading throughout Europe the musical style of which it treated. The courtly lyrics of Machaut, set to his music, have made a lasting place for themselves in the history of French song.

All of John's sons—Charles V, Louis duke of Anjou, John duke of Berry, and Philip the Bold—shared their father's interests and tastes, as also did Charles' second son Louis of Orléans. They were enthusiastic builders and collectors of books, illuminated manuscripts, paintings, tapestries, jewellery and other *objets d'art*, and they promoted at their courts many of the scholars and artists who produced them. Under Charles V the royal court, which was centred in and around Paris, reached new heights of splendour and magnificence, and the influence of its style was felt in many parts of Europe, from England to Bohemia. Charles completed the tower of Vincennes, begun by his father; he constructed the castle of Beauté-sur-Marne and his favourite residence the Hôtel Saint-Pol; and during his lifetime the Louvre (cf. pl. 55) was greatly enlarged by his master mason Raymond du Temple, and embellished with rich furnishings. The life of the king and his *entourage* was largely spent in these palaces, amid a *décor* hitherto unsurpassed in its riches: in rooms hung with tapestries or wainscotted, lit by stained-glass windows and containing other rich furnishings, *bric-à-brac* and books.

Charles was the first secular ruler to establish in France a more or less extensive library which, by the time of his death, consisted of some 1,200 manuscripts, many of them sumptuously bound and replete with masterpieces of illumination. The collection was housed in three well-equipped rooms in the Louvre, under the control

93. Surrender of a town; late fourteenth century. *London, British Museum Royal Ms 20 C VII, fo. 190.* (8 × 7.9).

Comment ceulr de poytiers et de thouars se rendi
rent francois a meffs les ducs de berry et de bour
goigne et au conestable. Et comment le duc de
bretaigne sist uenir les anglois en bretaigne.

E iour de la saint andry ensuiuant
meffs les ducs de berry et de bour
goigne le dit conestable et grant

C̄ſte feſte fut gr̄ad
et noble et tres plē
tureuſe ſicque par
hauant nauoit eſte
veue la pareille ou royaulme dan
gleterre. Et y vindrent le conte guil
laume de ijxnault et meſſire Iehā
ſon oncle auecq eulx grant quanti
te de baronnie et cheuallerie du pais
de ijxnault. Et tant que a ceſte
plentureuſe feſte furent douſe cō

tes huit cens cheualliers et cincq
cens dames que damoiſelles tou
tes de grant et hault lignauge la
quelle feſte fut Iouſtee z danſee p
leſpace de quinſe Iours. Mais
vng noble z Ieune bacheler fut
tue es Iouſtes qui eult grant plai
te. Ceſt aſſcauoir meſſire Iehā·
aiſne ſilz de meſſire henry viſcōte
de beaumont beau cheualier et
hardy qui ſarmoit dasur ſur

of a permanently employed librarian Sir Giles Malet, and it was enthusiastically commended by Christine de Pisan (*c.* 1364–*c.* 1433), the Italian born widow of one of Charles' secretaries, in her *Livre des fais et bonnes meurs du sage roy Charles V*. It was surprisingly representative of such non-Greek literature as was in vogue in the fourteenth century and that in practically all departments of knowledge: theology, philosophy, science, history and literature.

Christine de Pisan described in her *Livre des fais* a typical day in the life of the king. He rose between six and seven and, his toilet terminated, his chaplain assisted him in the recitation of the canonical hours, which was followed at about eight by solemn mass to music in his chapel. Thereafter, he heard requests from all kinds of people or attended his council. His first meal of the day was at about ten and it was concluded by soft music to 'revive his spirits'. Some two hours would then be spent in one of his great and richly-embellished rooms, when he held audience with princes, ambassadors, knights and other men who brought him news from all over the realm and from abroad. Some matters he dealt with immediately, others were passed on to the council. After an hour's siesta he spoke with his household staff and intimates and enjoyed his jewels and other works of art. There followed vespers and, in summer, a walk in his gardens where the queen and their children sometimes joined him. In winter this time was spent in reading and being read to; it was followed by a leisurely supper, when he conversed with his barons and knights, and he then retired for the night. Christine was anxious to emphasize the essential wisdom and moderation of the king, and Charles' weak constitution did inhibit him from indulging himself too greatly. Nevertheless, on important occasions even his court could rise to long meals interspersed with *entremets*, when theatrical turns were performed and fortresses and ships containing musicians and jugglers were wheeled into the rooms and, in the hands of the dukes of Burgundy and that *bon-viveur* the duke of Berry, such occasions, masked balls in great torchlit rooms and musical evenings became the order of the day.

The princely courts were held in almost equally magnificent surroundings. In the 1370s the duke of Berry employed Guy de Dammartin to restore the ancient palace of Poitiers burnt down by the Black Prince; he had the great hall erected there, with its stately fireplace and its statues of himself and his duchess, a beautiful image of courtliness and grace. He commissioned André Beauneveu to construct the magnificent palace of Mehun-sur-Yèvre, which became the home of the dauphin Charles after the Burgundian *coup* in Paris in 1418. Louis d'Orléans had many of his castles and country residences built or rebuilt: at La Ferté-Milon, Crépy, Béthisy, Pierrefonds and Coucy. Pierrefonds, an entirely new building constructed in an important strategic position near Compiègne, was the most splendid and up to date example of military architecture in its day (see above, p. 115). But it was not solely a military establishment; it was also a sumptuous residence which included a Hall of Heroines and a Hall of the Knights of the Round Table, each of them embellished with rich tapestries. Philip the Bold's court was centred on Dijon; but of all the buildings which he commissioned the great Chartreuse at nearby Champmol, a family mausoleum intended as the Saint-Denis of the dynasty, was one of the finest edifices of its day. Begun in 1383 to the design of Drouet de Dammartin, the brother of Guy, it provided such a quantity of work that it led to the emergence of a great school of sculptors—Jean de Marville, Claus Sluter and Claus de Werve—who, being regularly employed, were able to develop their own distinctive style whose influence was felt in distant Provence and even in England. In their hands Burgundian sculpture acquired a new vigour which was touched with earthy Netherlandish realism. Sluter was undoubtedly the greatest of the three. His magnificent tomb of the duke, with its procession of forty-one mourners around the base, and the so-called 'Well of Moses', originally designed as a pedestal for a

94. Jousting; Wavrin's Chronicles.
*Paris, Bibliothèque Nationale
Ms français 87, fo. 58v.*

crucifixion standing in a fountain in the cloister of Champmol, are among the most important surviving works of sculpture of the period north of the Alps.

Many of the royal and princely furnishings travelled with the court on its frequent journeys in chests or, in the case of tapestries which could easily be erected and dismantled, transported from palace to palace in great rolls. The weaving and dyeing of tapestries was particularly active in Paris and Arras from around 1300 and in the second half of the fifteenth century at Tournai and Brussels (cf. pls. 66, 71, 89). Executed in several panels which formed a *chambre*, they might cover the walls of one or several rooms, the artist frequently developing a particular theme. John II is said to have acquired at least 235 tapestries between 1350 and 1364, most of them of a relatively simple artistic quality, decked with fleurs-de-lys or armorial bearings. But, stemming from the patronage of Charles V and his brothers, much more ambitious schemes were undertaken and a thriving industry was brought into being which enjoyed a period of extraordinary prosperity in the years between 1360 and 1425. Charles is said to have collected over 200 tapestries during the course of his lifetime and his passion for them was shared in particular by Louis of Anjou and by Philip the Bold, who was reputed to have possessed one of the finest collections in Europe by 1400. All sorts of subjects were depicted: morality and religious scenes, historical, romantic, chivalrous, rustic, hunting, amorous and allegorical ones. Among the historical and legendry themes the most popular was the cycle of the Nine Worthies, to whom Du Guesclin was sometimes added. Next in popularity were those depicting the story of Charlemagne and his peers, and these were followed in general favour by scenes from the Trojan War and the Siege of Jerusalem.

Such tapestries were essentially court furnishings, but the finest of them were based on designs drawn up by some of the leading artists of the day. The chief Parisian tapestry weavers were Nicolas Bataille (d. 1400) and Jacques Dourdin (d. 1407) and they worked to the designs of artists like Jean Bandol of Bruges, Colart de Laon, André Beauneveu and Pol de Limbourg. Bataille was a *valet de chambre* of Louis of Anjou and is known to have been responsible for at least 250 tapestries in the thirteen years prior to his death. It has recently been shown that the astounding series of seven illustrating the *Apocalypse* (cf. pl. 62), which he was commissioned to produce for Louis of Anjou in the years 1373–80, was based on illustrations provided by Bandol, at the time one of Charles' official painters, from an illuminated manuscript of the Apocalypse in Charles' library (Bib. nat., ms. français 403). Philip the Bold was similarly provided with tapestries based on paintings, for one of which, executed to celebrate *la bataille de Roosebecke* in 1382, he paid Michel Bernat of Arras some 1,600 gold francs.

Illuminated manuscripts may also be regarded as a furnishing and an expression of court life and the production of them for the royal princes led to the invention of new techniques and the use of bold colours and designs by the artists of the epoch. During the course of the thirteenth century the copying and illustrating of such manuscripts had ceased to be a monastic monopoly and had become a well-paid secular profession. Paris had early acquired a reputation for their production. It was there that the distinguished illuminator Master Honoré, who had his own house in the rue Erembourc-de-Brie, set up his studio, turning out works for the courts of Philip III and Philip IV. With this well-grounded tradition, the French capital continued to dominate the field throughout the fourteenth century, furnishing employment for a number of illuminators' workshops. It was there in the 1320s that Jean Pucelle introduced into his miniatures a new modelling and perspective, and a use of light and shadow which undoubtedly owed something to Duccio and other Sienese painters, and opened the way for a less linear and two dimensional style. But fine as Pucelle's drawings and colourings were, his miniatures were still subordinate to the manuscript page, and were too tiny to permit of a full development of figures or space. However, during the last quarter of the fourteenth century a new advance in Parisian painting occurred as a result of the work of Flemish and Italian immigrants, who brought with them a more naturalistic tradition and a fresh treatment of volume and space. The most famous among them were the Limbourg brothers, André Beauneveu and Jacquemart de Hesdin, and they were actively patronized by the king and the royal dukes, above all by the duke of Berry (cf. pl. 18). In their works miniatures became practically independent pictures and separate from the text. Landscapes were now portrayed in depth, figures were presented in the round and great attention was given to detail. The most famous surviving production is the *Très Riches Heures du Duc de Berri*, begun for John, duke of Berry, in 1413 (cf. pls. 54, 55); but there were countless others as well. When transferred to larger surfaces, the new techniques brought about a revolution in northern painting during the second decade of the fifteenth century. With Jan van Eyck (*c.* 1390–1441) and Roger van der Weyden (*c.* 1400–64) a new and distinctively Netherlandish style emerged from international Gothic, just as in the same generation a new and distinctively Italian style emerged with Massacio and his contemporaries; but by then the prestige of Paris had been lost (cf. below, p. 190).

Fig. 51   Detail of a soldier from the tapestry *La Justice de Trajan et d' Archambault* (1455–61). *Berne, Historisches Museum.*

Charles V, besides collecting manuscripts, enjoyed reading them. We have already seen how he was in the habit of being read to before supper, and Christine de Pisan also observes that he was particularly fond of passages from the Holy Scriptures, Roman histories and philosophical works. He seems to have kept a reading-desk in each of his residences, with a clock, a table-lighter and an astrolabe. The books he used in the last year of his life were (apart from service books) all in French, which was clearly the one language he could read. They were nearly all devotional (including a French Bible which he always had with him) or concerned with astrology—which probably accounts for the astrolabes. But he had in his room at Saint-Germain-en-Laye a copy of the *Gouvernement des Princes* and the current *Grandes Chroniques de France* (cf. pls. 23, 37), already recording the events of his reign. He was interested in the theory as well as in the practice of kingship and, unable to read Aristotle in Latin, he had a French translation of the *Politics* made for his own use, probably by Raoul de Presles. Raoul is known to have translated a number of other works for Charles and for Louis of Anjou, including a treatise on the two Powers, and Augustine's *City of God*. Another translator who was active in royal service was the Hospitaller Simon de Hesdin, who was responsible for a rendering into French of Valerius Maximus. Philip the Bold preferred secular literature to theological writings, works on chivalry being the most common in his library. But the next three dukes added a great deal to his collection and they personally supervised many of the new purchases and the literary activity which went on around them. John the Fearless may have spent little time on intellectual pursuits, but Philip the Good devoted a good deal of time to study, especially in his old age; and according to Olivier de la Marche, Charles the Rash (cf. pl. 60), who is reputed to have been particularly scholarly in his youth, in his later years 'would never retire to bed until someone had read to him for two hours'. Louis of Anjou may have regarded his books primarily as precious objects, since of the forty-odd manuscripts which he took from the royal library on the death of Charles V (he was on good terms with the librarian Giles Malet), twenty-seven of the thirty-six we know of were richly bound with clasps of gold or silver and enamel; only ten had bindings of less value. But Louis' life was primarily that of a soldier and administrator, and the wealth he drew from his *apanage* cannot be compared with that of his brothers. He had fairly refined tastes, he kept a good table, he liked fine tapestries and gold and silver work (Bataille and Dino Rapondi were his chief suppliers), but it was his son (cf. pl. 90) who showed more intellectual pursuits. Louis II (1377–1417) had a number of scholars in his service—Pierre de Beauvau and Guillaume Saignet, who were respectively seneschal and chancellor of Provence, and Honoré Bonnet, a native of Provence and author of *L'Arbre des Batailles*—and he was in close contact with Guillaume Fillastre, who played an important role in the French Church and at the Council of Constance. He founded the University of Aix (1409) and we know that he had a retreat where he kept and read his personal books, which included Italian works.

The death of Charles V in 1380 was undoubtedly a blow for those artists and scholars who had enjoyed the enlightened patronage of his court, but it was not as disastrous as has sometimes been suggested. Although Charles VI was only a boy at the time of his accession and subsequently suffered from a recurrent mental illness, the patronage of the royal dukes continued unabated and was positively encouraged by the rivalry between them. Both the *Geste des ducs de Bourgogne* and the *Livre des faits du bon chevalier messire Jacques de Lalaing* were inspired to some extent by Burgundian propaganda and this tendency is particularly obvious in an anonymous poem called the *Pastoralet*, which aimed to bring discredit on the duke of Orléans and on everything connected with Burgundy's arch-enemy. The ambitions of the house of Burgundy are also reflected in the marked predilection for *Girart de Rousillon*, a work which belonged to *Burgundia* in the widest sense; and Jean Petit's *Justification*, in which he vindicated tyrannicide and commended the crime committed in 1407, is a most striking use of the literature of propaganda to suit the politics of the ducal house. Moreover, it was during the reign of Charles VI, and in particular during the first two decades of the fifteenth century, when the dukes were seeking to promote their protégés and partisans in almost every branch of the government, and when the whole position of the monarchy was brought into question, that we may discern the most intense period of humanist activities in Late Medieval France. Royal secretaries like Gontier Col (d. 1418) and Jean de Montreuil (d. 1418), who were deeply involved in politics and diplomacy and who, like Nicolas de Clamanges (d. 1437), had spent periods of their lives at Avignon or in Italy and correspond with the chancellor of Florence Coluccio Salutati (1331–1406), were called upon to defend the royal dynasty. It is often said that the royal library built up by Charles V was appropriated by the princes on his death; but less than two hundred works were lost, borrowed or stolen between 1380 and 1411 and Charles VI's purchases more than compensated for this. It was not until 1424 that the collection had dwindled to 843 items, and only in 1435, with the death of the duke of Bedford who had purchased them, that the collection was dispersed.

The decline of Paris and the French royal court as a centre of intellectual and cultural activity dates in fact from the accession of Philip the Good and the death of Charles VI. From that time there was no royal court in Paris and the centre of attraction for scholars and artists moved to the Low Countries where the Burgundian court was henceforward established at Ghent and Brussels. After the death of the duke of Berry and the assassination of John the Fearless, the most talented Flemish painters remained at home, where they enjoyed not only the patronage of the ducal court, but also that of the wealthy patricians and ecclesiastics of the most economically advanced cities north of the Alps. It is from 1420 that M. Coville has dated the decline of humanist activity in France and it was in that year that the long tradition of Saint-Denis as an official historiographical centre was interrupted. The greatest writers of the next generation—Enguerrand de Monstrelet, Mathieu d'Escouchy, Georges Chastellain and Olivier de la Marche—were all attracted to the Burgundian court. We have to wait until the 1440s for a temporary revival in 'French' painting with the appearance of Jean Fouquet, and it was not until the time of Louis XI that Philip de Commynes (cf. pl. 59) and Thomas Basin produced their masterly works (see below, p. 198).

After victory of the Burgundian party in 1418, the dauphin Charles established himself at Bourges and, from then until the end of the fifteenth century, the royal court remained in central France: in the castles of the Loire valley, the Orléanais and Touraine. It was a very different style of living from that of Charles V, centred on the old seigniorial residences near to the great forests—essential for the hunt. But although the court had now taken to the country, towns like Bourges, Moulins and Tours profited from the proximity of the princes. Houses were erected for nobles and rich merchants—like that of Jacques Coeur at Bourges (cf. pls. 19, 51)—and there was a growth in the commerce of luxury goods. The anonymous 'Master of Moulins', who painted the triptych in the cathedral there at the end of the fifteenth century, may have lived and worked at Moulins. The celebrated portrait of Charles VII's mistress, Agnes Sorel (cf. fig. 52), is to be found in the château country at Loches. It was at Tours that Jean Fouquet was born around the year 1420, and it is in the little parish church of Nouans, not forty miles away, that his great painting—the famous *Pièta*—is to be found. Fouquet was brought up in the Franco-Flemish tradition of miniature painting, was conversant with the works of Jan van Eyck and, after a journey to Italy in his early twenties, he absorbed Italian decorative motifs and developed a taste for linear perspective and a feeling for light. He is best known as a miniaturist, and his illumination of the *Hours of Etienne Chevalier*, a *Boccaccio* and a *Grandes Chroniques de France* are sufficient to establish his ability in that field. But his brilliance as a panel-painter is evident in his portraits of Charles VII (cf. pl. 20) and Juvénal des Ursins in the Louvre. The *Pièta* at Nouans is undoubtedly his finest surviving work, and the sculptured solidity which it demonstrates was an important milestone in French art. Fouquet was a painter in whom the traditions of North and South made contact, but he was unique in the France of his day: the centres of gravity had moved to the Netherlands and Italy.

One is immediately struck by the absence in England of a royal tradition of enlightened patronage of the arts such as existed in fourteenth-century France; for, unlike John II and his children, Edward III and his family are not especially noted for their intellectual and artistic pursuits. Edward's tastes were for the most part chivalrous and conventional. He planned to make Windsor the focus of his court and a great centre of chivalry, and his enormous expenditure on works there, which amounted to over £50,000, was the highest for any single royal building operation in medieval England. Much of this sum was spent on the great Round Hall, erected in 1344 to house the new chivalrous Order of the Round Table, and on the collegiate chapel of Saint George, founded to accommodate its successor, the Order of the Garter in 1348. In these buildings, and in his completion of Saint Stephen's Chapel at Westminster, Edward was clearly attempting to rival the house of Valois. Tournaments and joustings, hunting-parties and balls provided lavish entertainment for the aristocracy of the day, and the ring of satellite houses and hunting-lodges which he built around Windsor made it possible for him and the court to hunt in any part of the forest within easy reach of somewhere to eat and sleep. What cultural activity there was at his court was primarily due to Queen Philippa, who was herself of Valois stock on her mother's side, and whose family (with their court at Valenciennes) had shown a notable interest in the arts. Through her patronage a number of Hainaulters were attracted to the English court; they included, for a while, Jean Froissart (*c.* 1337–*c.* 1404), André Beauneveu of Valenciennes, and Jean (alias Hennequin) of Liège. Hennequin, who like Beauneveu had been drawn to the French court in 1364 by lavish commissions from Charles V, was responsible for the remarkable effigy of Philippa in Westminster Abbey (cf. fig. 53), an evident and unkind portrait carried out in her lifetime but one which, through the element of realism introduced into the treatment of the body, was to have its influence on subsequent royal effigies. Froissart spent most of the 1360s at the English court as a clerk of the queen's chamber, and possibly part of his childhood as well, and it was

Fig. 52   Portrait of Agnes Sorel, mistress of Charles VII. *Loches, Private Collection.*

through Philippa's patronage that he was able to travel to Scotland in 1365, to spend part of 1366 and 1367 at the Black Prince's court at Bordeaux, and to visit Italy in 1368–9. But it should be noted that after the queen's death in the latter year he was not kept on at the English court by Edward III, but obliged to return to Valenciennes, where he secured new patrons; and it was not until 1370 that he completed the first edition of his *Chronicle* at the request of Philippa's nephew Robert of Namur.

Although Froissart thought of himself primarily as a poet, it is as a chronicler that he is chiefly remembered and his great work, the four books of which cover the European field from about 1326 to the end of the fourteenth century, captured his contemporaries by its masterly narrative style and established itself as a repository of authenticated deeds of *noblesse*. It has been described as 'a kind of *Who's Who* or *Almanach de Gotha*' of gentlemen who sought 'to secure the immortality of a reference in his pages', and Froissart travelled far and wide to gather his information from them. Not unnaturally it reflects a view of the events that he describes which was favourable to his different patrons, and the textual problems of its various recensions are consequently such that there is still no complete scholarly edition of his work. But if Froissart cannot therefore always be trusted for his view of events—and he is notoriously inaccurate in matters of topography, chronology and numbers—as a literary work, and as a record of the *milieu* and *mores* of the chivalrous society of an age whose prejudices he shared, his *Chronicle* will stand for all time. For it opens the door to a vanished world and without it our knowledge of the fourteenth century would be infinitely less rich.

Apart from the activity of these Hainaulters at the English court, and the favour shown to Chaucer (cf. below, p. 195), there is not much evidence of royal interest in the arts in Edward's time and the lack of it continued to be felt. It may be that the destruction wrought by the Reformation and the passage of time have robbed us of much of the Late Medieval English achievement, and it must be admitted that we are seriously handicapped by the absence of detailed inventories of possessions in the royal households such as those compiled on the death of Charles V and his brothers in France, from which much of the information about their cultural activity has been drawn. But even bearing these factors in mind, the works of English artists seem to pale. London had no specialized *ateliers* to compare with those of Paris. The East Anglian psalters surviving from the beginning of the fourteenth century were the work of a group of travelling illuminators whom the needs of patrons assembled from time to time in different places and in different groupings. Even the deservedly famous manuscripts made for the Bohun family (*c.* 1365) cannot be attributed to a school of illuminators with a well-defined style of their own, let alone to any individual painter, and the quality of English manuscripts in the second half of the fourteenth century falls far below that of the French workshops. It has been suggested that the plague years caused a greater break in the continuity of English miniature-painting than they did in France; but it is significant that no Flemish artists appear to have been attracted to settle in London; that a psalter ordered by King John from 'Maistre Jean Langlois, escrivain', while he was a prisoner in the city in 1359, was not purchased when the king had seen it, but returned to the painter with a noble for his pains; and that when Froissart was having a copy of the first edition of his chronicles made for Richard II in 1381, he had it illuminated in Paris, where it was seized by Louis of Anjou.

The absence of any school with its own traditions and an evident centre may also be noted in the case of paintings on panel and of tapestries. Apart from the 'stained cloths' which hung on the walls of more modest households, the latter were all imported from the Continent, many were gifts from the kings of France and the dukes of Burgundy, and hence their English name 'arras'. A number of important paintings

Fig. 53   White marble effigy of Queen Philippa of Hainault (d. 1369) by Jean de Liège, Westminster Abbey, London.

survive from the last two decades of the fourteenth century, among them, a portrait of Richard II in Westminster Abbey (cf. fig. 54) and, much the most famous of them all, the Wilton Diptych in the National Gallery in London (cf. pls. 42, 44, 45). None of these can be attributed to a painter or a school. The superlative quality of the Wilton Diptych has tempted some writers to conclude that it is Franco-Flemish or French. Certainly, it has no particular local accent and its delicate style, which verges on affectation, combines the precise realism of Flanders with the courtly urbanity of France. But there are attendant problems to such an interpretation. The approximation of the physical types of Saint Edmund, Saint Edward and Saint John to the physical types of Edward II, Edward III and the Black Prince, and the evident portraiture of Richard II, suggest that it must have been painted in England. So also do the artist's conversancy with heraldic and other features. Richard's personal emblem of the white hart (first assumed in 1390) which is painted on the reverse side (cf. pl. 42), is also embroidered on the dresses of the eleven angels and appears on the scarlet gown of the king. The arms attributed to Edward the Confessor impaled with the quartered royal arms of France and England (which were a feature of the years between 1394 and 1399) are also to be found on the back of the diptych. The white hart on the reverse appears to be lying on the flattened branches of a bush of rosemary, known to have been the personal badge of Richard's first queen Anne of Bohemia (d. 1394). All this and other evidence suggest that it was painted between 1394 and 1399 and was of English provenance. It has been argued that no French painter would be likely to set three figures in a row and that the collars of broom-pods worn by Richard and the angels, and embroidered on the king's dress, may derive from an independent adoption of the *cosse de genêt* by Richard II as much as from a present of such collars from Charles VI in 1395–6 and their use by the Valois dynasty from 1378. If so, it is from Richard's reign that the idea of Plantagenet as a family name took its rise, and the adoption of the emblem may be associated with a conscious revival of claims going back to Geoffrey of Anjou, and thus represent an attempt to emulate rather than to imitate the house of Valois. But it is difficult to fit such an interpretation in with Richard's peace moves in the 1390s, with his plans for a French alliance and his marriage to Charles VI's daughter, Isabella, in 1396 (cf. above, p. 72). Two London painters called Gilbert Prince (d. 1396) and Thomas Prince of Litlington were commissioned to do a considerable amount of work for Richard in which they employed the white hart and broom-pods extensively as a decorative motif; but there is no evidence that they were responsible for the Wilton Diptych. The whole idea of the diptych is French; such compositions of a great man and his patron saint kneeling before the Virgin were not uncommon in the royal chapels of France at the time, such as those of the dukes of Burgundy and Berry. It has been argued that the diptych might well have been painted by an Englishman not unfamiliar with French painting; but it seems more likely that it was the work of a French or Flemish master in England. For the moment we can do no more than associate it with other unidentified paintings of the period, or simply label it 'international Gothic'.

The absence of detailed inventories is particularly exasperating in the case of books; but the published evidence strongly suggests that there was no royal library of any size in fourteenth-century England and, on the evidence of wills, the nobility were surprisingly unintellectual in their pursuits. There is no indication that Edward III was at all interested in books. Richard II, on the other hand, bought them fairly regularly and according to Froissart (who in 1395 presented him with a richly bound and illuminated book, apparently of his poems) he could speak and read French very well, and kept his volumes in his private chambers. We know of a number of other works presented to him, one of which includes a treatise on the duties of kings, a list of things seen in dreams and their interpretation, and a treatise

Fig. 54   Detail of a contemporary portrait on wood of Richard II by an unknown artist, Westminster Abbey, London.

entitled *Libellus Geomancie* compiled for the solace of Richard in March 1391 by *minimus servientum regis*. But although such works provide some commentary on the interests of the king and give a further insight into his fascinating psychology, they give us little idea of the number and range of the books which he may have possessed. We are on rather surer ground in the case of a knight of his household and sometime tutor, Sir Simon Burley, from an inventory of goods in his two London houses drawn up in 1388. This shows that he possessed a notable collection of books, which included nine French Romances, the *Chronicle of the Brut* and the *Prophecies of Merlin*, and a number of more serious works; only one volume—the *Romance of the Forester and the Wild Boar*—was in English and only one certainly in Latin. There are two other fourteenth-century inventories of laymen's libraries. One is of the library of Guy de Beauchamp, son and heir of the earl of Warwick, who died in 1360 leaving forty-two books to Bordesley Abbey in Worcestershire, of which nineteen were romances and the rest mainly devotional works. The other is that of the duke of Gloucester who had some eighty-three books at Pleshey, of which nineteen were romances, twenty-one devotional works, five law books, nine chronicles, two English Gospels and an English Bible. Apart from these, he had in his chapel a further two Bibles and thirty-nine service books.

Burley's library is likely to have represented his own interests and he may have purchased some of the volumes listed on his inventory while he was Richard's tutor; but it is interesting that it does not include any work of Chaucer's, for they must have known each other well. It is more difficult to assess how far Gloucester's collection reflected his own tastes, though it should perhaps be noted that the will of his wife Eleanor, who was the daughter and co-heir of Humphrey de Bohun, earl of Hereford (d. 1373), for whom the famous Bohun Psalters were executed, included thirteen works in French. Five of these were psalters, and three other works were on religious and moral subjects; but some of the others had evidently belonged to her husband and, like many of the tapestries which he possessed at Pleshey, were presents from Charles VI and Philip the Bold. It may be that Gloucester's intellectual interests, overridingly religious and chivalrous as they seem to have been, were derived from his father-in-law. He must have been trained for the office of constable, which he received in 1374, and Chaucer's knight bears testimony to Hereford's crusading reputation, which Gloucester tried to emulate, as did the earl of Arundel (doubly Hereford's brother-in-law) and Hereford's other son-in-law the earl of Derby, subsequently Henry IV. Though Gloucester and Derby cannot have known Hereford personally, his reputation was probably kept alive by his widow, a highly respected lady who was clearly interested in the education of Henry IV's children. The duchess of Gloucester and the countess of Derby both carried on their father's style in commissioning religious manuscripts, and it may be that Henry V's religious, crusading and literary interests were derived from his Bohun grandfather rather than from his Plantagenet one. All of Henry IV's children were interested in books, though Henry V had a bad record as a borrower and secured many of his volumes as plunder in the war. But much the most discerning of the three sons was Humphrey, duke of Gloucester. Like a few other aristocrats—for instance William Gray, bishop of Ely (who sent John Free to Italy), and John Tiptoft, earl of Worcester—he patronized humanists and collected Italian books. He counted the Italians Tito Livio Frulovisi and Antonio Beccaria among his secretaries and corresponded with Pier Candido; the bequest of his collection of books to the University of Oxford, and the building of a library to house them, was an important event for subsequent English scholarship.

Richard II's reign is usually regarded as the apogee of cultural activity in Late Medieval England and the last quarter of the fourteenth century was certainly a period of remarkable artistic and literary activity. We have already seen that a number of important paintings on panel date from that period. The new Westminster

Hall, with its traceried windows in the perpendicular manner by Henry Yevele, and Hugh Herland's great roof of timber arches with hammer beams and supporting angels, was begun in 1394 (cf. pl. 53). It was during the '80s and '90s, after two visits to Italy, that Chaucer's greatest works were written: *Troilus* and the *Legend of Good Women,* the *Astrolabe* and, above all, the *Canterbury Tales.* Richard has been regarded as being responsible for much of this achievement, harnessing the arts to the cause of the English royal prerogative and 'the divinity that doth hedge a king', spurning the martial exploits of his father and grandfather, seeking a peace with France, and building up the *mystique* of monarchy into something peculiarly his own. But it is difficult to document the king's personal involvement. The problems have already been noted with regard to his library and the Wilton Diptych, but in the obscurity which surrounds their contents and provenance they are certainly not unique. Nor can the work of Chaucer, Yevele and Herland be attributed to the king's patronage alone. Both Yevele (d. 1400) and Herland (d. *c.* 1406) had carried out extensive and important works during Edward III's reign and had been admitted to the royal household as early as 1360. The positions which they held as Master-Mason and Master-Carpenter in charge of the oversight of all the king's works were due to an administrative reform carried out during the king's minority and attributed to the treasurer of England Thomas Brantingham. It is largely a matter of chance that, whereas Edward III's extensive works at Westminster and Windsor have largely been demolished or built over, the Great Hall of Richard II remains much as it was at the time of his death.

Chaucer's career in royal service began as a valet of Queen Philippa in the 1360s (he married one of her ladies-in-waiting, Philippa Roet, possibly herself a native of Hainault) and after her death he owed as much to Edward III and John of Gaunt as he did to Richard. One of his earliest works, the *Book of the Duchess,* is a lament for Gaunt's first wife Blanche of Lancaster (d. 1369). It was in these earlier years that the annuities and grants of land which he enjoyed for the greater part of his life were bestowed upon him, that he saw active service in the war in France (1359–60 and 1369) and probably also in Spain (1366), and was sent on diplomatic missions to France (1368 and 1377) and Italy, when he visited Genoa and Florence (1372–3) and Lombardy (1378). But Chaucer was no mere court poet and the contacts of a practical life contributed greatly to his genius. As the son and grandson of London vintners, and subsequently controller of the petty custom on wine and merchandise in the port of London, he was conversant with the world of trade and business. He served his time as a justice of the peace and member of parliament for Kent; he had lived the life of a country gentleman, but London was his chosen home. He never went to a university, but he understood the issues which the clerks were debating in the schools; and whether or not he had a formal legal training, he knew the language of the law. The range of his reading is astonishing. He was well versed in the classical authors, was acquainted with the early medieval versions of the classical myths and the multifarious Latin literature of the Middle Ages, in its poetry, its history, its philosophy and its science. It has already been observed (above, p. 183) that he knew the work of his French contemporaries and after his first visit to Italy, he extended his knowledge to the works of Dante, Petrarch and Boccaccio. Chaucer did not invent his tales; but he told them as they had never been told before and in his hands the puppets of the *fabliaux* became living men and women. Unlike Froissart, whose interests and sympathies were limited to the aristocratic circles in which he moved, Chaucer was familiar with the lives and attitudes of all sections of society and it is his knowledge of the world, the enormous breadth of his reading, and his keen powers of observation, that are revealed so forcibly in the *Canterbury Tales.*

A striking feature of French royal patronage is its official nature. This is evident in varying degrees in all branches of the arts, but the positions which carried the greatest prestige and were among the earliest to acquire official standing were those of the master-masons and master-carpenters in charge of building works. The very scale of the enterprises they undertook, the financial outlay and engineering expertise that were involved, automatically placed them in a different category from other artists; the fact that buildings were in need of constant inspection and repair, and were continually being added to and altered, necessitated the early development of official and more or less permanent posts. During the course of the fourteenth century there was an increasing tendency towards specialization and centralization in the organization of royal building activities, which led to a more pronounced distinction between the administrative and technical sides of the various enterprises undertaken. Already in the early years of the fourteenth century the oversight of building administration was entrusted to a clerk of the king's works (*clerc payeur des oeuvres du roi*) who acted through a subordinate (*magister solutor operum*) in each *bailliage* and *sénéchaussée*. The purely technical officers, of whom a Master-Mason (like Raymond du Temple) and a Master-Carpenter were the most important, were in charge of most and ultimately all the royal building activity. They were what we might call the chief architects. The frequent employment of painters and sculptors also led to the early creation of more or less permanent offices (*pictores regis, peintres du roy, imagiers*). Already under John II two men held the title of king's painter: Girart d'Orléans from 1350 and Jean Coste from 1351. A similar development took place in Burgundy during the time of Philip the Bold. Jean de Marville was *ymagier et varlet de chambre* of the duke, and we have already seen how this became an official post (above, p. 187). Some of these men were attached to the royal and ducal households as *valets de chambre, ushers, esquires* and *familiares*. As early as 1313 an illuminator called Maciot was made a *valet* in the household of Philip the Fair and similar positions were subsequently given to other artists. On the accession of John, Girart d'Orléans, who had been employed on and off by the Crown from 1328 to 1350, was suddenly described as 'our beloved *familiaris...* painter and usher of our hall'. After the king's capture at Poitiers, when the household staff was necessarily reduced, Girart was nevertheless among those who accompanied the royal captive to England and he remained with the king throughout his captivity, first as a 'servant of the chamber' and then as his *valet de chambre*. It is clear that he was in some sense a personal companion of John and an insight into the nature of their relationship is perhaps revealed by the *jeu d'échecs* which he constructed for the king during the years of his captivity. On John's death in 1364 he was succeeded by Jean d'Orléans, *valet de chambre*, who in 1404 was succeeded by François d'Orléans, probably his son; clearly the three were related. But although Charles V retained the services of the family, he also appointed his own painters, like Jean Bandol of Bruges who became *peintre du roy* in 1368 and was probably admitted to the household in 1378 or 1379. By the end of the fourteenth century the position of *valet de chambre* had become a common appointment at the royal and princely courts for writers, artists and craftsmen who attracted their fancy: goldsmiths, *tapissiers*, illuminators, embroiderers and musicians.

The same tendency may be noted in historical writing. While the origins of the official element in French history are still somewhat mysterious, from some time in the thirteenth century the kings of France paid a monk of Saint-Denis as *chroniquer de France*, and this resulted in a steady stream of writings at the royal abbey down to 1420 (the *Grandes Chroniques* and the *Chronique du Religieux de Saint-Denis*). Although a break then occurred at the official historiographical centre (cf. above, p. 190), the Sandionysian tradition was continued in the *Latin* chronicle of Jean Chartier (d. 1464), which covers the years 1422 to 1450. From 1463 to 1476 the official chronicler was Jean Castel, a grandson of Christine de Pisan who was a monk of

Fig. 55   The siege of Calais in 1436; *Life and Acts of Richard Beauchamp, earl of Warwick*, by John Rous, *c.* 1485.
London, British Museum Cotton Ms Julius E IV Art VI, fo. 24v. (19.5 × 18.2)

Saint Martin des Champs and later abbot of Saint Maur des Fossés; but by then the
future lay with the memorialists—Thomas Basin (1412–91) and Philip de Commynes
(*c.* 1447–1511)—who, because of their proximity to the king, are to be considered in
close association with the official historians. A related, if somewhat different development, may be seen in Burgundy. Both Philip the Good and Charles the Rash
encouraged historical writing and had historians on their payrolls. If we cannot
discern their active patronage in the chivalrous chronicles of Enguerrand de
Monstrelet and the rather more talented Mathieu d'Escouchy who together took
Froissart's narrative down to 1460, the chronicles of Georges Chastellain and the
Mémoires of Olivier de la Marche were largely promoted by the dukes. Both of these
men's careers were made at the Burgundian court, where they held several
remunerative offices, and they were employed on several diplomatic missions.
In 1455 Chastellain was made permanent historiographer to the house of Burgundy

and was granted a residence in the duke's own Hôtel Salle-le-Comte at Valenciennes; under Charles the Rash he became a Knight of the Golden Fleece and was appointed historiographer of the Order. Although it would be wrong to think of these chroniclers as forming a 'Burgundian School', as Chastellain himself pointed out ('For I am not English, but French, neither Spanish nor Italian but French, and I have written of the exploits of two Frenchmen, one a king, the other a duke'), nevertheless, the fact that the dukes of Burgundy were lavish patrons inevitably meant that their

Fig. 56   A foot combat *en champs clos*– *Life and Acts of Richard Beauchamp, earl of Warwick*, by John Rous, *c.* 1485. London, British Museum Cotton Ms Julius E IV Art VI, fo. 7v. (18.1 × 17.5)

protégés saw events from a Burgundian angle and, as a matter of ducal policy, they were undoubtedly encouraged to do so. This in itself may have made it difficult for them to detach themselves from older attitudes to politics and the writing of history; but the new attitudes appeared in Basin's *Histoire de Charles VII et de Louis XI*, and in particular in Commynes' *Mémoires* of Louis XI and Charles VIII. These two memorialists were concerned with government in a new and imaginative way, and they showed an official knowledge and political awareness lacking in previous writers; yet their careers were remarkably different. Brought up in Normandy during the English occupation, Basin served the French Crown but in the end sought refuge with Burgundy. As we have seen (above, p. 138) he stood for the forces in France which resented and resisted the slowly-growing machinery of royal centralization. Commynes, on the other hand (cf. pl. 59), though like Chastellain he was born a subject of the house of Burgundy, and spent six years in the service of Charles the Rash, was enticed into the service of Louis XI. While he was aware of the dangers inherent in the new order, he was convinced that only a strong king could save France from internecine strife. What distinguishes both of these writers from their predecessors is their ability to extract a political message from the contemporary scene which they recorded.

There was nothing like these official appointments in England, with the important exception of building works, where the posts of Master-Mason and Master-Carpenter (who had general oversight of all the king's works) were set up in 1378. For although from the 1360s it became customary to admit writers (like Froissart and Chaucer) and later even painters (like Thomas Prince of Litlington, who accompanied Richard II to Ireland) into the royal household along with master-masons and master-carpenters (like Yevele and the Herlands), they do not seem to have held the official posts enjoyed by some of their contemporaries in France. Gilbert and Thomas Prince have sometimes been called 'the king's painters', by modern writers, but in the accounts for work carried out by them they are each referred to as *pictori London*. Thomas Gloucester appears to have held the office of 'king's painter' in the reign of Henry IV, but we have to wait until 1453 before another such person is known. As for historical writing, there was no official chronicle in Late Medieval England, and there were no memorialists like Basin and Commynes (though the employment of the Italian Tito Livio Frulovisi by Humphrey duke of Gloucester to write the biography of his brother Henry V is perhaps a remote parallel). London, on the other hand, produced numerous town chronicles which have no counterpart in Paris and in the fifteenth century we have the beginnings of a native antiquarian movement with William Worcester and with John Rous who wrote, among other things, the *Life and Acts of Richard Beauchamp, earl of Warwick* (cf. pl. 91 and figs. 20, 25, 40, 55).

It seems likely that English patronage of the arts and men of letters was at once less official, a little more old-fashioned and in many ways more broadly-based than was the case in France. Doubtless this was in part the result of a conjunction of circumstances, of past historical development, the war, and the entirely different position of the monarchy and the higher nobility in the two countries; but it was also the result of growing social differences and economic change. It has recently been suggested that, whereas the dominant position of the official historian in France reflects a self-conscious monarchy not to be found in England, the London chronicles might indicate the growing influence of the gentry and burgesses who in parliament were beginning to be coherent and vocal. It is surely not just a coincidence that in England the building and rebuilding of cathedral and parish churches in the new perpendicular style went on unabated, while France's greatest period of Gothic architecture for the most part lay in the past. The widespread foundation of chantries and collegiate churches, of hospitals and schools, of the Oxford and Cambridge colleges, and of parish churches with their rich stained-glass windows (cf. pls. 34, 46, 68), the product of a native school of glass-painters, is a striking feature of Late Medieval England and it reflects a very broad-based patronage. Many of these buildings, like the castles and manor-houses of the nobility and gentry and the houses of rich merchants, were the product of fortunes made in war and wool. We should be reminded of the Hundred Years War not only at Saint George's, Windsor, and at Henry V's foundations at Sheen and Sion, but also at Henry of Lancaster's collegiate church at Leicester (1356) and those of Sir Robert Knowles at Pontefract in Yorkshire (1385), of Sir Hugh Calveley at Bunbury in Cheshire (1386), of

Edward of York at Fotheringhay in Northamptonshire (1411); at John Lord Cobham's chantry college at Cobham in Kent (1370), and at Richard Beauchamp's chantry chapel at Warwick (1442–1465). It might also be recalled at the castles of John Lord Cobham at Cooling in Kent (1374–1375), of Sir Edward Dallingridge at Bodiam in Sussex (1386) (cf. pl. 36), of Sir John Fastolf at Caister in Norfolk (*c.* 1440), and of Lord Ralph Cromwell at Tattershall in Lincolnshire (begun in 1434). Many of these buildings still bear witness to the wealth and munificence of their founders and the skills of their builders. The series of English chantries (cf. pls. 35, 56) have been described as 'unique in the history of European art' and the Beauchamp chapel at Saint-Mary's, Warwick (cf. pl. 67), with its magnificent funeral effigy of Earl Richard adorned with weepers (cf. pls. 31, 43, 64) as 'the greatest achievement of mid-fifteenth-century English sculptors'. The tower of Fastolf's castle at Caister (cf. fig. 57), built with the ransom of the duke of Alençon whom he captured at the battle of Verneuil in 1424, originally had five stories of handsome rooms with arcaded fireplaces, and both summer and winter halls hung with rich tapestries. Like Tattershall (cf. fig. 58), with its domestic chapel, its collegiate church, its great fireplace, pleasances and fishponds, it was a home of ease and elegance rather than a fortified position. If we cannot always trace wealth derived from war in the land transactions of the period, it is everywhere apparent in the buildings of successful captains and in the rich furnishings, plate and jewellery recorded in their wills.

But we must not blind ourselves to the true proportions of the English achievement. Although the perpendicular style in architecture was peculiar to England, and was paralleled but not influenced by the flamboyant style in France, Sheen and Fotheringhay could hardly have vied with Beauté-sur-Marne and the Dijon Chartreuse, and there was no Lancastrian castle to match Pierrefonds or Mehun-sur-Yèvre. The East Anglian Psalters are not the *Très Riches Heures* and Warwick's funeral effigy, although certainly a landmark in fifteenth-century English funerary sculpture, does not bear comparison with Sluter's monumental effigy of Philip the Bold. There was only one court to speak of in Late Medieval England: that of the Crown. In France there was a profusion of courts: not simply of the royal dukes, but also of other territorial princes. There is therefore no English equivalent to the *Chronique du bon duc Loys de Bourbon, Le libvre du bon Jean, duc de Bretagne,* and the *Histoire de Gaston IV, comte de Foix,* by Leseur. And what English magnate could boast a court like that of Gaston Fébus, count of Foix and Béarn, at his Pyrénéan castle of Orthez? Although Froissart, who journeyed there in 1388, almost certainly exaggerated the role of Fébus as a patron of artists and men of letters—for the count's tastes, like those of the chronicler, were for the most part conventional—nevertheless, Fébus did possess a remarkable library and was himself something of a scholar. He could write good Latin as well as northern French and was fluent in the Iberian languages as well as in his native tongue. He was, moreover, the author of two remarkable works: the *Livre de Chasse,* which records his dominating passion for the hunt (cf. pl. 52), and the *Livre des Oraisons,* a devotional work written shortly after he had stabbed his son to death.

In part the reason for the greater French accomplishment lies in the relative size of the two countries, in the long history of provincial separatism in France, and the extraordinary independence of the French princes which had no parallel in England. For we can scarcely compare 'the duke of Lancaster that warred the Kynge of Spayne' or Gloucester in Hainault to great feudatories like Anjou, Burgundy, Berry and Orléans. In France, the provincial power of the territorial magnates re-vitalized the arts and the fifteenth-century schism in French politics encouraged the patronage of men of letters and developed the intellectual maturity of writers like Basin and Commynes.

Fig. 57 *Top* Caistor Castle, Norfolk.

Fig. 58 *Bottom* Tattershall Castle, Lincolnshire.

Genealogical table

The Houses of Plantagenet and Valois in the Fourteenth and Fifteenth Centuries

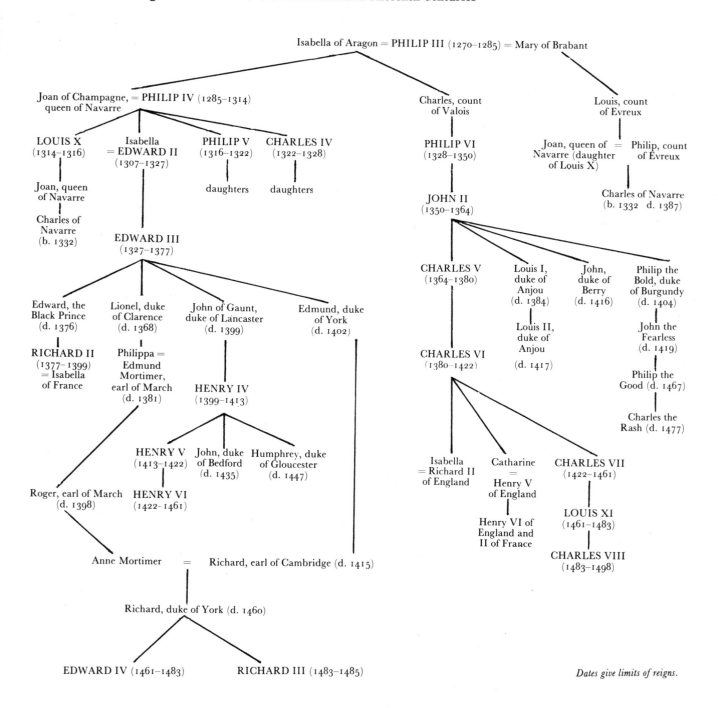

Dates give limits of reigns.

Epilogue

'Now you see the deaths of so many great men in so short a time, men who have worked so hard to become great and to win glory, and have thereby suffered so much from passions and cares and shortened their lives; and perchance their souls will pay for it . . . To speak plainly, as a man of no great learning but of some experience, might it not have been better for these men . . . to have chosen the middle way in things — that is, not to have cared so much and to have worked so hard, to have undertaken fewer enterprises, felt a livelier fear of offending God and persecuting people . . . and to have contented themselves with taking their ease and honest pleasure? Their lives would thereby have been longer, illness would have come later, their passing would have been more widely regretted and less desired, and they would have had less reason to dread death.'

In these words, Philip de Commynes reflected upon the happenings of the '70s and '80s of the fifteenth century: the death of Warwick 'the Kingmaker' on the battlefield of Barnet (14 April 1471), of the young Prince Edward at Tewkesbury (4 May 1471), and the murder of his father Henry VI in the Tower of London less than three weeks later (21 May 1471); the eclipse of the Burgundian state with the death of Charles the Rash (cf. pl. 60) at Nancy (5 January 1477), the death of Edward IV (cf. pl. 78) and Louis XI in 1483, the mysterious disappearance of the princes in the Tower and the death of Richard III (cf. pl. 79) on the battlefield of Bosworth two years later (22 August 1485). Between 1450 and 1500 the political map of western Europe changed dramatically; great royal and princely dynasties had reached the peak of fame only to fall in the turmoil of civil and foreign war, and two new royal houses were founded on the passing of the old.

The France and the England which emerged from the Hundred Years War were no longer tied together by a feudal bond, by language, or by culture; and the continuous hostilities had contributed to that conjuncture of circumstances—of plague, famine and economic decline—which characterized the Later Middle Ages throughout the greater part of Europe. Between 1300 and 1450 the population of France fell from around 21 million to around 14 million, that of England from around 4½ million to around 3 million and the effects were everywhere apparent. For while we must not ascribe to the Hundred Years War what was due to the 'hundred' years, it is difficult to escape the conclusion that it had contributed substantially to France's economic decline—*les bois sont venus en France par les Anglais*. Almost everywhere the ravages of the troops had brought ruin and depopulation, for although war killed fewer than the plague, the fall in population with all its attendant consequences was often set in motion by it. Politically, the result was to confirm, perhaps to hasten, the progress towards royal centralization and from centralization to the absolute monarchy of the *ancien régime*. For though the centralizing tendency was there before the war began, and thus did not represent a new departure, the powers now assumed by the king were in many instances the legacy of war. Between 1420 and 1430 the struggle between Plantagenet and Valois had come very close to destroying the French monarchy and the slow recovery after the appearance of Joan of Arc showed clearly that only the monarchy could effect a reconstruction. The reorganization of the army had strengthened the king's authority and brought into being a system of taxation free from such vague restraints as it had hitherto been subject to. The territorial magnates were no longer a political force in opposition to the king, for one by one the great fiefs were falling, to be annexed to the royal domain or used temporarily to endow some member of the royal family: Guyenne in 1453, Alençon in 1456, Roussillon and Cerdagne in 1463, the Armagnac lands in 1473, the duchy of Burgundy (and more to come) in 1477, the Angevin lands in 1481, and the duchy of Brittany ten years later. Those remaining were invaded by royal justice, royal taxation and royal military requirements. Clearly the day of the great independent fiefs, each having a political organization similar in kind to that of the kingdom, was over, and with their eclipse the nobility were increasingly thrown upon royal patronage and favour. Ruined by the wars, by the impoverishment of their estates, by the ending of their traditional role in society, and by the pace set by the royal court in luxury and extravagance, they were forced to enter the king's pay, to seek careers in the army and administration, or to wangle pensions in order to live nobly. Thus the France which emerged from the Hundred Years War was no longer a feudal kingdom, but a monarchy of a more modern type with a strong and now probably irreversible tendency towards centralization and absolutism.

Similar factors were at work in England—the decline of the nobility and the growth of royal authority with the ending of foreign and civil war—but in many respects her experiences had been different. For if the effects of the war on the redistribution of wealth have been exaggerated, if, as has been suggested, the Hundred Years War 'was at best a makeweight, not the mainspring of social change', in other ways its consequences were profound. The failure to develop a standing army had made unnecessary a system of arbitrary taxation such as was developed in France, while the extraordinary demand for money created by the war, for military expeditions and foreign occupation (cf. above, p. 138), had fostered the development of parliament and had done more than anything else, from the time of Edward III, to turn it into a body fundamentally different from that instrument of royal authority which had been brought into being in his grandfather's day. Already in the fifteenth century, Commynes noted the significance. Commenting upon an army being raised by Edward IV in 1474 to assist the duke of Burgundy, he wrote:

'But such things take a long time there [i.e. in England], for the king cannot undertake any war without assembling his parliament, which is like unto the three estates, and which is a very just and laudable custom; and the king is thereby stronger and better served in undertaking such enterprises. When these estates are assembled, he declares his intent and requests aid of his subjects; for no subsidies are levied in England unless it is to invade France or Scotland, or for similar enterprises; and then they are granted willingly and liberally, especially to pass into France.'

Although this was not the whole truth and, although with the ending of the war the representative body fell increasingly into abeyance, the pretensions which had been voiced by the Commons during the course of the fourteenth and fifteenth centuries, and the political experience that had been gained, were on record for future generations, and were among the more enduring legacies of Late Medieval England.

Fig. 59 Portrait of Charles VII (1422–61). *Musée de Versailles.*

Bibliography and notes

Introductory and Chapter I

For a convenient discussion of the origins of the war: G. Templeman in *Transactions of the Royal Historical Society* (*TRHS*), 5th ser., ii (1952), 69-88; P. Wolff in *Eventail de l'histoire vivante: homage à Lucien Febvre*, ii (1953), 141-8; J. Le Patourel in *History*, xliii (1958), 173 ff. and l (1965), 289-308. French title: J. W. McKenna in *Journ. Warburg and Courtauld Institutes*, xxviii (1965), 146, for Henry VI; Rymer's *Foedera* (original edit.), xii, 17 ff. (Picquigny), 223 ff. (Richard III), 490 (Henry VII), 497 ff. (Étaples), 592 ff. (confirmations). French succession: R. Cazelles, *La société politique . . . sous Philippe de Valois* (Paris, 1958), 35-52; J. Le Patourel in *History*, xliii (1958), 171-6; P. Chaplais (on Edward II's claim) in *Rev. du Nord*, xliii (1961), 145-8. Demography: P. Dollinger in *Rev. Historique*, ccxvi (1956), 35-45; G. Fourquin in *Le Moyen Age*, lxii (1956), 63-91; *Bordeaux sous les rois d'Angleterre*, ed. Y. Renouard (Bordeaux, 1965), 224; J. C. Russell, *British Medieval Population* (Albuquerque, 1948), but cf. J. Stengers in *Rev. Belge de Philologie et d'Histoire*, xxviii (1950), 605, and J. Krause in *Economic History Review* (*EcHR*), 2nd ser., ix (1957), for criticisms. Capetian kings: R. Fawtier, *Les Capétians et la France* (Paris, 1942; English trans., London, 1960). King's council: Cazelles, *op. cit.*, 36-7 and *passim*. French Estates: F. Lot and R. Fawtier, *Histoire des institutions françaises au moyen age*, ii (Paris, 1958), 547-77; P. S. Lewis in *Past and Present*, no. 23 (1962), 3-24; T. N. Bisson, *Assemblies and Representation in Languedoc in the Thirteenth Century* (Princeton, 1964); H. Gilles, *Les États de Languedoc au XVe siècle* (Toulouse, 1965), 23-8. King's conception of his realm: R. Fawtier in *Mélanges offerts à Paul E. Martin* (Geneva, 1961), 65-77. The countryside and the peasantry: convenient surveys and good bibliographies in J. Heers, *L'occident aux XIVe et XVe siècles* (Paris, 1963), livre II, ch. 1, and *The Cambridge Economic History of Europe* (*CEH*), i, ed. M. M. Postan (2nd ed., Cambridge, 1966), ch. vii. French nobility: G. Duby in *Rev. Historique*, ccxxvi (1961), 1-22; E. Perroy (on Forez) in *Past and Present*, no. 21 (1962), 25-38; J. Le Patourel in *Europe in the Late Middle Ages*, ed. J. Hale and others (London, 1965), 155-83. Paris and the Ile-de-France: F. Lehoux, *Le bourg de Saint-Germain-des-Prés* (Paris, 1951); G. Fourquin, *Les campagnes de la région Parisienne à la fin du moyen age* (Paris, 1964), ch. 1. London: T. F. Tout in *Proc. Brit. Academy*, x (1921-3), 487-511; E. L. Sabine in *Speculum*, viii (1933), 335-53, ix (1934), 303-21, xii (1937), 19-43; S. Thrupp, *The Merchant Class of Medieval London* (Chicago, 1948); R. Bird, *The Turbulent London of Richard II* (London, 1948). English nobility: F. M. Powicke, *The Thirteenth Century* (Oxford, 1953), 541, on number of knights; G. Holmes, *The Estates of the Higher Nobility in Fourteenth-Century England* (Cambridge, 1957). Retaining: K. B. McFarlane in *Bulletin of the Institute of Historical Research* (*BIHR*), xx (1943-5), 161-80, N. B. Lewis in *TRHS*, 4th ser., xxvii (1945), 29-39, and G. Holmes, *op. cit.*, ch. 3, for England; P. S. Lewis in *BIHR*, xxxvii (1964), 157-84, for France. Baronial incomes: H. L. Gray in *The English Historical Review* (*EHR*), xlix (1934), 607-39, and T. B. Pugh and C. D. Ross in *BIHR*, xxvi (1953), 1-28, and *EcHR*, 2nd ser., vi (1954), 185-94, for England. E. Perroy in *Past and Present*, no. 21 (1962), 25-38, for France. Plantagenet dominions: J. Le Patourel in *History*, l (1965), 289-308. Bordeaux, Gascony and the wine trade: *Bordeaux sous les rois d'Angleterre*, *cit. supra.*, livre iii; R. Boutruche, *La crise d'une société. Seigneurs et paysans du Bordelais pendant la Guerre de Cent Ans* (Paris, 1947), livre i, especially chs. i, iii and vi. Bastides: C. Higounet in *Le Moyen Age*, liv (1948), 113-31; J. P. Trabut-Cussac in *Le Moyen Age*, lx (1954), 81-135. Gascon administration: F. M. Powicke, *The Thirteenth Century* (Oxford, 1953), ch. vii; Y. Renouard in *Histoire des institutions françaises, cit supra.*, i (Paris, 1957), ch. vii; P. Chaplais in *Studies Presented to Sir Hilary Jenkinson*, ed. J. Conway Davies (Oxford, 1957), 61-96, and in *Annales du Midi*, lxix (1957), 5-38, and lxx (1958), 135-60; J. Le Patourel in *Europe in the Late Middle Ages, cit. supra.*, 159-63; E. Lodge, *Gascony Under*

English Rule (London, 1926), ch. vii, has been largely superseded, but her articles in *History*, xix (1934), 131-40, and *EHR*, l (1935), 225-41, are still useful. Treaty of 1259 and problem of sovereignty: M. Gavrilovitch, *Étude sur le traité de Paris de 1259* (Paris, 1899); W. Ullman in *EHR*, lxiv (1949), 1-33; P. Chaplais in *BIHR*, xxi (1948), 203-13, and in *Le Moyen Age*, lvii (1951), 269-302, lxi (1955), 121-37, lxix (1963), 449-69; M. David, *La souveraineté et les limites juridiques du pouvoir monarchique du IXe au XVe siècle* (Paris, 1954). Judicial Processes: G. P. Cuttino, *English Diplomatic Administration, 1259-1339* (Oxford, 1940), and in *Speculum*, xix (1944), 161-78. Scotland: R. Nicholson, *Edward III and the Scots* (Oxford, 1965). Crusade: A. Luttrell in *Europe in the Late Middle Ages, cit. supra.*, 133-4. Low Countries: H. S. Lucas, *The Low Countries and the Hundred Years War, 1326-1347* (Ann Arbor, 1929). Quotations: *Berners' Froissart*, ed. W. P. Ker, iv (London, 1902), 223-4; Michael de Northburgh in *Robertus de Avesbury. De Gestis Mirabilibus Regis Edwardi Tertii*, ed. E. M. Thompson (RS, London, 1889), 358-9; Juvénal des Ursins and Jean de Rély from P. S. Lewis in *Medium Aevum*, xxxiv (1965), 103; on English forests from W. G. Hoskins, *The Making of the English Landscape* (London, 1955), 69.

Chapter II

General: The only comprehensive survey of the entire war is E. Perroy, *La guerre de Cent ans* (Paris, 1945; Eng. trans., London, 1951). Diplomatic preparations and the early campaigns are the subject of E. Déprez, *Les préliminaires de la guerre de Cent ans, 1328-1342* (Paris, 1902), and H. S. Lucas, *op. cit*. There is no satisfactory study of Edward III's reign, but much of the history of the war during the second half of the fourteenth century is covered in R. Delachenal, *Histoire de Charles V* (5 vols., Paris, 1909-31), and P. E. Russell, *The English Intervention in Spain and Portugal in the Time of Edward III and Richard II* (Oxford, 1955). S. Armitage-Smith, *John of Gaunt* (London, 1904; reprinted 1964) has been largely superseded on military and diplomatic affairs by these two works. A. Steel, *Richard II* (Cambridge, 1941; reprinted 1962) sadly neglects them; but H. Wallon, *Richard II* (2 vols., Paris, 1864) may still be profitably consulted on Anglo-French relations. H. J. Hewitt, *The Black Prince's Expedition of 1355-1357* (Manchester, 1958) is an excellent study of an individual campaign; further detailed accounts are to be found in K. A. Fowler, *Henry of Grosmont, First Duke of Lancaster, 1310-1361* (unpublished Ph.D. thesis, University of Leeds, 1961), and A. F. Alexander, *The War in France in 1377* (unpublished Ph.D. thesis, University of London, 1934). On Burgundy, J. Calmette's *Les grands ducs de Bourgogne* (Paris, 1949; Eng. trans., London, 1962) should now be supplemented with R. Vaughan, *Philip the Bold* (London, 1962) and *John the Fearless* (London, 1966), the first half of a projected four-volume study of the dukes. M. R. Thielemans, *Bourgogne et Angleterre, 1435-1467* (Brussels, 1966) is a comprehensive and well-documented survey of Anglo-Burgundian political and economic relations after the treaty of Troyes. Various aspects of Charles VI's reign are treated in M. Nordberg, *Les ducs et la royauté. Etudes sur la rivalité des ducs d'Orléans et de Bourgogne, 1392-1407* (Uppsala, 1964); P. Bonenfant, *Du meurtre de Montereau au traité de Troyes* (Brussels, 1958); M. Rey, *Les finances royales sous Charles VI, 1388-1413* (Paris, 1965), and *Le domaine du roi et les finances extraordinaires sous Charles VI, 1388-1413* (Paris, 1965). M. McKisack, *The Fourteenth Century* (Oxford, 1959) and E. F. Jacob, *The Fifteenth Century* (Oxford, 1961) are the most recent surveys of English history during the period, but J. H. Ramsay, *The Genesis of Lancaster* (2 vols., Oxford, 1913) and *Lancaster and York* (2 vols., Oxford, 1892) may still be profitably consulted for foreign affairs. J. H. Wylie, *Henry IV* (4 vols., London, 1884-98) and, with W. T. Waugh, *Henry V* (3 vols., London, 1914-29) give very full accounts of the political history of the two reigns; similarly C. L. Scofield, *Edward IV* (2 vols., London, 1923). A short survey

204

of Henry V's military career is given in E. F. Jacob, *Henry V and the Invasion of France* (London, 1947), and a more detailed account in R. A. Newhall, *The English Conquest of Normandy, 1416-1424* (New Haven, 1924). E. Carleton Williams, *My Lord of Bedford* (London, 1963) traces the duke's career in France, but the articles of B. J. H. Rowe and R. A. Newhall in *EHR*, xxxvi (1921), xlvi (1931), xlvii (1932), l (1935), and in *Essays Presented to H. E. Salter* (Oxford, 1934) remain indispensable. G. du Fresne de Beaucourt, *Histoire de Charles VII* (6 vols., Paris, 1881-91), gives a comprehensive account of Anglo-French affairs. The *Procès de condamnation et réhabilitation de Jeanne d'Arc* has been published by J. Quicherat (5 vols., SHF, Paris, 1841-9), and the *Procès de condamnation* (with a French translation) by P. Champion (2 vols., Paris, 1920-1); a new edition is being prepared by P. Tisset (vol. I, SHF, Paris, 1960). For fifteenth-century English accounts of her, see W. T. Waugh in *Historical Essays in Honour of James Tait*, ed. J. G. Edwards and others (Manchester, 1933). The Congress of Arras is the subject of a book by J. G. Dickinson (Oxford, 1955), and J. Calmette and G. Perinelle, *Louis XI et l'Angleterre* (Paris, 1930), covers the final phases of the war. Edward III's policy: J. Le Patourel in *History*, xliii (1958), 176; M. McKisack, *ibid.*, xlv (1960), 15, and *The Fourteenth Century*, 147; R. Nicholson, *op. cit.*, 106-7; E. Perroy, *op. cit.* (Eng. trans.), 69, 116 and *passim*; G. Templeman in *TRHS*, 5th ser., ii (1952), 87; and (on destructiveness of his campaigns) H. J. Hewitt, *The Organization of War Under Edward III* (Manchester, 1966), 116. Philip VI: Cazelles, *op. cit.* Invasion threats: *R. de Avesbury, op. cit.*, 363-7 (ordinance); Bib. nat. (Paris), Pièces orig., vol. 265, doss. Behuchet, nos. 12-14 (1337); Arch. dép. Côte-d'Or (Dijon), B11715 and 11875 (1339); Arch. dép. Basses-Pyrénées (Pau), E31 (Edward's letter). Revolts: J. Le Patourel in *History*, xliii (1958), 179-89. Projected Franco-Aragonese invasion of Aquitaine: Delachenal, *op. cit.*, III, 270, and Arch. dép. Basses-Pyrénées, E520 (prince's foreknowledge). Rinel and Calot: J. Otway-Ruthven, *The King's Secretary and the Signet Office in the XV Century* (Cambridge, 1939), 89-105 and 156; B. A. Pocquet du Haut-Jussé, *La France gouvernée par Jean Sans Peur* (Paris, 1959), *passim*; Dickinson, *op. cit.*, xi and 47; etc. Budgeting (1433-4): *Letters and Papers Illustrative of the Wars of the English in France*, ed. J. Stevenson (2 vols., RS, London 1861-4), II, ii [547-74], and J. L. Kirby in *BIHR*, xxiv (1951).

Chapter III

English military organization: M. Powicke, *Military Obligation in Medieval England* (Oxford, 1962), and the works of N. B. Lewis, R. A. Newhall and A. E. Prince cited there (pp. 160 and 168); cf. also J. W. Sherborne in *EHR*, lxxix (1964), 718-46, on strength of expeditionary forces, and K. A. Fowler in *Les Cahiers Vernonnais* (*Actes du Colloque International de Cocherel*), no. 4 (1964), 55-84, on military finance and discipline. There is no comprehensive account of French military organization; but cf. Lot and Fawtier, *Hist. des instits. françaises*, ii, livre 5, ch. i (L'Armée) and the works cited there. The most helpful recent studies are by P. Contamine in *Cahiers Vernonnais*, no. 4 (1964), 19-32, *Azincourt* (Paris, 1964), and M. Rey, *Les finances royales*, 355-435. P. C. Timbal, *La guerre de Cent ans vue à travers les registres du parlement, 1337-1369* (Paris, 1961), is a useful collection of documents and an analysis of the problems of military obligation which they raise. The accounts of the treasurers-of-wars, from which a very detailed picture of French military organization could have been gleaned, were for the most part destroyed during the Revolution; but sufficient extracts from them remain (cf. L. Mirot in *BEC*, lxxxvi, 1925, 245-379), together with a large number of subsidiary documents (cf. Rey, *op. cit.*, 356-7), upon which this survey is based. I hope to examine the entire subject in depth in a forthcoming work on *War and Society in Fourteenth-Century France*. French military reforms: *Ordonnances des rois de France de la troisième race*, iv, 67-70 (1351); v, 645-51 and 657-61 (1373 and 1374); xiii, 306-13 (1439); xiv, 1-5 (1448); cf. below for those of 1363 and 1444. Arms, armour and artillery: J. Hewitt, *Ancient Armour and Weapons in Europe* (3 vols., London, 1855-60); C. Ffoulkes, *Armour and Weapons* (Oxford, 1909), *The Armourer and His Craft* (London, 1912), 13-15 and *passim*, *The Gun-Founders of England* (Cambridge, 1937), and numerous other works by the same author; *Le compte du Clos des Galées de Rouen, 1382-1384*, ed. C. Bréard (Mélanges Soc. de l'Hist. de Normandie, Rouen, 1893), 63-154; T. F. Tout (on firearms) in *EHR*, xxvi (1911), 666-702; W. Y. Carman, *A History of Firearms* (London, 1955), 22-38; O. F. G. Hogg, *English Artillery* (London, 1963), chs. i-v; B. H. St. J. O'Neill, *Castles and Cannon* (Oxford, 1960), chs. i-ii; Newhall, *Conquest*, 262-3; Rey. *op. cit.*, 427-30; J. Hale (on bastion) in *Europe in the Late Middle Ages*, ch. xvi.

Quotations from L. Delisle, *Histoire . . . de Saint-Sauveur-Le-Vicomte* (Valognes, 1867), P. J., n. 159, on guns at Saint-Sauveur; *Issue Rolls of the Exchequer*, ed. F. Devon (London, 1837), 212, on guns at Cherbourg; *The History of The King's Works*, ed. H. M. Colvin (2 vols., HMSO, London, 1963), ii, 802, no. 2, on Queenborough. Constables and marshals: G. Le Barrois d'Orgeval, *Le maréchalat de France* (2 vols., Paris, 1932), i, 9-332, and ii, 186-205 (list of marshals); J. Mitchell, *The Court of the Connétable* (New Haven, 1947), 5-14; G. D. Squibb, *The High Court of Chivalry* (Oxford, 1959), ch. i. Constable's Powers: G. Daniel, *Histoire de la milice françoise* (2 vols., Amsterdam, 1724), i, 127-31 (Clisson), and Bib. nat., français 5241, fos. 30r-2r (Le Tur). Biographies: S. Luce, *Histoire de Bertrand du Guesclin* (Paris, 1876); E. Molinier, *Étude sur la vie d'Arnoul d'Audrehem* (Paris, 1883); E. Cosneau, *Le connétable de Richemont* (Paris, 1886); E. Bossard, *Gilles de Rais* (Paris, 1886); A. Lefranc, *Olivier de Clisson* (Paris, 1898); A. de Bouillé, *Le maréchal de La Fayette* (Lyon, 1955); E. Garnier (on Fiennes) in *BEC*, xiii (1852), 23-52; and the following positions des thèses de l'École des Chartes: P. Durrieu, *Bernard VII, comte d'Armagnac, connétable de France* (1877); G. Lefèvre-Pontalis, *Jean de Villiers, sire de l'Isle-Adam, maréchal de France* (1883); M. de Bengy-Puyvallée, *Louis de Sancerre, connétable de France* (1904). Captains and Lieutenants: this survey is based upon commissions and mandates mainly in the Treaty Rolls (C76) and Gascon Rolls (C61) in the Public Record Office (PRO) in London, the series of Chancery Registers (JJ) in the Archives Nationales and the collections Clairambault and Pièces Originales in the Bibliothèque Nationale in Paris. Many of the English commissions have been published in Rymer's *Foedera*. On the French side, cf. the lists of officers in G. Dupont-Ferrier, *Gallia Regia* (6 vols., Paris, 1942-61), and unpublished documents and other materials in K. A. Fowler, *Henry of Grosmont*, Appendix B. Many of the biographies cited above are also relevant, together with L. Flourac, *Jean Ier, comte de Foix* (Paris, 1884); A. Walckenaer, *Louis Ier, duc d'Anjou* (positions des thèses, 1890); and J. Chavanon, *Renaud VI de Pons* (La Rochelle, 1903). Quotation: Berners' *Froissart*, ii, 359 (ed. Macaulay, London, 1895, 203). Frontier and occupied territories: Fowler in *Cahiers Vernonnais* and M. Rey, *op. cit.*, 364-85. Military finance, muster and review: *Ordonnances* and works by Fowler, Mirot and Rey cit. supra; R. A. Newhall, *Muster and Review* (Cambridge, Mass., 1940); H. Moranvillé, *Étude sur la vie de Jean le Mercier* (Paris, 1888). Quotation: *La complainte*, ed. C. de Robillard de Beaurepaire in *BEC*, xii (1851), 257 ff. Standing army: *Arch. admin. de Reims*, ed. P. Varin (10 vols., Docs. Inédits, Paris, 1839-53), iii, no. DCCLVI, for *ordonnance* of 1363; *Mandements de Charles V*, ed. L. Delisle (Docs. Inédits, Paris, 1874), nos. 562 and 679, for its implementation; P. Chaplais in *Camden Miscellany*, xix (Roy. Hist. Soc., London, 1952), 47, for John's proposals to Edward; Arch. dép. Nord (Lille), B319, no. 15798, for 1444 taxation scheme; De Beaucourt, *op. cit.*, iii, ch. xv, and iv, ch. xiv, for *ordonnances* of 1439, 1444 and 1448. Quotations: Thomas Basin, *Histoire de Charles VII*, ed. C. Samaran (2 vols., Paris, 1933 and 1944), ii, 28-9 and 32-5.

Chapter IV

Heralds: M. Keen, *The Laws of War in the Late Middle Ages* (London, 1965), 194-5; *Chroniques de Jean Froissart*, ed. S. Luce and others (14 vols., SHF, Paris, 1869-1966), I, i, 1 and 209, vi, 210, vii, 455; *La Chronique d'Enguerran de Monstrelet*, ed. L. Douët-d'Arcq (6 vols., SHF, Paris, 1857-62), i, 3-4; *The Essential Portions of Nicholas Upton's De Studio Militari*, ed. F. P. Barnard (Oxford, 1931), 1-3; Bib. nat., français 25186, fo. 57 ff. (manual). Laudatory biographies: *The Life and Feats of Arms of Edward The Black Prince*, ed. Francisque-Michel (London and Paris, 1883), 5-6; *Chronique de Bertrand du Guesclin par Cuvelier*, ed. E. Charrière (2 vols., Docs. Inédits, Paris, 1839), i, 3; *Le livre des faits du bon chevalier Messire Jacques de Lalaing*, ed. Kervyn de Lettenhove in *Oeuvres de Georges Chastellain* (8 vols., Brussels, 1863-6), viii, 1-259; *Le Livre des faicts du bon Messire Jean le Maingre, dit Boucicaut*, ed. M. Petitot (2 vols., Coll. Mémoires relatifs à l'hist. de France, Iière sér., vi and vii, Paris, 1819), i, 3 ff. Chivalric orders and vows: J. Huizinga, *The Waning of the Middle Ages* (Penguin Books, 1955, etc.), chs. iv, vi and vii; Y. Renouard in *Le Moyen Age*, lv (1949), 281-300; P. S. Lewis in *Annales du Midi*, lxxvi (1964), 77-84, and works cited there; J. Armstrong in *Britain and the Netherlands*, ii, ed. J. S. Bromley and E. H. Kossmann (Groningen, 1964), 9-32. Ransoms and booty: M. Postan in *EcHR*, xii (1942), 7 ff. and *Past and Present*, no. 27 (1964), 34-53; E. Perroy in *Mélanges d'histoire du Moyen Age dédiés à la mémoire de Louis Halphen* (Paris, 1951), 573-80; D. Hay in *TRHS*, 5th ser., iv (1954), 91-109; K. B. McFarlane in *ibid.*, vii (1957),

91-116, and in *Past and Present*, no. 22 (1962), 3-18; Hewitt, *The Black Prince's Expedition*, 152-65; Fowler, *Henry of Grosmont*, 285-303 and Appendix G; Timbal, *op. cit.*, 305-74; C. T. Allmand in *History Today*, xv (1965), 762-9; Arch. dép. Eure-et-Loir (Chartres), E2725, fo. 28v, and Bib. nat., français 4736, fo. 21 ff., for butiners; M. Keen in *History*, xlvii (1962), 1-17, and K. B. McFarlane in *EHR*, lxxviii (1963), 290-310, on brothers-in-arms; *Froissart*, ed. Luce, iv, 16; *Thomae Walsingham, Historia Anglicana*, ed. H. T. Riley (2 vols., RS, London, 1863-4), i, 272. Devastation of the countryside: Basin, *op. cit.*, i, 84-8; Boutruche, *op. cit.*, 166 and 170; J. Monicat, *Les Grandes Compagnies en Velay, 1358-1392* (Paris, 1928), 178-9 and 187-8; Fourquin, *Les campagnes*, 290; L. Genicot in *CEH*, i (2nd ed.), ch. viii; *Journal d'un bourgeois de Paris, 1405-1449*, ed. A. Tuetey (Paris, 1881); A. Blanchet, *Les souterrains refuges de la France* (Paris, 1923); letter of prior of Brailet ed. J. Quicherat in *BEC*, xviii (1857), 357-60. Thiérache campaign: *Avesbury, op. cit.*, 304-5, for Edward's letter; L. Carolus-Barré in *Mélanges d'archéologie et d'histoire* (École française de Rome, lxii, 1950), 165-232, on Carit's mission. Black Prince's campaign: *Avesbury, op. cit.*, 434-7 and 439-43 (letters of prince and Wengfield); Hewitt, *The Black Prince's Expedition*, 74-5. Reims campaign: *The Chronicle of Jean de Venette*, ed. R. A. Newhall (New York, 1953), 98-9. Campaigns of 1370s: Delachenal, *op. cit.*, iv, chs. ix and xii, v, ch. vii; Armitage-Smith, *op. cit.*, ch. v. Fastolf's advice: *Letters and Papers, cit. supra.*, II, ii, 579-82. Poitevin frontier: *Froissart*, ed. Luce, viii, 19. Raencons, appatiz and safe-conducts: Fowler in *Cahiers Vernonnais*, no. 4 (1964), 55-84, for fourteenth century, also E. Labroue, *Le Livre de Vie*. *Les seigneurs et les capitaines de Périgord Blanc au XIVe siècle* (Bordeaux and Paris, 1891), 13, and *Bergerac sous les Anglais* (Bordeaux and Paris, 1893), 183, for Bergerac, and PRO, E101/174/6, nos. 1-5, 7, 9-10, 16-18, for Brittany; Arch. dép. Manche (St-Lô), H15014 and 15357, for Mont Saint-Michel; Arch. dép. Eure-et-Loir (Chartres), E2725, fos. 17v, 32v, 36v, 48r, 50v, 55r, 64r, for Châteaudun; Arch. nat., KK324, and R. Triger, *Fresnay-le-Vicomte de 1417 à 1450* (Mamers, 1886), 116-8, for Maine; H. Denifle, *La désolation des églises, monastères et hôpitaux en France pendant la guerre de Cent ans* (2 vols., Paris, 1897-9), i, 498-9 and 506-7, for Juvénal des Ursins; *Froissart*, ed. Luce, v, 121, and Luce, *Du Guesclin*, 271, for safe-conducts. Routiers: A. Bossuat, *Perrinet Gressart et François de Surienne* (Paris, 1936); A. Chérest, *L'Archiprêtre* (Paris, 1879); E. de Fréville in *BEC*, iii (1841-2), 258-81, and v (1843-4), 232-53; G. Guigue, *Les Tard-Venus en Lyonais, Forez et Beaujolais, 1356-1369* (Lyon, 1886); Labroue, *Le Livre de Vie*, and p. 49 for the quotation; Monicat, *op. cit*; J. Quicherat, *Rodrigue de Villandrando* (Paris, 1879); A. Tuetey, *Les Écorcheurs sous Charles VII* (2 vols., Montbéliard, 1874); *Froissart*, ed. Luce, vi, pp. xviii-xxiii, notes; Denifle, *op. cit.*, ii, 179-307 and 380-1; Arch. dép. Loire-Atlantique (Nantes), E119/12 and 13, for English *routes*. Military discipline: Fowler in *Cahiers Vernonnais*, no. 4 (1964), 74-81, for English armies in fourteenth century; Keen, *op. cit.*, on law of arms; Squibb, Orgeval and Mitchell, *loc. cit.*, on courts of constable and marshals; Arch. dép. Tarn-et-Garonne (Montauban), A26, and Arch. nat., J865/26, for subsidiary prévôts; B. J. H. Rowe in *EHR*, xlvi (1931), 194-208, on fifteenth-century Normandy. Estates and routiers: Monicat, *op. cit.*, is the best account of the evacuation of one province; Arch. dép. Aveyron (Rodez), C1335-9, 1354 and 1386-7, are treasurers' accounts for the evacuation of Rouergue, and C1336, fo. 27r ff. for Armagnac's annuities to routiers; Arch. dép. Basses-Pyrénées, E48-9, for general patis; Arch. dép. Eure-et-Loir, E2724, fo. 10r, and Arch. dép. Manche, H15014, for centralization of control in north. Social tensions: Timbal, *op. cit.*, *passim*; P. S. Lewis in *TRHS*, 5th ser., xv (1965), 1-21, on propaganda. Quotations: *La complainte*, ed. C. de Robillard de Beaurepaire in *BEC*, xii (1851), 257 ff; Juvénal des Ursins from Lefranc, *op. cit.*, 159, n. 3; *Chronicle of Jean de Venette*, 111-3; *Tragicum argumentum* in *Bull. hist. et philologique du comité des travaux historiques et scientifiques* (1862), 173-7; *Alain Chartier, Le Quadrilogue Invectif*, ed. E. Droz (Classiques franç. du Moyen Age, Paris, 1950), 20-33; *Le Jouvencel par Jean de Bueil*, ed. C. Favre and L. Lecestre (2 vols., SHF, Paris, 1887-9), ii, 20-21.

Chapter V and Epilogue

General: H. Focillon, *Art d'Occident* (2 vols., Paris, 1938; Eng. trans., London, 1963), i; L. Lefrançois-Pillion and J. Lafond, *L'art du XIVe siècle en France* (Paris, 1954); J. Evans, *Art in Mediaeval France* (London and New York, 1948), and *English Art, 1307-1461* (Oxford, 1949), have good bibliographies. Relevant volumes in the Pelican History of Art are: M. Rickert, *Painting in Britain: the Middle Ages* (1954); L. Stone, *Sculpture in Britain: the Middle Ages* (1955); G. Webb, *Architecture in Britain: the Middle Ages* (1956); P. Frankl, *Gothic Architecture* (1962). Relevant volumes in the Contact History of Art, ed. A. Held and D. W. Bloemena are: *Gothic Painting* and *Medieval Manuscript Painting* (London, 1965). H. S. Bennett, *Chaucer and the Fourteenth Century*, and E. K. Chambers, *English Literature at the Close of the Middle Ages* (Oxford Hist. Eng. Lit., ii, 1945-7), are the standard works on English literature; cf. also the bibliographies in the relevant vols. of the *Cambridge History of English Literature*. For France, J. Bedier and P. Hazard, *Histoire de la littérature française*, i (Paris, 1926), and G. Cohen, *La vie littéraire en France* (Paris, 1953) are useful. Anglo-Norman: M. D. Legge in *History*, xxvi (1941), 163-75; H. Suggett in *TRHS*, 4th ser., xxviii (1946), 61-83. Flemish artists: R. M. Tovell, *Flemish Artists of the Valois Courts* (London, 1950), *passim*. Avignon: A. Coville, *Gontier et Pierre Col et l'humanisme en France au temps de Charles VI* (Paris, 1934), ch. viii; F. Simone, *Il rinascimento Francese* (Turin, 1961), ch. i. Royal and princely buildings: Delachenal, *Charles V*, iii, 105 ff. and 107 for Christine de Pisan; O. Cartellieri, *The Court of Burgundy* (Eng. trans. of *Am Hofe der Herzöge von Burgund*, London, 1929), ch. ii; F. D. S. Darwin, *Louis d'Orléans* (London, 1933), 104-5; *The King's Works*, i, 162-3, 515 ff. and 870 ff., and Evans, *English Art*, 46-8, for Edward III's works; J. Harvey, *Henry Yevele* (London, 1944), and *The King's Works*, 174, no. 8, 189-90, 209-11 and 220-1 for Yevele, Herland and the positions they held. Libraries: L. Delisle, *Recherches sur la librairie de Charles V* (Paris, 1907), 220-3 and *passim*; Darwin, *op. cit.*, 91 ff. and 211-20; A. Coville, *La vie intellectuelle dans les domaines d'Anjou-Provence de 1380 à 1485* (Paris, 1941), 10-35, and *Gontier et Pierre Col*, 15-19; Cartellieri, *op. cit.*, ch. ix; J. Labarte, *Inventaire du mobilier de Charles V* (Docs. inédits, Paris, 1879), nos. 1990 and *passim* for astrolabes, 2089 for *Gouvernement des Princes* and 2099 for *Grandes Chroniques*; Calmette, *Golden Age of Burgundy*, 209, for quotation from De la Marche; A. Luttrell in *Recherches de théologie ancienne et médiévale*, xxxi (Louvain, 1964), 138, on Hesdin; M. V. Clarke, *Fourteenth Century Studies* (Oxford, 1937), 120-2, for English libraries; *Testamenta Vetusta*, ed. N. H. Nicolas (2 vols., London, 1826), i, 146-9, for will of duchess of Gloucester; Berners' *Froissart*, ed. Macaulay, 430, on Richard II, and MS. Bodley 581 for volumes presented to him. Tapestries: R.-A. d'Hulst, *Tapisseries Flamandes* (Brussels, 1960), 1-6, and *passim*; Darwin, *op. cit.*, 208-10. Illuminated manuscripts and paintings on panel: K. Morand, *Jean Pucelle* (Oxford, 1962); Tovell and Contact History *cit. supra*; Evans, *English Art*, 10-11, 95-6 and 100-4; Coville, *La vie intellectuelle*, 16-17, for seizure of Froissart's Chronicles; T. Cox, *Jehan Foucquet, native of Tours* (London, 1931); J. Harvey in *Archaeologia*, 98 (1961), 1-28, and works on Wilton Diptych cited there. Beauneveu and Liège: Evans, *English Art*, 84 and 100; Froissart, *Voyage en Béarn*, ed. A. H. Diverres (Manchester, 1953), and bibliography pp. 128-9; A. H. Diverres in *Medieval Miscellany Presented to Eugène Vinaver*, ed. F. Whitehead and others (Manchester, 1965), 97 ff; M. Galway in *University of Birmingham Hist. Journ.*, 7 (1959-60), 18-35; A. Molinier, *Les sources de l'histoire de France* (6 vols., Paris, 1901-6), iv, 4-18; D. Hay in *BIHR*, xxxv (1962), 114, for the quotation. Chaucer: standard edit. by W. W. Skeat (7 vols., Oxford, 1897); modern English version of *Canterbury Tales* by N. Coghill (Penguin Books, 1951); biographical material in *Life Records of Chaucer* (Chaucer Soc., 2nd ser., xii, xiv, xxi-xxii, 1875-1900), ed. R. E. G. Kirk and others; J. M. Manly, *Some New Light On Chaucer* (New York, 1926); S. Honoré-Duvergé on Chaucer in Spain in *Recueil de travaux offert à Clovis Brunel* (1955), 9-13; *John of Gaunt's Register*, ed. S. Armitage-Smith, I, i (Camden Third Series, xx), no. 608, for patronage of Philippa and Gaunt. Official patronage: A. Martindale in *The Flowering of the Middle Ages*, ed. J. Evans (London, 1966), 281 ff; M. Rey, *Le domaine du roi*, 156-7, for king's works; Hay, *loc. cit.*, 116 ff. and Calmette, *Golden Age*, ch. ix, on historical writing; H. d'Orléans, duc d'Aumale, in *Miscellanies of the Philobiblon Society*, ii (London, 1856), 30-1 and 47, on Girart d'Orléans; J. Harvey in *Archaeologia*, 98 (1961), 7, notes 2 and 3, and *The King's Works*, 227, on the Princes and Gloucester. Chantries and colleges: Evans, *English Art*, ch. ix and 181 for quotation; G. H. Cook, *English Collegiate Churches* (London, 1959), and *Mediaeval Chantries and Chantry Chapels* (rev. ed., London, 1963), *passim*; Stone, *op. cit.*, 207 for quotation on Beauchamp Chapel. Princely courts: P. Tucoo-Chala, *Gaston Fébus et la vicomté de Béarn* (Bordeaux, 1960), 263-81; *La Chronique du bon duc Loys de Bourbon*, ed. A.-M. Chazaud (SHF, Paris, 1876); *Le libvre du bon Jean*, ed. A. Charrière in *Chronique de Bertrand du Guesclin*, ii, 421 ff; *Histoire de Gaston IV*, ed. H. Courteault (2 vols., SHF, Paris, 1893-6). Epilogue: *Mémoires de Philippe de Commynes*, ed. J. Calmette (3 vols., Classiques de l'hist. de France au Moyen Age, Paris, 1924-5), ii, 8 and 340-1.

Index

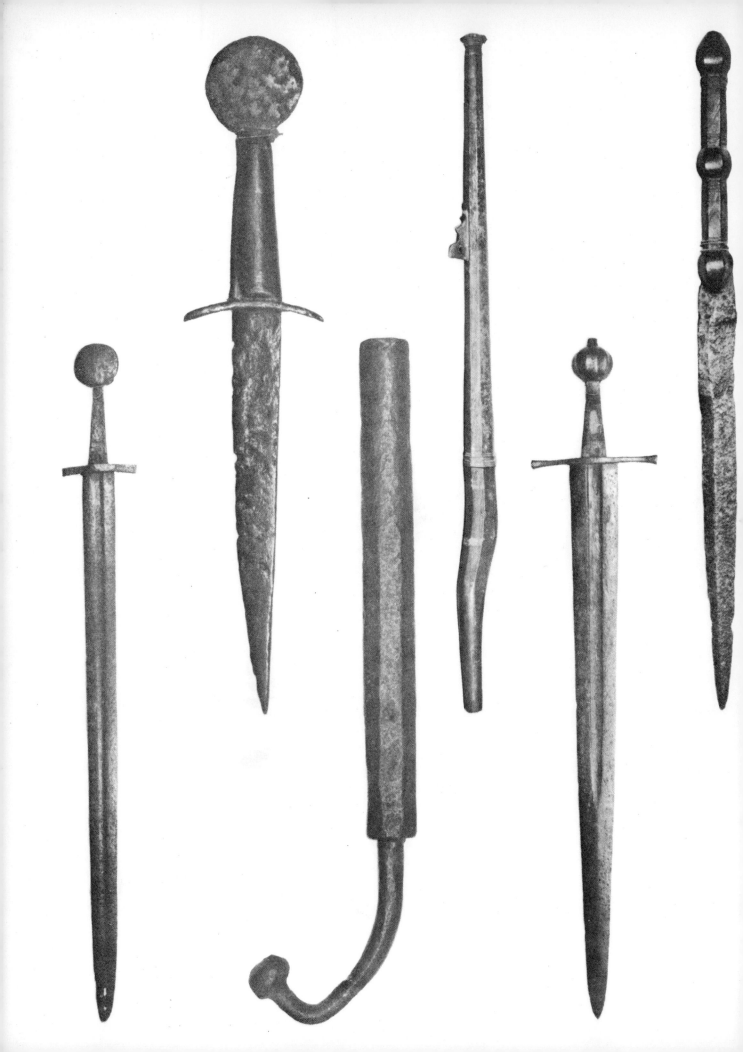